D1552499

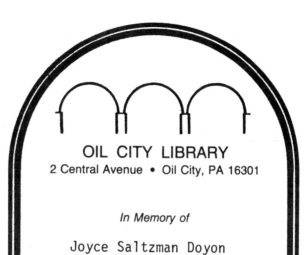

OIL CITY LIBRARY
2 Central Avenue • Oil City, PA 16301

In Memory of

Joyce Saltzman Doyon

Presented by

Flower Garden Bowling League

Fordson, Farmall, and Poppin' Johnny

Fordson, Farmall, and Poppin' Johnny

A History of the
Farm Tractor and Its Impact
on America

Robert C. Williams

UNIVERSITY OF ILLINOIS PRESS
Urbana and Chicago

This book is printed on acid-free paper.

Library of Congress Cataloging-in-Publication Data

Williams, Robert C. (Robert Charles), 1944–
   Fordson, Farmall, and Poppin' Johnny.

   Bibliography: p.
   Includes index.
   1. Farm tractors—United States—History. 2. Farm
tractors—Canada—History. 3. Agriculture—United
States—History. 4. Agriculture—Canada—History.
I. Title.
S711.W54   1987   631.3′72′0973   86-1359
ISBN 0-252-01328-X

Contents

Preface

Most people realize that between the end of the First World War and the proliferation of television sets there was a profound change in American society. During that period, most Americans migrated from the farm to the city. The "why" and "how" of that movement merit more attention, because an ever-shrinking percentage of the population managed to produce ever-larger quantities of food for the swelling cities. The tractor was a major factor in allowing production to expand while the labor supply contracted. It was not the only reason, but it was a major one. A biography of the tractor is as useful in understanding the United States in the twentieth century as a biography of Talleyrand is in understanding the era of the French Revolution and Napoleon in Europe.

The tractor is, of course, worthy of study on its own merit. Many folks—even those from urban backgrounds—are fascinated by the machine. It is a symbol of power. It is a case study in mechanical development and adaptation. For some older Americans, the tractor may seem to be a demon that destroyed their way of life and drove them from the farm. To others of the same generation, it is a deliverer that liberated them from some of the Adamic curse—the painful toil and "sweat-of-the-brow"—that blistered hands, warped backbones, and numbed minds. For young farmers, the tractor is a tool in which they will spend a large portion of their waking hours for many years to come. And for everyone, the tractor is an important link in the production chain that furnishes cheap food and fiber—commodities that the thoughtful person does not take for granted.

The tractor is a dramatic machine, and it played an important role in American history. It has attracted some previous historical attention. R. B. Gray's *Development of the Agricultural Tractor in the United States* (1974) is essentially a field guide with notes on the mechanical details of some models. Michael Williams's *Farm Tractors in Color* (1974) is a very pretty picture book. However, both books are primarily visual in nature, whereas this book is a narrative of the tractor's development and its impact on American society.

Anyone seriously interested in the history of the tractor must examine the background and environment surrounding the machine. In his article "The Impact of Technological Change on American Agriculture" (*Journal of Economic History*, December 1962), Wayne D. Rasmussan suggested that there were two major revolutions in American agriculture: one occurred when horses and mules replaced hand tools and human muscle, and a second one when engines replaced equine muscle. In the same issue, Clarence Danhoff took issue with the term *revolutionary*, preferring instead the word *evolutionary*. Yet, semantics aside, both articles documented that the changes were of first magnitude.

The classic account of early farm mechanization is Fred Shannon's *The Farmer's Last Frontier, Agriculture, 1860–1897* (1945). For the era of farm technology most closely preceeding the tractor, the prevailing expert is Reynold Wik. His *Steam Power on the American Farm* (1953) is a definitive study of the tractor's external combustion antecedent. His 1972 book, *Henry Ford and Grass-Roots America*, describes the car maker's introduction of mass production into the tractor industry, but it also offers valuable insight into the character of the father of the Fordson tractor.

This book is a biography of the tractor. It is divided into two sections. The first (chapters 1 through 6) traces the chronological development of the tractor. The second (chapters 7 through 9) describes some of the social and economic consequences of the tractor and examines its impact on the farm and the individual farmer.

The term *tractor* is used here in a specialized sense to describe primarily the common American wheeled farm tractor. Industrial, highway, aviation, and other nonagricultural tractors are largely ignored. Foreign and track-type tractors are noted only to the extent that they directly impinge on the American farm. The United States and Canada are treated without distinction, because they constitute a single market for tractors and farm equipment, and because the border is an artificial line through what is otherwise a common agricultural area. Until recently, other foreign countries have had little influence on North American machinery, manufacturers, or society, except for occasional cross-fertilizations from Great Britain and for European and Far Eastern imports in the 1970s and 1980s. Track-type tractors ("Caterpillars") never constituted a significant segment of the farm fleet, except in very localized areas where special conditions prevailed. This is the story of the "ordinary" tractor.

The interminable evolution of this book has been assisted by an army of helpful people. Some have been from academic circles, some from industry, some from the farm. Probably none of them would agree with everything in the book, yet all have made a contribution. To acknowledge and thank all would take as many pages as a normal chapter, but I would like each of you to know that I do appreciate your help. Dr. Seymour V. Connor, the late Dr. Charles Wood, and Dr. Joseph King all helped immeasurably with their advice. Mrs. Gloria Lyerla and her staff at the Texas Tech University Library were consistently solicitous and worked minor miracles in finding and obtaining materials.

Before I wrote this book, I thought that acknowledgments were quaint, trite conventions. I now know better. A book may be the product of its author, but it would not exist if the writer were not assisted, encouraged, and accommodated. Books are the result of more travail than the reader would ever guess, but the author's discomfort may well be less than that of the constellation of people surrounding him.

This book would never have been published if it were not for the support and encouragement provided by my wife, Lynne Williams. My children often suppressed their enormous energy to provide a few moments of constructive peace and quiet at critical times. My mother, Margaret Williams, made a tremendous contribution at the keyboard and in proofreading. At the age of seventy-five she bravely took on the challenge of learning a wordprocessing program and manipulating a microcomputer. That she prevailed is evidenced by the existence of this text. I hope that my family knows how much I appreciated their effort and perseverance.

I

The Development of the Tractor

1
The Roots of American Agricultural Technology

In one generation between 1920 and 1950, most farms in the United States changed from dependence on draft animals to dependence on mechanical power. That change was a profound one. It forced the farmer to change most of the production techniques that he had already perfected and to begin experimenting with new equipment and new methods. Yet he bought the tractor anyway, plunging headlong into a new technological era. The farmer did not hesitate because he had become accustomed, perhaps even addicted, to new machinery and new techniques.

A great many farmers in the United States in the first half of the twentieth century were far removed from the stolid conservatism of some of their medieval ancestors. Many farmers in many cultures have found change threatening. To them the status quo was the result of generations of trial and error and the chances of improving on it seemed improbable. However, to most recent American farmers, change was routine. American agriculture was fluid by nature. It borrowed, adapted, and incorporated new elements in a constant process of metamorphosis. To the American farmer, change was traditional.[1]

In order to understand the tradition of constant change, it is necessary to examine the heritage of American agriculture and technology. When seen in the context of its background, the rapid adoption of the tractor is far more comprehensible. The broadest context includes the entire metamorphosis of Western society since the fifteenth century and the more localized economic and technological changes in the United

States that are popularly called the *Industrial Revolution*. But the specific context is the accelerating development of agriculture in the period after Independence.

In the northern colonies at about the time that insurgents began calling for separation from England, "two men and a boy, using 2 or 3 good horses or 4 or 6 oxen could scratch over 1 or 2 acres a day."[2] The farmer or local woodworker generally fashioned a primitive wooden plow for himself or for local barter. The plow was cheap, but it wore out quickly and demanded tremendous brute strength to drag it through the soil. Yet despite the device's primitive form, plowing was an improvement over hand cultivation, which was even less efficient.

The staple crop throughout the colonies was corn, adopted by earlier colonists from the Indians, who had developed innumerable varieties. The early colonists also adopted the Indian practice of clean cultivation and adapted the plow to that use as well.[3]

American agriculture at the time of the rebellion was gradually becoming eclectic. The plow then in use was a legacy of medieval Europe and had scarcely been improved. The optimistic and experimental spirit that pervaded the new nation after independence unleashed what would eventually become a flood of inventiveness, and in a society overwhelmingly composed of farmers, it was natural that inventors would turn to the plow.

Among the first Americans to attack the shortcomings of the plow on a theoretical level was a noted politician, philosopher, farmer, architect, and inventor named Thomas Jefferson. Jefferson set out to derive through mathematics an efficient curve along which to contour a moldboard. After comparing Jefferson to Leonardo da Vinci, David E. Smith, a modern mathematician, concluded that "The curve[d] surface which he proposed (1788) for the moldboard was the first important step in the modern development of this agricultural implement." Even though Jefferson's theoretical design did not prove successful in practice, it pioneered the search for an engineered plow shape.[4]

Between Jefferson's death in 1826 and the end of Reconstruction in 1877, a space of less than one average lifetime, men altered their tools so completely that a major historian of the era termed it a "near revolutionary" change.[5] The tempo of invention was quickening. The transportation revolution that influenced canals, steamboats, and railroads not only introduced new technologies—some of which were transferable—but it also effectively disseminated new technology quite rapidly. Farming operations were changing.

By 1819 Jethro Wood had altered the irreparable nature of the cast iron plow by building it of several standardized cast iron parts. Any broken or worn segments could then be replaced, and the cast iron plow gradually conquered the loamy soils of the East.

The prairie sod of the Midwest with its thickly matted grass stalled cast iron plow bottoms. This dark, sticky soil did not scour across rough and porous cast iron, and grass fibers clogged the plow's leading edge. The plains soil locked away the golden treasure of today's cornbelt until someone developed an implement formidable enough to slice through the plains' topsoil. That plow was not long in coming. Inventive farmers and blacksmiths worked on the problem almost as soon as they encountered the stubborn soil. By 1833, John Lane was experimenting with steel plow bottoms. He succeeded in his experiments, but apparently failed to transform his discovery into a commercial success. Less than a decade later, John Deere began selling steel plows on an ever-growing commercial scale. So great was the impact of Deere's production that for generations Deere and Company advertisements featured a picture of Deere with the caption and motto "He gave to the world the steel plow."[6] Farmers apparently took such innovation for granted, since they cracked that "He may have given it to the world, but I had to buy mine!" Nevertheless, the steel plow not only built an industrial empire for Deere and Company, but it also opened up the Midwest to farming.

Within a decade, John Deere plows faced strong competition from Oliver Chilled Plows and others. James Oliver overcame the metallurgical problem that plagued all the steel plow companies. Oliver perfected a process that prevented the moldboard from warping during the tempering process. He went on to devise a process for chilling the surface of the plow while allowing the core to cool more slowly. Oliver's process made the plow's face hard so that it wore well, but left the inner portion of the metal soft and resilient so that it resisted breakage. At the same time, Oliver, Deere and others began to fashion their plows with a distinct twist to the moldboard, so that as a ribbon of earth passed over the moldboard it was stressed and pulverized. The twist resulted in better prepared soil than wedge-shaped plows produced.

Improvements in plow design during the first half of the nineteenth century were quite rapid. Less obvious were the small-scale improvements, the removal of those little imperfections that prevented brilliant but crude prototypes from being as satisfactory as their designers had hoped. Such small-scale improvements were made while farmers considered new-fangled contraptions, and helped smooth the way for widespread adoption. Minor changes also provided loopholes by which competitors squeezed past patent restrictions. Implement prices declined. Fierce competition and sophisticated manufacturing processes drove the industry from the village blacksmith shop into huge urban factory compounds that gradually changed family owners into stockholders in large corporations. By the time of the Civil War, building farm equipment required capital and organization on a scale available only to major corporations.[7]

The same competition that squeezed the blacksmith shop out of implement manufacturing encouraged the new farm machinery corporations to introduce new machines. Oliver mounted a plow on two wheels, which reduced draft, and then placed a seat on the wooden plow beam. Both horse and farmer benefited from reduced exertion, and the plow moved through the field faster because it was no longer restrained by the farmer's tired plodding. Deere and other implement works responded by adding a third wheel that stabilized the rig and took some of the weight off of the tongue. Competition prompted the replacement of the wooden beam with steel. From there it was a simple step to provide for two more horses and a second plow bottom. With that development, the farmer could purchase an implement that would double his hourly productivity— no small improvement.[8]

Farmers adopted new equipment for a variety of motives. In the case of the riding plow, there was the promise of creature comforts. But there were other incentives. The agricultural press, land grant colleges, and farming societies all urged the farmer to be "modern." And the farmer could see around him a society that was being transformed by machines. It was natural that he wanted to participate in the modernization process. There was ample opportunity for him to do so.

Improving plowing operations did not offer too much advantage if the farmer could not cultivate or harvest as much land as he could plow. Crop production is an integrated, sequential system. The limiting factor in that system is whatever operation restricts total production. Often improvement in one area only revealed a bottleneck in another area, so one invention frequently called for another.

The men and women who farmed in the 1940s witnessed in their lifetime a steady succession of improved cultivators, for example. As children, many of them had cultivated the young corn crop with a Georgia stock—essentially a blade set below the junction of triangular handles. With two to four trips per row (depending on row width), the youngster could "plow out" the weeds between the growing cornstalks. A "gee-whiz" cultivator had the same basic plow frame, but the working portion looked more like an overgrown spade fork. Generally it did the work of a Georgia stock in half the time. So did a "double shovel," which was more or less two Georgia stock bottoms placed on a single frame. No doubt the teen-age laborers welcomed such new improvements. But real progress came with the introduction of riding cultivators that cut the weeds and tilled the soil of an entire row in one trip. By moving his posterior, the young adult could keep the "wiggletail" cultivator close to the growing stalks— but not too close. And if two horses could pull a one-row cultivator, why not add two more horses and double the size of the entire rig? Obviously by purchasing a two-row cultivator the farmer and his wife doubled the effectiveness of each hour in the field.

This hypothetical couple may have "headed" goose-neck maize in their youth, walking down each row cutting each seedhead with a knife and dropping it into a tow sack. What an improvement when the owner purchased or (more likely) hired a custom operator with a row binder! Binders were highly sophisticated and highly complicated devices that cut each row of corn or milo and bunched the stalks together, and then tied each bundle with twine. Some models even carried a number of bundles until enough had been gathered for a shock. The mechanism that bound the bundles was susceptible to several maladjustments, which could cause intense annoyance in even the most placid personalities and sometimes provoked irritable farmers into paroxysms of vitriolic eloquence. But row binders cut the time required to harvest corn by substantial margins.

The tying technology that row binders employed was transferred from broadcast binders developed for small grains. Naturally, these had a history of their own. Cyrus McCormick and Obed Hussey are justifiably renowned for developing their early reapers that caught farmers' fancies (and their dollars) in large numbers after the Civil War. Instead of having to cut wheat with scythes or sickles, the farmer walked beside a reaper and raked the grain and straw off in bunches. Other workers then picked the bunches up and tied them manually. Soon self-raking reapers ap-peared, and eventually inventors added a binding mechanism to automate one more step in the harvesting process. Each step in the process, of course, reduced labor requirements.

Whether the farmer raised wheat or grain sorghum, the bundles had to be threshed. In the early national period threshing was done as it had been for ages, with flails, sledges or animal hooves. But even before the Civil War, experimenters worked on machines to separate the grain from the straw or stalks. Early machines used horsepower through contrivances that were more clever than durable, but they at least replaced hard labor. By the time steam locomotives could cross the continent, portable steam engines became common power sources for custom threshing operations. In the Red River Valley and in the far West the process of harvesting wheat had been further consolidated with horsedrawn combines. Virtually every aspect of crop production had been changed by machinery.

One of the ironies of the tractor is that it came so late in the process of farm mechanization. Most of the machinery in use in the field in the 1980s had horsedrawn antecedents prior to the advent of the tractor. There are exceptions such as forage harvesters, module makers, and rotary shredders, but such implements are the exception rather than the rule. That is not to say that all of those early machines worked well using horsepower—many did not. In most cases the addition of the tractor's internal combustion power improved the functioning of preexisting but redesigned machinery. Yet, paradoxically, the tractor was more fundamentally revolutionary than any of the machinery that preceded it.

Every contraption that farmers adopted and retained in the era before the tractor increased farm efficiency. Each reduced the number of man hours necessary to produce a given amount of produce. The United States Department of Agriculture's 1941 *Yearbook* estimated that it had required fifty to sixty hours to produce twenty bushels of wheat on an acre of land in 1822. By 1890 the same yield on an acre required eight to ten man-hours. The tractor and associated equipment would continue the trend. All the equipment that farmers adopted between 1822 and 1890 cost money, so the capital necessary to compete in farming increased steadily. If mechanization was the price of efficiency, an increased capital requirement was the cost of mechanization. But American farmers, like American manufacturers, had become accustomed to invention and innovation.

Just as much of America's nineteenth-century industry depended on steam power, so too did those farmers who first used mechanical power to augment human and animal muscle. In a typical application of steam power on the farm, a portable engine was linked to a separator ("threshing machine") by a leather or canvas belt that was several rods long. The exposed belt was a safety hazard, and workers also had to guard against the constant danger of sparks escaping into the dry stubble field or the straw stack. Nevertheless, steam appeared to be the only suitable power source for threshers.

The word *portable* as applied to early steam engines was a relative term, intended to contrast with huge stationary units built on stone bases. When the thresherman finished his job at a farm, he had to prepare his "portable" thresher engine for moving by removing various extensions and packing some parts away. In some cases, the boiler's smokestack had to be removed and stowed before a tongue and trees were attached so that a team of horses could drag the monster to the next farm. Such a move was not made any easier by the incredible weight of the steam engine which mired into every wet spot and threatened many bridges. In an era when only impoverished local governments provided funds for most roads, and provided little money even then, the collapse of a bridge under a steam engine was all too common. While the horses attached to the engine strained and tugged, other teams were needed to move the separator, bundle wagons, water tank, coal wagon, and sometimes even a sort of primeval camper. The delays involved in moving the heavy equipment cost the operator, tired his stock, and suggested that additional power was needed to move the steam engine.

One obvious solution to the problem of limited portability was self-propulsion. And some threshermen altered their engines to do just that. Soon manufacturers copied the idea of self-propulsion, starting with the Merrit and Kellogg Company of Battle Creek, Michigan and the G. and C. Cooper Company of Mt. Vernon, Ohio.[9] By the early 1880s, nearly all the engine manufacturers listed self-propelled models in their annual catalogs.

The mechanical expedients used to transfer power from the flywheel to the engine's wheels were often intricate, sometimes ingenious, and occasionally effective. Curiously enough, even though the engines moved themselves, a team of horses was often retained in front of the steamer to steer and assist through soft spots. The presence of horses was also thought to have a reassuring effect on the teams of passing wagons and buggies. Nevertheless, manufacturers eventually phased out hitches in favor of mechanical steering.

As soon as steam engines became self-propelled, experimenters began trying to plow with them, a development that manufacturers watched with keen interest. That was not the first effort to plow with steam, though. In England, early experimenters mounted winches on portable engines and pulled plows across the small fields with cables. Such cable plows, however, never succeeded in the United States where larger fields demanded excessively long cables. The new self-propelled engines seemed

to offer a better solution. A steam engine dragging a plow behind it was
not limited to small plots of land. In fact, because of the machines' huge
size and cost, steam plowing was successful only on giant farms. Even so,
early models often broke down. Factories soon reinforced drivetrains and
added stronger towbars, measures that certainly made the product better
suited for traction work, but that also added further to weight and cost.
Implement makers, likewise, began to produce heavy gang plows specifically designed for steam plowing. But there were too few large farms to
provide much of a market for steam plowing machinery.[10]

Despite its failure to provide plowing power for the average farm,
the steam engine played an important role in farm mechanization. Threshing engines awakened farmers to the potential of mechanical power in
other farming operations. Of course, plowing was one of the most power-
intensive of such operations. At the time, one expert estimated that plowing consumed 60 percent of the total energy used to produce a crop of
wheat.[11] Even if steam was not the ultimate fulfillment of the farmer's
need for plowing power, it did put farmers on the lookout for some
alternative.

Threshing and similar jobs created a market for a surprisingly large
number of steam engines in agriculture during the period from 1885 to
about 1920. At its peak in 1910, steam power furnished 3.6 million horsepower out of a total of just above 21 million in all forms on American
farms.[12] That was about 17 percent of the power available, a surprisingly
large percentage considering that many if not most of the engines belonged
to custom operators. But the engines' impact may have been even larger.
In his classic study of steam power, Reynold Wik reached a number of
conclusions. He noted that steam was the first sizable inanimate power
source on the farm, and for a long time the only non-muscular source.[13]
Steam made large-scale farming possible, but the high initial cost of steam
engines and the expense of purchasing off-farm fuel began the trend away
from self-sufficiency. When farm power came exclusively from human and
animal muscle, market prices were important but not crucial, because the
farm furnished food for both man and beast. When steam power arrived
on the farm, it brought bigger mortgages and greater indebtedness. That
meant that a farmer was compelled to raise stated amounts of cash, no
matter what happened to mercurial farm prices. And the cash outlay for
production increased as well, because fuel no longer came exclusively
from the farm's own hay meadow, oat field, and garden. In addition, with
increasingly complex machinery, "down time" became critical as repair

parts for untimely breakdowns came not from the neighborhood shop, but from factories in Racine, Wisconsin or Waterloo, Iowa. Steam engines accelerated the development of commercial farming and inducted the farmer into a mechanical and corporate world. In this, and by introducing the farmer to mechanical power, the steam engine prepared the way for the later appearance of gasoline tractors.

Finally, steam developed a reservoir of mechanical training for the operators, mechanics, and engineers who would later be necessary for tractors. Even though external and internal combustion engines differ in significant details, they operate upon similar principles. Mechanics who mastered steam engines undoubtedly found gasoline machinery less alien than those who had no such introduction. And most of the theories of thermodynamics were calculated and refined before engineers were called upon to estimate the energy of a quantity of burning kerosene in the cylinder of a tractor.

The experience with steam also aided tractor manufacturers in the area of marketing. According to Wik, it was the threshing engine manufacturers and implement makers who first developed the distribution network of branch houses, dealers, and salespeople that is usually credited to the automotive industry. In time, that distribution network played a major role in the rapid adoption of the internal combustion tractor when mass production began.[14]

The steam traction engine was a trailblazer, preparing the way for internal combustion. That particular role is so obvious that it would be easy to underemphasize it. Perhaps the best description of its significance was given by one of the men who later played a central role in the introduction of the tractor. Writing about fifty years after the event, Henry Ford still remembered in graphic detail the occasion of his first encounter with a self-propelled engine:

> The biggest event of those early years was meeting with a road engine about eight miles out of Detroit one day when we were driving to town. I was then twelve years old. The second biggest event was getting a watch—which happened the same year. I remember that engine as though I had seen it only yesterday, for it was the first vehicle other than horse-drawn that I had ever seen. It was intended primarily for driving threshing machines and saw mills and was simply a portable engine and boiler mounted on wheels with a water tank and coal cart trailing behind. I had seen plenty of these engines hauled around by horses, but this one had a chain that made a connection between the engine and rear wheels of the wagon-like frame on which the

boiler was mounted. The engine was placed over the boiler and one man standing on a platform behind the boiler shovelled coal, managed the the throttle, and did the steering. It had been made by Nichols, Shepard & Company of Battle Creek. I found this out at once. The engine had stopped to let us pass with our horses and I was off the wagon and talking to the engineer before my father, who was driving, knew what I was up to. The engineer was very glad to explain the whole affair. He was proud of it. He showed me how the chain was disconnected from the propelling wheel and a belt put on to drive other machinery. He told me that the engine made two hundred revolutions a minute and that the chain pinion could be shifted to let the wagon stop while the engine was running. This last is a feature which, although in a different fashion, is incorporated into modern automobiles. It was not important with steam engines, which are easily stopped and started, but it became very important with the gasoline engine. It was that engine which took me into automotive transportation. I tried to make models of it and some years later made one that ran very well, but from the time I saw that road engine as a boy of twelve right forward to today, my great interest has been in making a machine that would travel roads. . . .[15]

Significantly, Ford's narrative is bracketed by condemnations of farm work as containing "too much hard labour." It was written only a few years after Ford introduced his first tractor. In the half-century between Ford's boyhood meeting with the Nichols-Shepard and his entry into the tractor business, other innovators—many of them in the employ of threshing machine companies or farm implement manufacturers—had built experimental, prototype, and limited production traction engines, determining through trial and error the general parameters of good tractor design. Yet from the beginning these experimenters worked with a sound knowledge of mechanics, a knowledge derived largely from from experience with steam engines. They experimented knowing that farmers were interested in the potential of mechanical power. When Cyrus Gordon Williams (my grandfather and one of the first tractor farmers in his area) bought his first tractor shortly after World War I, it undoubtedly appeared to be the logical thing to do. His Concho County, Texas, farm was large enough to justify a tractor, and his experience indicated that mechanization was profitable. He was, like many other farmers of the era, ready for mechanical power.

NOTES

1. From the perspective of the present, some of the farmers of the past seem to have been slow to adopt new devices. That perspective is well expressed in Earl W. Hayter, *The Troubled Farmer: Rural Adjustment to Industrialism, 1850–*

1900 (DeKalb: Northern Illinois University Press, 1968). The question is largely one of whether nineteenth-century farmers are compared to their ancestors or to their descendants.

2. Percy Wells Bidwell and John I. Falconer, *History of Agriculture in the Northern United States, 1620–1860* (New York: Peter Smith, 1941), 124.

3. Lyman Carrier, *The Beginnings of American Agriculture* (New York: McGraw-Hill, 1923), 93–95. Carrier emphasizes that clean cultivation and inter-tillage in America antedates such practices in Europe. These techniques "had been commonly practiced in America by white men more than one-hundred years when Jethro Tull in England wrote his *Horse Hoeing Husbandry* and had been in use by the Indians untold centuries before." Tull's book was published in 1731. Writing of Tull, another historian commented that "He tried to impress on farmers the necessity of cleaning between rows of crops, and it was to simplify the work of hoeing that he advocated the use of mechanical drills which sowed seed in parallel rows," Charles Singer, et al. eds., *A History of Technology*, vol. 4 (Oxford: Clarendon Press, 1957), 5–6. Row cultivation in Europe may have been used in horticulture in the United Provinces (Holland?), but does not appear to have been a widespread practice in European field crops (Singer et al. *Technology*, vol. 3, 13).

4. David Eugene Smith, *Thomas Jefferson and Mathematics* (New York: Scripta Mathmatica, n.d.), 3; G. E. Fussel, *The Farmer's Tools 1500–1900* (London: Andrew Melrose, 1952), 45. Fussell related a "romantic story" which alleged that Jefferson plagiarized his formula from an English plow brought to the New World either through Scotland or Holland. This seems improbable. The existence of the plow was not proven, and no explanation was given about how Jefferson derived the mathematical formula from the object itself. Finally, had Jefferson plagiarized the design, he surely would not have then submitted it to the British Board of Agriculture, the very agency most likely to discover his alleged theft.

5. Clarence H. Danhof, *Changes in Agriculture: The Northern United States, 1820–1870* (Cambridge: Harvard University Press, 1969), viii. The account that follows uses Danhoff, *Changes*, and Bidwell and Falconer, *History of Agriculture*.

6. See almost any Deere catalog prior to the 1950s. See also Wayne Broehl, *John Deere's Company* (Garden City, N. Y.: Doubleday and Co., 1984).

7. Cyrus McCormick's Company illustrates both the competition and the coporate development of a relatively typical farm implement company in the period, even though McCormick was not a major plow manufacturer at that time, William T. Hutchinson, *Cyrus Hall McCormick* (New York: DaCappo Press, 1968 [reprint New York: D. Appleton-Century Co., 1935]).

8. The evolution of the plow in this period is well represented in the artifacts and catalogs of the Lubbock County (Texas) Museum or similar collections. The macroeconomic consequences of such technology (in the entire economy, not just agriculture) are considered in Nathan Rosenburg, *Technology and American Economic Growth* (New York: Harper & Row, 1972).

9. Reynold M. Wik, *Steam Power on the American Farm* (Philadelphia: University of Pennsylvania Press, 1953), 18–19, 61, 71, 76; Jack Norbeck, *Encyclopedia of American Steam Traction Engines* (Glen Ellyn, Ill.: Crestline Pub-

lishing Co., n.d.), 106, 172; R. B. Gray, *Development of the Farm Tractor in the United States* (St. Joseph, Mich.: American Society of Agricultural Engineers, 1974), 3–6.

10. Hiram M. Drache, *The Day of the Bonanza: A History of Bonanza Farming in the Red River Valley of the North* (Fargo, N. D.: Institute for Regional Studies, 1964).

11. Bradford Brinton, "Some Suggestions for Tractor Plowmen," *Threshermen's Review and Power Farming* (March 1914): 7.

12. W. M. Hurst and L. M. Church, *United States Department of Agriculture Miscellaneous Publication*, No. 157, "Power and Machinery in Agriculture" (Washington: United States Department of Agriculture, April, 1933), 11–12.

13. Wik, *Steam Power*, 209. In this he overlooked the role of the windmill, not only for pumping water, but also as a general source of farm power for grinding, milling, sawing, churning, and other jobs.

14. Wik, *Steam Power*, 155, 211, 213.

15. Henry Ford and Samuel Crowther, *My Life and Work* (Garden City, N.Y.: Garden City Publishing Co., 1922), 22–25.

2
The Birth of the Tractor

In 1892 when John Froelich built the first mechanically successful gasoline tractor, he explored a new technology. The Otto four-stroke cycle engine was only sixteen years old.[1] Internal combustion was something of a novelty even in the industrialized areas of Europe and North America. The work of automotive pioneers like Gottlieb Daimler, Karl Benz, René Panhard and the Peugot firm in Europe, and Charles Duryea in the United States was either in the earliest experimental stage, or still in the future. Ransom Olds was experimenting with a gasoline fueled steamer, and Henry Ford would not be ready to test his first horseless carriage for another year.[2] Yet in Iowa, during the autumn of 1892, Froelich built a gasoline traction engine that powered a thresher and pulled the rig from field to field.[3]

John Froelich's life is shrouded in obscurity, and his role in the history of the tractor is little more than a bit part. He pieced together a tractor from components made by other people, than vanished into other, less noteworthy interests. Froelich built his tractor by mounting a gasoline engine manufactured by the Van Duzen Gas and Gasoline Engine Company on a steam traction engine chasis made by Robinson and Company.[4] The following year (1893) Froelich incorporated the Waterloo Gasoline Traction Engine Company of Waterloo, Iowa. The company experimented with tractors for several years but sold only gasoline engines. Two years after incorporation, the Waterloo Gasoline Traction Engine Company became the Waterloo Gasoline Engine Company, the name change reflecting their major product. Froelich, who was more interested in tractors than engines, was vexed by the change. He withdrew during the reorganization and had little, if any, subsequent impact on tractor development.

Froelich's abrupt departure and the reorganization of the Waterloo company did not mean that the entire company had abandoned the concept of an agricultural tractor. Six or seven years later, the Waterloo Gasoline Company ventured into the tractor market and gradually established itself as a major tractor manufacturer. In 1918—twenty-five years after Froelich organized the company—the Waterloo firm was absorbed by Deere and Company.[5] Apparently along with the Waterloo Engine works, Deere also acquired its now-familiar green-and-yellow trademark color scheme.

While the Waterloo Gasoline Engine Company grew from a struggling seedling to a viable business, other firms experimented with the concept of an internal combustion traction engine. In 1892, William Patterson built a custom-designed tractor for evaluation by J. I. Case, but it apparently had little, if any, influence on the company. The Van Duzen Company, which furnished Froelich his engine, may have learned of tractor experiments through Patterson or by other means. In any case, the engine maker tested a tractor in 1893 that was similar to Froelich's. So did the Otto Gas Engine Company. Apparently neither experiment produced a viable commercial product. There is no record of anything developing from the Otto Company. Eventually, Van Duzen's design rights were sold to the Huber Manufacturing Company, an established name in steam tractors. The Huber Company then introduced a single-cylinder tractor with a transmission adapted from its steam tractor design. Huber built about thirty tractors the first year, but none of the early hybrid tractors were commercial successes. Neither Van Duzen, Otto, nor Huber received enough return from their investments to stay in the gasoline tractor business, and all withdrew before a salable design developed.

The first men to build commercially successful tractors were two young upstarts at Charles City, Iowa, less than sixty miles north of Waterloo on the Cedar River. According to an Horatio Alger-like article, Charles W. Hart dreamed from his early youth of motorizing farming, and he methodically set out to achieve that goal.[6] When the professors at Iowa State College of Agriculture and Mechanical Arts were unwilling or unable to help him along, Hart transferred to the University of Wisconsin where he apparently found a more congenial faculty. There he met Charles H. Parr, another engineering student, who was infected by Hart's dream. In 1897, while still students, they formed the Hart-Parr Gasoline Engine Company and began manufacturing stationary engines. The youths de-

veloped a successful business, but could not enlist local capital in a tractor
venture. Consequently, they moved back to Hart's hometown of Charles
City, where they built their first tractor in 1902. Their apprenticeship in
the engine business must have been good training, for their prototype
(which they sold that year) worked for seventeen years or longer. The
following year they sold fifteen Hart-Parr tractors, of which five were still
in operation in 1930. Hart-Parr soon led the tractor market. Reynold Wik
asserted that by 1907 about one-third of the nation's six hundred tractors
were built by Hart-Parr. Only Kinnard-Haines and International Harvester were large competitors.[7]

Hart-Parr's tractors were the most popular brand during the first
decade of the twentieth century, but tractors in use by 1907, if evenly
distributed, would have averaged only about one for each ten thousand
farms.[8] Nevertheless, because of its priority and its productivity, Hart-
Parr earned the right to be considered the founder of the gasoline tractor
industry. Their successors proudly claim that the "manufacturing plant
founded by Hart and Parr has been in continuous operation since
1901. . . ."[9]

Hart-Parr was not long without competition in the tractor market.
In 1902, with the assistance of George Perkins of the House of Morgan,
McCormick and Deering, the two largest harvesting machinery companies, merged. Together with a few smaller firms, they formed a large trust
that achieved an unparalleled horizontal integration of the industry. Almost immediately the new giant, christened the International Harvester
Company, began consolidating and rationalizing its production. While
consolidating model lines, the new company continued the process of
vertical integration begun by the Deering Company. International Harvester also began to expand the range of its products. The Chicago-based
firm thus helped to establish the trend toward "long-line" implement
companies—a trend that continued.[10]

Because harvesters, binders, and threshing machinery were closely
associated with traction engines, it is not surprising that International was
among the first implement companies to enter the tractor market. International and eleven other companies simultaneously began making tractors
in 1906.[11]

Something of the state of the art is apparent from the description of
International's 1906 tractor. It had a single-cylinder engine mounted on
rollers so that it could engage a friction drive mechanism. The crankcase
was open, cooling was furnished by a spray tank, and the ignition was a

primitive "make-and-break" system. Like the boll weevil in the ballad, the crude machine had trouble finding a home. In less than two years, International Harvester moved its tractor-building program from Upper Sandusky, Ohio to Akron, then to Milwaukee. With the final move, Harvester upgraded the design, replacing the crude friction drive with a geared transmission. By 1910, International Harvester became the country's leading producer, and by 1911 furnished about one-third of the United States' production. Yet the status of the tractor industry was such that even the largest manufacturer produced essentially a shop-made machine. Twenty years later, Harvester's president, Cyrus McCormick, recalled that the earliest plant "bore only slight resenblance to what would now be considered a mass-production shop." By 1912 International's annual production had increased to a few thousand units per year. Rumely and Hart-Parr, the next largest producers, produced even fewer tractors. Those numbers appear miniscule in retrospect, but they constituted the peak of a boom cycle. However in 1912, tractor production perched precariously on the edge of a bust, and soon collapsed.[12]

The boom-bust cycle of 1907–12 was a complex phenomenon. One obvious factor was the crude, experimental status of technology. Less obvious was the rapidity with which supplies of a new device satisfied and then exceeded demand, a factor that had two complicating parts.

First, several large, established companies staged a precipitous entry into the market, causing a rapid expansion of productive capability. For example, the Rumely Company, already well established in steam and threshing machines, began building their soon-to-be-famous "Oil Pull" in 1909. At the same time, the old implement manufacturing firm of B. F. Avery began selling tractors through its dealer network. The following year, the old, powerful steam traction company of Aultman-Taylor began manufacturing tractors. International also introduced its "Mogul" in 1910. Even companies outside of the implement industry were attracted to tractors. For example, the Minneapolis Steel and Machinery Company, later to be a part of Minneapolis-Moline, began selling tractors. In 1911, the huge railroad supply and windmill company of Fairbanks-Morse started building tractors. Finally, one of the largest steam engine makers, the J. I. Case Threshing Machine Company, also climbed on the tractor-drawn bandwagon.[13]

All of these companies were old, established firms. They were well financed and capable of concentrating enough capital to embark on substantial production runs which, although small in absolute numbers, were huge in relation to previous output. Even though these companies had organized marketing structures, they soon discovered that collectively they had oversupplied the market.

Smaller companies also contributed to the sudden swamping of the market. In Cleveland, the puny shop of the Morgan Engine Works dabbled in tractor making. Its product was statistically insignificant by itself, but was typical of innumerable overly optimistic and under capitalized enterprises that cumulatively rivaled some of the larger producers. The Morgan Engine Works is unusual in that it survived to become a part of J. I. Case's Wallis tractor facility, a very significant entity at a later period.

The small companies that plunged into tractor manufacturing before 1912 were attracted to an industry that seemed deceptively easy to enter. Like later aspirants, they purchased off-the-shelf components from various manufacturers and combined them with shop-built assemblies to form a tractor. Sometimes the combination worked; sometimes it was a mechanical Frankenstein. Even if the tractor worked well, however, the company frequently had problems with distribution and marketing. Unless it quickly found an unfilled niche, the prognosis for new entrants was grim. A few who concentrated on specialized or peculiar markets managed to survive.

The second factor that intensified the boom-and-bust cycle was the large size of the tractors produced in relation to the scale of most contemporary farms.[14] Most of the early tractors borrowed from steam traction engine design. *Scientific American* described in 1908 a twenty-two horsepower tractor that could pull six fourteen-inch moldboard plows and weighed "only 19,000 pounds." The article did not report the number of acres required for turning this sprightly behemoth. In 1908 the contestants at the Winnipeg tractor trials weighed in at some 537 pounds per horsepower.[15] Naturally, such dinosaurs were ill-adapted to farms in the United States, which then averaged less than fifty acres of harvested cropland per farm.

Cyrus McCormick, grandson of the inventor and president of International Harvester, stated that his company understood the problem and would have preferred to produce a smaller tractor, however the market demand was for big tractors. The firm's best seller was a giant of sixty horsepower.[16] Farmers in Canada and those in the Dakotas wanted large tractors that could drag huge gang plows through the virgin prairie sod. They, rather than the average farmer, had the motivation and money to purchase tractors. Their farms were large enough to accommodate the huge turning radius and general clumsiness of sixty-horsepower machines. Unfortunately for the implement manufacturers, the number of large farms was limited, and in due time even many of these abandoned tractors after their first one. Some three years later in 1915, two researchers from the Department of Agriculture, Arnold P. Yerkes and H. H. Mowry, dissected the pre-1912 boom. They methodically questioned tractor owners and analyzed their replies. The investigators learned that many early tractor purchasers found little use for their tractors after breaking the land for the first time. They estimated that more than four hundred farmers who had used tractors now recommended horses. In retrospect, they diagnosed the cause of the boom, using words of calculated precision. The "rapid growth of the gas tractor was not due to its superiority over the horse but to the fact that large tracts of unbroken prairie land were being opened up in the West and that sufficient horses were not available. . . . Where tractors had been used to any great extent or for a considerable length of time the business interests have become prejudiced against them and believe they have had an injurious effect on the farming community and general prosperity of the community . . . most businessmen do not consider the tractor a good investment for the average farmer."[17]

The men from the Department of Agriculture also concluded that tractors replaced only a negligible number of horses. They did qualify their conclusions, however, by reminding the reader that the tractor was still in the process of development, and that the early operators were not sufficiently familiar with the mechanisms involved. Repairs were a major expense, according to their survey, and they surmised that inefficient use, negligence, and unwitting abuse were often part of the reason for high repair costs. Their surmise is not subject to statistical proof, but it is reasonable given the novelty of internal combustion engines in that first decade of the twentieth century and given the frequent lubrication and adjustment requirements of early equipment. Yerkes and Mowry concluded that notwithstanding their criticisms of the tractor, its future was bright. "With the decrease in the price of farm tractors and an increase in their mechanical efficiency, simplicity and durability, all of which seem to be assured, together with more efficient operation by men who have been properly trained for their work, it is safe to predict that the tractor will soon become an important factor in reducing the cost of crop production on the average farm."[18]

The prognostication proved remarkably accurate, although it at first appears contradictory to much of the data and many of the conclusions in the bulletin. On closer examination, it shows how discriminating and thoughtful Yerkes and Mowry were in analyzing the evidence at hand. Such cheerful prophecies were made in 1915, however, well after the manufacturers had closed their books on the years from 1907 to 1912.

Even before tractors became widely used, most of the coverage of tractors by the nation's periodicals was distinctly positive. Although there were occasional derogatory articles, most journalists seem to have accepted an unstated premise that the tractor was a mechanical inevitability, destined to succeed eventually despite short-term weaknesses. Such an attitude reflected the general temper of the times, but when repeated in print countless times, such an outlook reinforced prevailing opinions and materially fostered tractor development. Public expectations compounded by the favorable attitude of the press became a self-fulfilling prophecy—the tractor had to succeed because people believed that it must.

The nature of the tractor's press coverage can be gauged by a sampling of articles from the time. A "golly gee" kind of article in a 1901 edition of the *Scientific American Supplement* described an "agricultural automobile" at the Pan-American Exposition in Buffalo. In an article in the *World's Work* two years later, the author somewhat prematurely hailed the automobile plow as "the latest successful invention in agricultural machinery." *Scientific American Supplement* again lauded an "agricultural gasoline automobile" in October 1905.[19] Two months later the popular magazine offered a hypothetical account of the expenses involved in "motor cultivation" compared to "horse cultivation." Such cost estimates, augmented later by edited and condensed records, became a popular form of comparison. Some three years later in 1908 a similar comparison "based on average North Dakota conditions" vindicated the kerosene tractor in competition with a coal burning steamer. Steam and "gasolene" were also compared in *The Engineering Magazine* in 1911, with the advantage given to the internal combustion machine.[20] The article—an abstract of a paper read to the American Society of Mechanical Engineers by Lynn Webster Ellis—warned that the United States was on the verge of becoming a net food importer unless something corrected the developing trend. He continued: "The farm field is the last and greatest stronghold of the horse and the most difficult place for the substitution of mechanical power. The farm tractor is the solution to the immediate problem." Ellis pointed out that animal feed alone cost the United States some $1.25 billion annually.[21]

Journal articles also contributed to the refinement of tractor design. For example, Lynn Ellis wrote a description of the engineering goals and the design criteria of a small tractor, anticipating the elements that were necessary to make it successful. Ellis understood the engineering and economic problems involved, however, and began the article with the sobering observation that "the scrap heaps of large tractor factories of solid reputation are strewn with small tractor failures." Before setting forth his criteria, Ellis cautioned that "Building a small farm tractor is no child's play, but ten times harder than building a big one . . . ," and agricultural editors called for small farm tractors even before the debacle of the big tractors. Ellis's article is similar to countless others of the period. The abundance and variety of press coverage strongly indicates that journalism helped create a climate of opinion from which tractors emerged. Farm papers and technical journals apparently helped formulate what the tractor would be and served as a communication medium—from consumer to producer, from manufacturer to potential customer, from thoughtful observer to designer, and from manufacturer to manufacturer. It is also noteworthy that although articles on tractors were common in farm papers, they were not parochial items restricted to the agricultural press and engineering sector, but rather generated sufficient general interest to be featured in all classes of magazines and papers.

The publicity that the press furnished the tractor was augmented by the great public tractor shows, the foremost of which was the Winnipeg show in 1908. Those responsible for the fair at Winnipeg, Manitoba, sought some method of boosting attendance at the fair and hatched the idea of a tractor contest. Initially, the competition was popular and unscientific, because it was calculated primarily to draw crowds. At first, manufacturers responded in a lighthearted vein, allowing their local dealers to participate in the event without factory support.[22]

As a device for drawing crowds, the Winnipeg contest was at best only a modest success, but as a method of disseminating information on tractors, it exceeded all expectations. It allowed farmers to actually see machinery at work, to touch sample tractors, and later to talk directly to laboratory engineers. After the first year, no one, including manufacturers, took the fair lightly.

In its second and third years, the contest became something of a showdown between internal combustion and steam. Steam engines were permitted for the first time in 1909. In 1910, the show delivered a decisive victory to the internal combustion camp. The age of steam was over, and the Winnipeg Tractor Trials had become exceedingly important to the industry, the press, and the farmer alike.[23] By 1912, tractor companies were spending an average of $1,800 to exhibit at Winnipeg, emptying office and factory so that managers and employees could observe the trials and evaluate the relative merits of various machines and components.[24] Farmers had the opportunity to compare machinery, and reportedly trusted those products that won no prizes above those that were not even entered. Above all else, the contest promoted the tractor, reason enough for manufacturer participation. According to the Avery Company, "We think these things promote the use of the tractor and consequently help sales."[25] Not surprisingly, the Winnipeg show first indicated the new direction in which the tractor industry was moving in 1913 when emphasis shifted to smaller, more versatile tractors:

> Manufacturers and farmers both are taking the smaller type of tractor seriously. . . . Interest is undeniably focused upon the more complicated situation on the average farm, where plowing is succeeded by disking, harrowing, and seeding, hauling and harvesting, where threshing is merely one of the short big jobs for the stationary engine and the lighter work of pumping, grinding, baling, shelling corn, etc. must be taken care of without too great a loss in mechanical efficiency.

> It is a nice nut for the manufacturer to crack, this actual replacing of the horse. Many farmers are doing it, with the very types of tractors that have been shown at Winnipeg in the last few years. But the public trial at Winnipeg or elsewhere, is a more convincing demonstration, and we venture to predict that the motor contests of the future will seek to bring out the greater factor of versatility rather than minute technical differences. Certainly such a wonderful educational force as the public motor competition will not have served its purpose to either the maker or the buyer until the last great question is solved and the unquestioned superiority of the general purpose tractor over the horse is demonstrated in a clear, convincing and absolutely impartial way.[26]

Tractor designers after 1912 turned toward two distinct but related goals. First, they tried to plan lighter, cheaper, better designed, more efficient, more agile tractors that were more nearly suited to the average, relatively small farm. Second, they began to seek a design versatile enough to replace the horse completely in all phases of farm production. There was almost unanimous agreement on the former goal. Vehement differences of opinion persisted on the latter.

In 1913, the Bull Tractor Company unveiled a new tractor that rattled the industry. The "Bull with a Pull" was a trim, agile, athletic youngster when compared to the doddering mammoths that it competed against.

The Bull was a fraction of the weight of older tractors, yet delivered five horsepower at the drawbar and twelve on the belt.[27] The tricycle tractor's single drivewheel was on the rear at the right side so that it ran in the furrow, a fact that caused early speculation about potential problems with soil compaction. But the iron ox's finest attribute was its price, variously reported between $395 and $800.[28] Cyrus McCormick, an official in the competing International Harvester Company, later summed up the little Bull tractor with concise sagacity. "It was never," he wrote, "a mechanically sound product, but its commercial popularity was such that it swept the field."[29]

In 1914 the Bull Tractor Company held first place in tractor production, falling to second place in 1915, fourth in 1916, and seventh in 1917. The Bull tractor died in 1918, followed by the parent company within two years. Ironically, the corporate officers and the Toro engine subsidiary survived, albeit outside the tractor industry. Even the Bull Tractor Company's brief success is somewhat remarkable. The Bull Tractor Company itself did little if any actual manufacturing. The tractors were farmed out to be manufactured by the Minneapolis Steel and Machinery Company. The company used engines from a variety of suppliers, but when engine suppliers could not meet Bull's needs, the Toro Manufacturing Company was formed to supply engines. After the parent company died, Toro grew into a major supplier of park and lawn equipment, irrigation hardware and other products.[30]

The instant success of the Bull Tractor Company influenced the tractor industry far more than the firm's eventual failure. Almost immediately, other manufacturers rushed out their own light tractors. Unfortunately, many of the smaller companies also copied the weaknesses of Bull's business organization. They lacked the vast, long-term capital and financial flexibility to survive, and like the Bull Tractor Company, ended their existence in a financial junk heap. Others reckoned the boom in small tractors to be a passing fad and remained devoted to large traction engines. The small tractor survived, however, even when many of the small companies did not.

One of the more successful companies in building small tractors was the Wallis Tractor Company, an enterprise associated with the J. I. Case Plow Works. In 1913, it introduced a tractor that was substantially more expensive than the Bull, but was far better designed and better built. For some time the Wallis people had built and sold a large tractor that they named the "Bear." Logically, then, when their small tractor emerged from the factory den, it was dubbed the "Cub."

The Wallis Cub initiated a configuration that became almost normative in the tractor industry. Much of that design showed obvious kinship to the automotive industry, but some elements were fresh and unique. Like most automobiles of the day, the Cub had a multicylinder engine set in front with its crankshaft parallel to the long axis of the machine. Behind the engine, the Cub had a transmission containing machined steel gears that ran in a sealed oil bath. The transmission was connected to the rear axle with an automotive-type propeller shaft. Both of the rear wheels were powered. The tractor's bearings were the latest roller type, not crude babbit. And like good quality cars, the Cub had pedals that operated the brakes and clutch. In all of the automobile-like features, the Cub differed from common tractor design, borrowing automotive features. Many previous tractors had one- or two-cylinder engines, that were often set crosswise in the frame. Many had exposed cast iron gears and chain drive, features vulnerable to sand and dust. Some even used friction drives.

In two significant features, the Cub departed from automobile design and from common practice in tractor construction. It had no frame in the conventional sense. The lower portion of the engine was a curved section of boiler plate, that connected to the front end assembly on one end and to the transmission on the other. The frameless design became an industry standard in subsequent years. The other significant feature in Cub design was its single front wheel. It was not copied widely immediately, but in the period between the introduction of the row-crop tractor and the introduction of power steering, the single-wheel or narrow front end became the "conventional" steering gear for tractors.

In nearly all of these matters, both automotive and unconventional, the Wallis factory anticipated later design trends. The Cub was recommended by an engineer as an exemplary design in 1918, some five years after its introduction.[31]

The engineers and managers in the tractor industry were well aware of the rapidly changing nature of tractor design. They pointed out that such variation and experimentation was not surprising, because "the first tractor propelled by an internal combustion engine was placed on the market 23 years ago."[32] So drastic were the changes in scale and sophistication as tractors were shrunk in size and price and expanded in quality, that the United States Department of Agriculture reports carefully distinguished between the older and new generations. In 1915, the department carefully noted the existence of newer, smaller tractors that "may fairly be considered as belonging to a different class than those under discussion in this bulletin," and suggested that the new class promised to be far more satisfactory than older tractors, but warned that "they have not been in actual use under service conditions for a sufficient length of time to demonstrate their utility conclusively."[33] The researchers cautioned at the end of their report that the data given represented "a machine in the process of development and not the record of a completed and perfected outfit." A year later, the same agency issued a report on tractors less than three years old in an attempt to supply current information available on the rapidly evolving field.[34] By 1918 Arnold Yerkes and L. M. Church had completed a report on the newer, smaller tractors, which the Department of Agriculture issued that summer.[35] This report was far more favorable to the tractor than earlier bulletins. It clearly reflected the rapid improvement of the rolling power plants.

The rapid development and notable improvement in tractors did not mean that there was any appreciable agreement on the best configuration for small tractors. Some had one drive wheel, others had two. A few had four drivers, while at least a few used a huge drum to transmit power to the ground. Drive wheels were located to the side, in front, and in the rear. In 1916, C. M. Eason, an engineer himself, tried to describe the prevailing thinking in tractor manufacturing circles. After noting the general reduction in size and the improvement in reliability, Eason despaired of selecting the particular design that would eventually predominate. He simply observed that there were more than 150 tractors on the market, and "no two of them alike." He suggested that engineers from various firms cooperate. "If all would work together more closely on this problem," he wrote, "a lot of freak failures would be avoided, the manufacturers would save money and the farmer would get the ultimate tractor sooner."[36] No such cooperation was forthcoming, but tractor designs did gradually begin to converge along common lines by the end of the First World War.

In 1915 and 1916, the three-wheel tractor with one drive member was popular with designers. The success of the Bull tractor no doubt led others to plagiarize that general approach. It was also very appealing in that such a system eliminated the need for a differential, thus simplifying the whole machine. The single-drive system was vulnerable to ambush from any devious mudhole or lurking sandy spot, however, and was utterly devoid of symmetry or aesthetic appeal. It was gradually left behind by two-wheel drive competitors.

Two or three seasons after Eason's appraisal of the zany variety in tractor designs, Raymond Olney was able to describe an emerging consensus that was consolidated to about two patterns. "It would appear," wrote the editor of *Power Farming*, that "the day of the freak tractor is past and that the evolution has advanced to a stage where the ideas as to the ultimate type or types center around only a few existing types." In 1918, Olney hailed a more or less standardized format for tractor design. Most had four wheels with the two rear wheels powered. Most had a four-cylinder engine, automotive-type transmission and more dirt-proofing.[37] The tractor was coming of age.

As has been suggested, the convergence of tractor designs was accompanied by an appreciable refinement of various components. Just as there was a period of rapid progress in basic configuration between 1916 and 1918, there were similar improvements in the tractor's constituent parts. In 1916, in a paper read before the Society of Automotive Engineers, Philip A. Rose described the state of the art in tractor design. Most used babbit bearings, exposed cast semisteel gear trains, and primitive transmissions. A few still used make-and-break ignition, and a few used chain drive. Some tractors still had single-cylinder engines with heavy flywheels, a design that made the tractor heavy in relation to its horsepower. The remainder were a fair mixture of two- and four-cylinder engines, some with the cylinders inline, others with them opposed to each other.[38]

Tractor design obviously lagged behind prevailing practices in the automotive field, a gap noted by other engineers as well. One of these engineers listed five criteria for a practical farm tractor: (1) it must be universally adaptable to all sorts of farm chores, (2) it must have a good power-to-weight ratio, (3) it must have a large area of contact between drive wheels and ground, (4) it must be cheap to operate (which necessitated an efficient transmission and a cheap fuel such as kerosene), and (5) it must be light and easy to operate and maintain. All of these criteria except the third and fifth might be assisted by borrowing automotive technology. Such a borrowing process was encouraged by popular demand as well as by economic interests.[39]

The convergence of tractor design and automotive design was hastened in 1917 when the Society of Tractor Engineers merged into the far larger Society of Automotive Engineers. Cyrus McCormick, apparently writing from personal experience, declared that "Immediately the tractor companies gained the benefit of the experience-earned knowledge of the automotive world."[40] Judging by the speed at which changes appeared in nearly all tractors between 1916 and 1918, McCormick's term *immediately* was no exaggeration. Primitive make-and-break ignitions, chain drives, and babbit bearings were quickly replaced in many models, or old models were replaced entirely. That autumn of 1917 *Power Farming* congratulated the Society of Automotive Engineers for their contribution to the tractor field, especially in the area of standardization.[41]

The rapid development of the tractor during the middle teens was not accompanied at first by a commensurate improvement in tillage tools and other field equipment.[42] Farmers were often forced to adapt existing equipment originally designed for horses. In the case of many drag-type tools—harrows, disks, drags and some plows—a change in motive power made little difference. In others (such as grain drills, a few plows, and binders), the machinery functioned well enough, but the farmer realized little net savings. Two workers were still required for the operation: one to run the tractor, the other to run the implement. Because tractors ran faster than a plodding team, machinery usually wore out quickly when used with the new power source. And horse-drawn implements were often too weak for satisfactory conversion, because a tractor, unlike horses, did not hesitate or slow down under the strain of rough going.[43] Undoubtedly the imcompatibility of horse-drawn implements with tractor power retarded the adoption of the tractor until the systematic development of new tools.

The mismatching of tractor and implement was slowly overcome as manufacturers gradually designed compatibility into power machinery. As tractors became more popular, implement manufacturers designed equipment for tractor use, finally building a specific plow for a given model tractor.[44] Almost from the first, for example, a few custom plows were available with some form of power lift, and some offered a primitive form of draft control. But such designing increased the expense of power farming, because every change of tractors meant a new set of implements.[45] Such costs may explain the popularity of clumsy, drag-type equipment and help to explain why the tractor remained primarily a source of power just for plowing. Tractors seldom hauled wagons or performed other diversified jobs.[46]

Tractor designers were consistantly tempted to increase the size of their tractors. One engineer wrote succinctly, with at least a touch of frustration, that "For many years the tendency has been to keep increasing or trying to do just a little more, no matter what size [tractor] you started with. . . . One of the hardest things in the tractor business is to have the nerve to stand pat and build one size and not keep constantly increasing the size so that it will do a little more work."[47] The tractor designers' temptation to increase capacity was probably due in part to feedback from the farm. In a 1920 survey that included tractors built and sold as much as five years earlier, a sizable percentage of farmers surveyed recommended a tractor one size larger than the one that they owned. Their opinion was well known at factory drafting tables.

Farmers also wanted lower-priced tractors. Here their demands were probably easier to resist. Until the advent of mass production, costs remained relatively high, due in part to the expense involved in piecemeal construction. There had been a dramatic decrease in the average price during the mid-teens, but prices began inching up again before the war. Probably few people were surprised at the results of Yerkes and Church's survey, which suggested that medium-priced tractors were the best investment.[48] The more expensive units were overpriced relative to their working ability, whereas the cheaper tractors were not sufficiently well built. A tractor that struck a happy medium between the two extremes was the best investment.

The farmers' economic plight pressured the planners to include one other interesting specification in their design criteria. For a little time, before the development and widespread adoption of the catalytic cracking techniques by the petroleum industry, gasoline was a relatively expensive fuel, one for which the farmer was forced to compete with the motorist. Hart-Parr confronted this expense by introducing a kerosene-burning tractor.[49] Many, and perhaps most, tractor models were soon designed or altered to become "dual fuel" engines—starting on gasoline but running on kerosene once the manifold was hot enough to vaporize the heavier fuel. But kerosene also had disadvantages. When using the cheaper fuels, engines frequently required a water injection system to prevent overheating, and sometimes as much as 25 percent more kerosene than gas was required to do a given amount of work.[50] In the large, early tractors, kerosene appeared to be more advantageous as a fuel than it did in smaller tractors, but it remained a common fuel almost three decades after the advent of the small tractor.[51]

Most people doubted the efficiency and flexibility of the tractor in doing light work such as cultivating, mowing, and similar jobs that were generally regarded as the permanent and indisputable property of the horse. Such pessimism afflicted even the most cheerful tractor propagandists. Lynn W. Ellis and Edward A. Rumely in their classic *Power and the Plow* foresaw much of what transpired in mechanization, yet they wrote: "It is doubtful if the really efficient farm tractor can be an all-around machine. The requirements of the farm as to power are far too widely separated."[52] Ellis and Rumely did note, however, that a tractor had recently been introduced that was designed essentially for cultivation.

The cultivation of intertilled crops constituted a mechanical stumbling block for early tractors. Perhaps no better description can be found of this shortcoming than that implied in a laudatory description in *Scientific American*: "Every operation in the handling of wheat crops, oats and flax can be done with the tractor. Everything in connection with the corn crop up to the moment of planting can now successfully and economically be done by this revolutionary engine, and its work begins again with the harvest of the crop, the filling of the silo, the shelling of the corn and the shredding and baling of fodder."[53]

Obviously, tractors were more beneficial to small-grain farmers than to those in the vast corn and cotton belts. There, "Few if any, tractors . . . are utilized for such work [cultivation] with entire satisfaction."[54]

Some daring innovators soon attempted to adapt both tractor and farming practices to mechanical cultivation. One claimed that he cultivated better with mechanical power because he only had to watch the ground and was not distracted by managing a team of horses.[55] His particular accomplishment was all the more surprising, because his tractor appears to have been a ponderous Heider Rock Island. Fortunately, manufacturers were experimenting as well, and one—Moline—soon tried out a much more nimble machine.

The Moline "Universals" were bizarre-looking contraptions. Their dominant feature was a pair of large steel wheels mounted on either side of a frame and were placed at the front of the structure. In order to keep the chassis level, the left wheel could be raised or lowered to adjust to the job the machine was performing. If the tractor was plowing, the right wheel rolled in the furrow, and the left wheel was raised to level the entire structure. When cultivating, the left wheel was lowered to the same plane as the right.

Early models of the Universal were powered by a two-cylinder, horizontally opposed engine. The cylinders were parallel to the long axis of the tractor. The skeletal frame was hinged behind the engine and drive wheels, the front section bearing a small gear that articulated upon a rack to pivot the aft frame. Although the rear portion could be supported by a dolly, it was intended to rest upon whatever implement was in use, at least in normal use.

The driver's seat was suspended over the extreme rear, directly over or behind most implements, where both tractor controls and implement levers were in easy reach of the operator. When the tractor was furnished with the factory-built plow, the controls included a power-lift for the plow.[56] The object of the deliberately unorthodox design was simple: The Moline Universal was intended to replace the horse in all farm operations including cultivation. Apparently it was tolerably successful in achieving its designers' goals. It undoubtedly was a commercial success, because Moline Plow Company planned production of twenty thousand tractors annually by 1918.[57] Its unique design was consistently complimented in trade publications, which pointed out the benefits of the weight distribution of a two-wheel drive tractor.

In 1918 Moline engineers incorporated electric starters, electric lights, and an electric governor on their tractor. Electric starters were not common then even in automobiles. It was a revolutionary advance, but it did not catch on for many years. Moline enclosed all components of the drive system to protect them from harmful abrasions and provided an up-to-date four-cylinder, inline power plant.[58] The Moline Universal model "D" soon afterwards enjoyed the flattery of imitation when Allis-Chalmers and others introduced look-alikes. Allis-Chalmers's price of $790 was undoubtedly an unwelcome competition as was the advent of the first mass-produced tractor at about the same time.[59] Had the Moline Universal been backed by a healthy corporate structure, however, its technical excellence might have given it a distinct advantage over new competitors. But the Universal died in the wreckage of the Moline Plow Company. The company was headed by John N. Willys of automotive fame and staffed by unquestionably talented men like George N. Peek, the author of the Peek Plan for agricultural relief, and Hugh S. Johnson, later master of the NRA Blue Eagle. But in the postwar agricultural depression the Moline Plow Company went into receivership, and the Universal tractor died.[60] The concept of an all-purpose tractor—although not mortally wounded—suffered from the debacle as well, at least temporarily. An engineer who was a lifelong observer of the tractor industry described the reaction. Although the Moline Universal died for reasons that had nothing to do with the features that made it an " 'all-purpose' machine," P. M. Holdt and some other commentators felt that its demise reinforced industry opposition to the idea of a general purpose tractor.[61]

The eccentric appearance and early death of the Moline Universal should not obscure its long-term contribution to the development of the agricultural tractor. Many thousands of the little tractors were built; so many, in fact, that they appear in a disproportionate number of photographs from the era. For many farmers, particularly in the corn belt and in specialty crop areas, the Moline Universal was the first tractor to succeed in their area, and it furnished them with their first favorable impression of mechanical power. More important, the Moline Universal pointed the way toward the all-purpose or row-crop tractor that emerged several years later.

About the time that the Universal Tractor Company began its work on its versatile machine, other engineers in other companies were exploring an alternative technique for horseless farming: a machine designed exclusively to cultivate and do nothing else.[62]

Unlike the Moline Universal, the new machines were designed not for versatility, but were totally specialized. They were popularly and quite accurately called "motor cultivators."[63] Around 1914, Allis Chalmers, Avery, Bailor, Emerson-Brantingham, and a number of other manufacturers brought out relatively similar designs. An extant Emerson-Brantingham motor cultivator is typical of such machines. It was powered by a four-cyliner, in-line, water-cooled gasoling engine built by LeRoi. A single front wheel was mounted in front of the machine and served to steer it. The rear of the implement rested on what appeared to be a reinforced version of an EB two-row horse-drawn cultivator modified slightly to incorporate shafts and chains to drive the rear wheels. In lieu of a clutch and transmission, Emerson-Brantingham substituted a large friction disk that engaged a sliding drum when the machine was in motion. The drum could be moved close to the center of the drive disk for a low drive ratio, or out toward the edge for a higher ratio. The operator sat suspended behind the cultivator, surrounded with an abundance of wheels and levers. He operated both power unit and implement without hired help. His position doubtless provided him with a copious coating of dust to help absorb his perspiration.[64] Indefatigable pollsters Yerkes and Church apparently had high hopes for such specialized contraptions, speculating that such outfits might become "valuable auxiliaries to the tractor" that might result in "a much greater displacement of horses than . . . the tractor alone. . . ."[65]

Motorized cultivators ultimately did not justify the high hopes of their backers. Unlike plowing, cultivating was not a power-intensive operation, and thus it did not justify a heavy investment in specialized equipment. A few affluent farmers purchased the machines and presumably disposed of their horseflesh. But for most farmers, the purchase of both a tractor with related equipment and a motorized cultivator was a capital investment of impossible proportions.[66] Yet even in retail failure the motor cultivator injured the future prospects of the farm horse, for if farming without draftstock was possible with a motor cultivator, it was possible with other, less specialized equipment. What was needed was not more specialized equipment with minimal versatility, but less specialized equipment with maximum versatility. The industry awaited the development of the technological capability to build a general purpose tractor, and the popular cognizance of the need for it. L. W. Ellis summarized the problem with an admirable combination of brevity and completeness, "The ultimate need is for a durable, self-contained power plant, so light as neither to waste power in moving it nor to compress the ground in passing over it, capable of performing every operation from driving stationary machines, to plowing, pulverizing, seeding, cultivating, harvesting and hauling the crop. It must be low in cost, both initial and operative, economical of labor and repairs, and capable of utilizing economically whatever fuel may be most abundant and easily procurable."[67]

In the period from the birth of the tractor to the entry of the United States into the First World War, farmers watched the development of tractors with keen interest tempered with realistic skepticism. But farmers did not rush to town and purchase tractors because of several serious defects. At first tractors were too large and too expensive for the average farmer. They could not cultivate. And farmers only gradually learned to apply the tractor to farm tasks. As these problems were gradually and partially solved, tractors became more popular.

After the large tractors were discredited in 1912 and 1913, tractor manufacturers were forced to redesign and refine their tractors, changes that farmers appear to have appreciated almost immediately.[68] Between 1915 and 1918, farmers' attitudes seem to have changed at least as fast, if not faster, than the mechanical development of the tractor. In 1915, Yerkes and Mowry stated flatly that "the tractor appears to have made for itself no important place in the agricultural economy of the country."[69] By 1919 Yerkes and Church reported that it had already proved very valuable "under some circumstances, even though the machine was still mutating and developing." They cautioned potential buyers that the tractor had not, at that time, "assumed a fixed place in general farm practice."[70] But just as the manufacturers were gradually tailoring the tractor more closely to the farmer's needs, farmers were learning to adapt their practices to efficient tractor use. For most farmers, the learning process involved secondhand information, because few could afford to experiment in their own farming operations. On January 1, 1917, for example, there were about 127 farms per tractor in use.[71] Each time the tractor farmer took his machine to the field, neighbors paused to watch his trials and his successes. Fenceline observation and chatter quickly revealed which tasks the tractor could do efficiently, and which it could not. Many farmers were well justified in delaying their tractor purchases until the machine was better refined.

A few farmers were simply prejudiced against gasoline plow horses. For several years the Port Huron Company offered remanufactured steam engines in advertisements that prominently featured the phrase "Steam—the Dependable Power."[72] The advertisement obviously implied that the alternative mechanical power source—internal combustion—was *not* reliable. It played on farmers' suspicions of the internal combustion tractor. Even many of the skeptics were cautious in their criticism, however. One wrote the *Breeder's Gazette,* "I am watching the development of the tractor with great interest but shall certainly not buy one until a better type has been put on the market. . . ." He wanted a tractor that could reduce the number of horses on his farm.[73] Although he himself was pleased with his tractor, dairy farmer B. J. Rutenik reported that his neighbors still viewed his tractor with "a good deal of doubt and misapprehension."[74]

Some caution and skepticism persisted, but opposition to the tractor gradually dwindled. Many opponents, like the ones above, more or less reserved the right to adopt the machine later. Apparently some of the people who still preferred horses or mules had become convinced that the tractor was inevitable.[75] Arnold P. Yerkes, in an article in which he criticized some of the more exaggerated claims of tractor advocates, concluded that he and those whom he criticized were in agreement that the tractor would eventually be standard equipment on the ordinary farm.[76] Arthur L. Dahl, writing in *The Independent,* equated the use of the tractor with up-to-date farming.[77] Apparently, by the time America entered the First World War, an ubiquitous if somewhat nebulous concensus prevailed: Draft animals were old fashioned—tractors owned the future.

Acceptance of the tractor concept—if not the tractor itself—was promoted immeasurably by the evangelistic enthusiasm of many early owners. But the motives behind their advocacy are not always obvious. One opponent of the tractor ascribed many of the pro-tractor letters to "inspired sources," with the obvious implication that the inspiration was not divine but derived from vested interests.[78] Undoubtedly, some new tractor owners were defensive about their novel innovation and preached the gospel of mechanization as a way of justifying their own actions. Yet, in countless letters from tractor owners, there shone a genuine and unaffected enthusiasm for the tractor. In April 1917, *Power Farming* published in one issue letters from fifteen farmers who used tractors. Even though they were probably solicited, these letters, like dozens of others at the time, urged other farmers to adopt the gospel of labor-saving devices and buy a tractor.[79]

A more direct index of and stimulus for acceptance of tractors by farmers came when those who had experimented with the first light tractors purchased their second tractor—either for expansion or replacement. Such financial commitment probably spoke far more eloquently than dozens of letters to the editor.[80]

Another factor that increased acceptance of tractors by farmers was the increasing versatility of the tractor. Some of that versatility was due to the more maneuverable size and the refinement of general design. Even more was due to the farmers' developing awareness of the tractor's potential. The United States constituted virtually a continental market—but a market that could be exploited only by machinery adaptable enough to work a staggering variety of crops. To achieve full market potential, the same tractor had to work tropical sugar cane and sub-Arctic wheat, Atlantic coast truck farms, midwestern corn fields, irrigated southwestern cotton fields, and apple orchards in the Pacific Northwest. Once the engineers developed a compromise design adaptable to such a variety of conditions, the farmers still had to apply the technology on a practical level. By 1918 that application was well under way. Tractors were used in the soggy rice fields of California and the Deep South. Tractors worked in Minnesota, Texas, the Dakotas, Kansas, and Canada.[81] The tractor was no longer a laboratory prototype, but had moved to on-the-job field tests across the United States.

The popular enthusiasm for tractors even worried some of the backers of mechanical power. A writer in *Power Farming* contended that the tractor's most dangerous enemy was the "blue sky" salesman. Such overly enthusiastic talkers made exaggerated claims for the tractor, and consequently gave farmers expectations that no tractor could satisfy. The subsequent disappointment, he said, harmed the power implement industry more than the furious opposition of diehard horse lovers.[82]

About the time the first tractors began sprouting on prairie farms, the small, portable internal combustion engine made its debut. Because little, one-cylinder power plants were smaller investments and cheaper to operate, they were much more rapidly adopted than tractors. Small gasoline engines were handy power sources for corn shellers, feed grinders, washing machines and milking machines. As early as 1910, farmers used some six hundred thousand or more small engines. One writer claimed that the small engines produced more horsepower for American farms than all the power used in American industry.[83] Such small engines preceded the tractor or the automobile on many farms. On even more farms, portable engines arrived at about the same time as the first car or tractor. In either case, the gasoline engines of less than a dozen horsepower were often the teaching machines or laboratory specimens that familiarized many farmer-mechanics with the rudiments of internal combustion. They made farmers more familiar with spark plugs, valves, gasoline, and other mysteries of the smelly world of petroleum-fueled power. Familiarity with small engines made larger ones—such as those found on tractors—seem less alien and less sinister. Beyond that, relationships between tractors and single-cylinder engines are hardly demonstrable, but the increasing use of both power sources suggests that the two complemented each other more than they competed. Certainly each in its separate way assisted the farmer in his chores and caused him to rely on more and more mechanical power.

The young men who sought agricultural deferments on the eve of American entry into World War I were approximately the same age as the tractor. As they had matured, so had the farm tractor. The machine had matured from a cumbersome, clumsy toddler into a lithe, agile (but smaller) mechanical servant. At about the same time that that generation of boys faced the prospects of confronting the technology of mass destruction, the tractor was being prepared for the initiation rites of industrial maturity—the beginning of mass production.

NOTES

1. C. Lyle Cummins, Jr., *Internal Fire* (Lake Oswego, Ore.: Carlot Press, 1976), 160–78.

2. Allan Nevins, *Ford: the Times, the Man, the Company* (New York: Charles Scribner's Sons, 1954), 125–35; "A Gasoline Steam Carriage," *Scientific American* (May 21, 1892): 239. See also Glen A. Niemeyer, *The Automotive Career of Ransom E. Olds* (East Lansing: Michigan State University Business Studies, 1963), 8–9.

3. E. Wennergran, "His Neighbors Laughed, but John Froelich Invented a Tractor Anyway," *Wallace's Farmer and Iowa Homestead* (March 18, 1950): 380–81.

4. Froelich was not the first to attempt an internal combustion tractor as the Charter Gas Engine Company had mounted some of their engines on Rumely trucks as early as 1889, but these were apparently unsuccessful. For this and much of the following paragraph, see Roy Burton Gray, *Development of the Agricultural Tractor in the United States* (St. Joseph, Mich.: American Society of Agricultural Engineers, 1974), 13–14, 20–21.

5. Florence L. Clark, "Marker for Iowan Who Built First Tractor," *Hoard's Dairyman* (October 25, 1939): 566.

6. Edward Mott Wooley, "Secrets of Business Success," *The World's Work* (January 1914): 346–52.

7. Reynold M. Wik, *Henry Ford and Grass-Roots America* (Ann Arbor: University of Michigan Press, 1972), 84; Gray, *Development of the Agricultural Tractor*, 17, relates the traditional story of W. H. Williams of Hart-Parr coining the term *tractor* in 1906. Gray then shows that it was used as early as 1890 in a patent application. Wik, *Grass-Roots*, p. 245n, shows that the term is at least as old as 1856. The term is used consistently without definition in "The Scott Gasoline-Motor-Propelled Agricultural Tractor," *Scientific American Supplement* (November 4, 1905): 24948–49. However, seven years later *Scientific American* found it necessary to explain: "What is the tractor? The Term 'tractor' is merely a newer and more convenient term to designate the traction engine. . . ," "The Winnipeg Motor Contest: A Motor Show for Farmers," *Scientific American* (June 29, 1912): 583.

8. The United States' Census of 1900 listed 5,737,372 farms with 283,218,000 acres of cropland harvested. The 1910 census figures were 6,361,502 farms, with 311,293,000 acres harvested. See *Agricultural Statistics 1950* (Washinton: United States Department of Agriculture, 1950), 565.

9. White Motor Corporation, *Progress . . . [sic] in Tractor Power from 1898: Charles City Plant, White Farm Equipment, (Form No. R-1673)* (Charles City: White Motor Corporation, March 1975), 2. The factory's products have successively born the trade names of Hart-Parr, Oliver, and finally White Tractor Company.

10. A brief contemporary description of the merger and its general impact may be seen in W. B. Thornton, "Revolution by Farm Machinery," *The World's Work*, vol. 6 (August 1903), 3766–79. A description of the merger itself, written by an interested, partisan commentator can be found in Cyrus McCormick, *The Century of the Reaper* (Boston: Houghton Mifflin Co., 1931), 111–27. Gray, *Development of the Agricultural Tractor*, 15, states that the Massey-Harris Company also started producing a tractor in 1902, the Wallis "Bear." This appears to be incorrect. Massey-Harris did not acquire Wallis products until they purchased the assets of the J. I. Case Plow Works in 1928. See *Report of the Federal Trade Commission on Manufacture and Distribution of Farm Implements* (Washington: Federal Trade Commission, 1948), 59, 61. Also neither of the corporate histories of Massey-Harris/Massey-Ferguson mention the 1902 tractor, and in fact, both comment on Massey-Harris's first tractor in 1919 (which was a failure) and the advantages of acquiring the J. I. Case Plow Works' Wallis tractor in 1928: E. P. Neufeld, *A Global Corporation* (Toronto: University of Toronto Press, 1969);

Merrill Denison, *Harvest Triumphant: The Story of Massey-Harris.* (New York: Dodd, Mead and Co. 1949).

11. McCormick, *Century of the Reaper*, 124, 130, 132, 155–56.

12. Reynold M. Wik, "Henry Ford's Tractors and American Agriculture," *Agricultural History* 38 (April 1964): 81 and McCormick, *Century of the Reaper*, 159 both have good accounts of this bust. For a near-contemporary account see C. M. Eason, "The Tendency in Farm Tractor Design," *Power Farming* (February 1916): 9.

13. Not to be confused with the J. I. Case Plow Works, a separate concern and subsequent producer of the Wallis tractors.

14. Gray, *Development of the Agricultural Tractor*, 17–19. A good example of the oversized and cumbersome machinery of this first generation of tractors is described and pictured in Perkins, "A Gasoline Tractor of 100 Horsepower Capacity," *Scientific American Supplement* (March 18, 1911): 168. For a more complete description of some of the more extreme monsters on the era see Reynold Wik, "Mechanization of the American Farm," *Technology in Western Civilization*, vol. 2: *The Twentieth Century*, eds. Melvin Kranzberg and Carroll W. Pursell (New York: Oxford University Press, 1967), 360.

15. Frank C. Perkins, "The Modern Farmer's Tireless Horse," *Scientific American* (June 27, 1908): 453, 458; McCormick, *Century of the Reaper*, 157. See figures for 1900 and 1910, *Agricultural Statistics 1950*, 565.

16. See McCormick, *Century of the Reaper*, 156–58.

17. Arnold P. Yerkes and H. H. Mowry, "Farm Experiences with the Tractor," *Bulletin* No. 174 (Washington: United States Department of Agriculture, April 15, 1915), 4–9, 37,38.

18. Yerkes and Mowry, "Farm Experiences," 41; Wik, *Grass-Roots*, 85.

19. "Automobiles in Agriculture," *Scientific American Supplement* (March 16, 1901): 21078; Thornton, "Revolution," 3775; "The Agricultural Application of the Gasoline Automobile," *Scientific American Supplement* (October 21, 1905): 24917.

20. "The Scott Gasoline-Motor-Propelled Agricultural Tractor," *Scientific American Supplement* (November 4, 1905): 24949; Perkins, "Tireless Horse," 453, 458; L[ynn] W[ebster] Ellis, "Economic Importance of the Farm Tractor," *The Engineering Magazine* (May 1911) 335–38. Ellis was an engineer, and his spelling is consistent with other petroleum compounds, if not common usage.

21. Lynn W. Ellis, "The Problem of the Small Farm Tractor," *Scientific American* (June 7, 1913): 518–19, 525, 528.

22. For a good description and history of the Winnipeg contest, see L. W. Chase, "The Motor Contest," *The American Society of Agricultural Engineers— Transactions* 6 (December 1912): 55–86; McCormick, *Century of the Reaper*, 157–58; also L. W. Ellis and E. A. Rumely, *Power and the Plow*, (Garden City, N.Y.: Doubleday, Page and Co. 1911), 3,4.

23. L. W. Ellis, "The Winnipeg Tractor Trials: Sixth Annual Event Shows Farmers Ready for General-Purpose Engines," *Scientific American* (September 6, 1913): 202.

24. Chase, "Motor Contest," 56–62.

25. J. B. Bartholomew, "Discussion on the Motor Contest," *American Society of Agricultural Engineers—Transactions* 6 (December 1912): 201.

26. Ellis, "Winnipeg," 204.

27. Wik, *Grass-Roots*, 87; Gray, *Development of the Agricultural Tractor* 22, fig. 23.

28. Ellis, "Problem," 307; retraction, "The Tractor with Drive Wheel in the Furrow," *Scientific American* (May 13, 1916): 512. Prices from, respectively, McCormick, *Century*, 159, 160; Wik, *Grass-Roots*, 87; and Norman F. Thomas, *Minneapolis-Moline: A History of Its Formation and Operations* (New York: Arno Press, 1976), 243.

29. McCormick, *Century of the Reaper*, 159, 160.

30. Gray, *Development of the Agricultural Tractor*, 28. For a good con-temporary description, see P. M. Heldt, "Tractor Activities in the Twin Cities," *Automotive Industries* (October 24, 1918): 702–5; Thomas, *Minneapolis-Moline*, 243. The Bull/Toro story would appear to have the potential for an interesting corporate history.

31. Victor W. Page, "The Motor Driven Commercial Vehicle: Distinctive Agricultural Tractor Design," *Scientific American* (May 18, 1918): 458. The tractor is not identified in the article, but is unmistakably a Wallis "Cub".

32. Victor W. Page, "Modern Agricultural Tractor Design," *Scientific American* (July 29, 1916): 100, 101.

33. Yerkes and Mowry, "Farm Experience," 2, 3.

34. Arnold P. Yerkes and L. M. Church, "An Economic Study of the Farm Tractor in the Corn Belt," *Farmer's Bulletin* 719 (Washington: United States Department of Agriculture, May 1916), 1. L. M. Church may have been Lilian M. Church, a remarkable woman who transcended some of the sexual stereotypes of her day, but who remains relatively obscure today.

35. Arnold P. Yerkes and L. M. Church, "Tractor Experience in Illinois: A study of the Farm Tractor under Cornbelt Conditions," *Farmer's Bulletin* 963 (Washington: United States Department of Agriculture, June 1918), 5.

36. C. M. Eason, "The Tendency in Farm Tractor Design," *Power Farming* (February 1916): 9.

37. Raymond Olney, "Signs of Progress in the Farm Tractor Field," *Power Farming* (October 1918): 10, 11.

38. Philip S. Rose, "Farm Tractors," *Scientific American Supplement* (April 29, 1916): 282–83.

39. Page, "Modern Agricultural Tractor Design," 100. A particularly inter-esting convergence of such interests is seen in an article in a farm journal by an official of the SKF Ball Bearing Company, Horace Niles Trumbull, "Why Use Anti-Friction Bearings on the Tractor," *Power Farming* (September 1916): 34.

40. McCormick, *Century of the Reaper*, 163.

41. Raymond Olney, "A New Chapter in Farm Tractor Development," *Power Farming* (September 1917): 7–9.

42. Yerkes and Church, "Economic Study of the Tractor in the Corn Belt," 24.

43. For a brief description of the problems of redesigning horse-drawn

mowers and binders, see the last two paragraphs of David Beecroft, "Fifty Tractors in National Demonstration at Salina," *Automotive Industries* (August 1, 1918): 213.

44. This can be readily seen from the catalog of almost any manufacturer of the time. In many of the tractor descriptions, the plow was sold with the tractor. Such was the case with the Hoosier tractor, which came with a custom-built Grand Detour plow, "Hoosier Farm Tractor," *Automotive Industries* (January 10, 1918): 132–33.

45. The author's grandfather, Cyrus Gordon Williams, owned successively three different tractors: a Fordson, a Farmall "Regular," and a John Deere A. With each purchase he was forced to replace much if not all of his mounted tillage tools and planters (John D. Williams, interview, Wickett, Texas, August 1978).

46. Arnold P. Yerkes and L. M. Church, "The Farm Tractor in the Dakotas," *Farmer's Bulletin* 1035 (Washington: United States Department of Agriculture, 1919), 18.

47. George T. Strite, "Fundamentals of Tractor Design," *Automotive Industries* (February 14, 1918): 354.

48. Yerkes and Church, "Farm Tractor in the Dakotas," 9.

49. Edward Mott Woolley, "Secrets of Business Success," *The World's Work* (January 1914): 346–49.

50. Rose, "Farm Tractors," 283.

51. Yerkes and Mowry, "Farm Experiences," 18–19; Yerkes and Church, "An Economic Study," 18.

52. Ellis and Rumely, *Power and the Plow*, 105, 327, 328. Edward Aloysius Rumely was born in 1882 in La Porte, Indiana to the well-known thresher-manufacturing family. In 1906 he received his M. D. degree from Freiburg University. The following year he founded Interlaken School. He worked for the M. Rumely Company from 1907 to 1914. While there, he actively supported Theodore Roosevelt's 1912 campaign and other liberal causes.

In 1915 Rumely bought the New York *Evening Mail* and served as its editor and publisher until 1918. During World War I he was convicted of violating the Trading with the Enemy Act because he had purchased the *Evening Mail* with German funds. Rumely was pardoned by President Coolidge after wartime fervor had waned.

Rumely spent the twenties researching and promoting vitamens. With the collapse of the economy during the depression, Rumely returned to politics as a supporter of Franklin Delano Roosevelt, becoming an economic adviser to the president during the early New Deal. However, after he and the president quarreled vigorously, Rumely helped found the Committee for Constitutional Government in 1937.

During the McCarthy era, Rumely was convicted of contempt of Congress for refusing to reveal the names of subscribers to committee literature. The case was fought all the way to the Supreme Court, which unanimously ruled in favor of the former farm machinery manufacturer. Rumely, who spent much of his life in New York, returned to LaPorte around 1959 and died there on November 26, 1964, after 82 eventful years. He published books on farm machinery, education, nutrition and health, and politics.

53. "The Winnipeg Motor Contest," 583. The baling referred to here involved the use of a hay press, manually fed and manually tied; the pick-up, self-tying baler did not become popular until after World War II.

54. Yerkes and Church, "An Economic Study," 21.

55. F. M. Henderson, "Farming with a Gas Tractor in Indiana," *Power Farming* (September 1916): 7, 8, 53; C. H. Eason, "The General Purpose Farm Tractor," *Journal of the American Society of Automotive Engineers* 12 (June, 1923): 602.

56. This description is based on an extant artifact in the Lubbock County Museum, Shallowater, Texas. Ironically, perhaps, with the introduction of the huge four-wheel-drive tractors in the 1960s and 1970s, many manufacturers have returned to an articulating frame that bends the tractor in the middle to turn it. Undoubtedly, modern hydraulics perform the task with considerably less exertion by the driver than was necessary on the old Universal.

57. The Moline Plow Company, *Minute Books*, May 10, 1917, as cited in Thomas, *Minneapolis-Moline*, 127.

58. "Remy System Combines Governor with Generator," *Automotive Industries* (May 2, 1918): 862–63; P. M. Heldt, "Moline Model D Tractor," *Automotive Industries* (June 6, 1918): 1091.

59. Allis Chalmers Company, "Here It Is!" [advertisement], *Orange Judd Farmer* (November 30, 1918): 508–9. Also see Thomas, *Minneapolis-Moline*, 129.

60. Thomas, *Minneapolis-Moline*, 147–77.

61. P. M. Heldt, "Varied Types of Farm Work Handled by Air-Tired, All-Purpose Tractors," *Automotive Industries* (December 28, 1935): 854.

62. Ellis, "Problem of the Small Farm Tractor," 526.

63. Gray, *Development of the Agricultural Tractor*, 23, fig. 30, gives a brief general description of motor cultivators.

64. For a description of one of the first motor cultivators, see Jacques Boyer, "An Automobile Hoe," *Scientific American* (November 28, 1908): 376. For a description at the height of the machine's limited popularity, see "Among the Manufacturers: The Avery Corn Cultivator," *Power Farming* (July 1916): 62.

65. Yerkes and Church, "Tractor Experiences in Illnois," 26.

66. For an almost eloquent analysis of the failure of the motor cultivator, see Olney, "Signs of Progress," 10.

67. Ellis, "Economic Importance," 336 Cf. C. M. Eason, "Tendency in Farm tractor Design," *Power Farming* (March 1916): 43.

68. Yerkes and Church, "The Farm Tractor in the Dakotas," 3, 4.

69. Yerkes and Mowry, "Farm Experiences with the Tractor," 44.

70. Yerkes and Church, "Tractor Experiences in Illinois," 4.

71. There were an estimated fifty-one thousand tractors on 6,478,000 farms, the average size farm was 144 acres, Bureau of the Census, *Historical Statistics of the United States [from] Colonial Times to 1970*, Part 1 (Washington: United States Department of Commerce, September 1975), 457, 469. Another estimate places the number of tractors at ninety thousand, but that would almost necessarily have included all the tractors manufactured to 1917—including those abandoned or scrapped, Wik, "Mechanization," 360.

72. Port Huron Engine and Thresher Company, "Attention! Steam, the Dependable Power," [advertisement], *Power Farming* (October 1916): 46.

73. H. C. Taylor, "Difficulties in Using Tractors," *Breeder's Gazette* (May 16, 1918): 1036.

74. B. J. Rutenik, "The Efficiency of the Farm Tractor," *Hoard's Dairyman* (July 28, 1916): 5, 14.

75. RWC [*sic*] "Horses, Mules and Tractors," *Breeder's Gazette* (October 14, 1915): 660.

76. Arnold P. Yerkes, "The Tractor and Farm Management," *Power Farming* (March 1916): 66.

77. Arthur L. Dahl, "The Tractor That Never Tires," *The Independent* (May 25, 1918): 321, 339.

78. J. F. Dyer, "Experience with Tractors," *Breeder's Gazette* (February 10, 1916): 307.

79. *Power Farming* (April 1917): 12–13, 51–55.

80. Rutenik, "Efficiency," 5.

81. Arthur L. Dahl, "The Tractor's Place in the Rice Fields," *Power Farming* (July 1918): 13; C. V. Hull, "Power Farming America's Vast Prairies," *Power Farming* (October 1916): 7.

82. H. N. Fullenweider, "Mixing Common Sense with Tractor Operation," *Power Farming* (June 1917): 9.

83. Edward A. Rumely, "The Passing of the Man with the Hoe," *World's Work* (August 1910): 1324–58; "Farmers' Power Plant," *Literary Digest* (November 27, 1915): 1219–20.

The Nichols Shepard Steam Engine that inspired young Henry Ford was fairly typical of the external combustion antecedents of the tractor. (Stemgas Publishing Company, Lancaster, Penn.)

A reproduction of Froelich's 1892 tractor. (Deere & Company)

John Froelich, one of the first men to build a tractor. (Deere & Company)

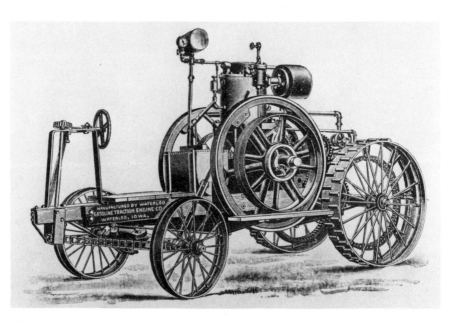

The Waterloo Traction Engine was the direct descendent of the Froelich traction engine and an ancestor of modern John Deere tractors. (Deere & Company)

This Hart-Parr tractor in the Smithsonian Institution is one of the oldest extant tractors. (National Museum of American History, Washington, D.C.)

"The Bull with the Pull" was the first inexpensive tractor. Although it sold well for a few months, its single drive wheel provided such poor traction that the design soon failed.

Emerson-Brantingham Motorized Cultivator. Before agile tractors were developed, row-crop farmers either had to retain horses for cultivation or purchase a specialized, self-propelled cultivator such as this one. The expense involved in buying and maintaining two separate machines (tractor and cultivator) made them unfeasible economically. (Lubbock County Museum, Shallowater, Tex.)

The Moline Universal tractor was the first mechanically successful row-crop or general purpose tractor. Unfortunately, it did not survive the plunging farm prices that followed the end of World War I. (Lubbock County Museum, Shallowater, Tex.)

3
The Fordson Era

On June 28, 1914, most American farmers were busy at their usual summer tasks. It was haying time in many sections of the country; corn-belt farmers rushed to get their fields cultivated, and many southern farmers were planting their cotton crops. Nationwide, few farmers had time to ponder the significance of the dramatic events being reported in the newspapers—news of the assassination of Crown Prince Franz Ferdinand. The Austrian heir-apparent had died in a small Balkan town whose name most farmers could not pronounce in a province that seemed totally removed from Iowa or Georgia.

Gradually, as the nations of Europe mobilized for war, Americans began to sense that something important was happening. By planting time in 1915, it had become clear that events in Sarajevo, Bosnia, had a direct influence on farm prices in DeKalb, Illinois. Nor were demands for grain and meat the only effects of World War I on the American farmer. The incomprehensibly bloody carnage in the fields of France and the fringes of Russia was deadly not only for human draftees, but also for hapless draft animals. The horses and mules that pulled the wagons, caissons, ambulances, and hearses suffered a high mortality rate that soon resulted in a world-wide shortage of horses. As early as 1915, *Scientific American* predicted that an "enormous drain on America's horse supply . . . will hasten the adoption of tractors hitherto accepted with some hesitation."[1]

Europe at war was far from self-sufficient, and the unparalleled expenditures of the combatants benefited American farmers. Cotton, for example, was necessary for uniforms, tents and even the nitrocellulose that fired naval guns. And in total war, wheat for bread was almost as much a weapon as powder. Farm produce prices soared, war stimulated business, and farmers expanded.

Three years later the war moved closer. On April 6, 1917, the United States declared war on Germany, and the farmers who sold their grain and hogs for eventual consumption in Europe now faced the prospect of seeing their sons, hired hands, and neighbors exported to feed the conflict. If the farmer escaped the pointed finger of the draft—and chances were good that he would—he had to compete for hired labor against wages paid in "the feverish activity in the industrial centers, with their constant call for fresh laborers." Labor, like horses, became scarce. Farmers paid more than twice as much in wages in 1919 as they had in 1909. The combination of a horse shortage and a labor shortage was joined by the threat of a national food shortage. It was a staggering prospect.[2]

Tractor promoters used the threat of shortages to full advantage. Beginning in May 1917, Raymond Olney, the editor of *Power Farming*, pleaded with farmers to use tractors to release men for the armed services and to provide the food the allies needed. Even non-farm journals sounded a similar plea. Tractors were good for the nation, and farmers who bought tractors helped win the war.[3]

Using income from wartime prices, farmers responded to 1917 pro-mechanization propaganda by ordering tractors. Demand for the machines soared. Farmers purchased 49,504 tractors for use in the United States.[4]

Tractor manufacturers were overwhelmed by the increased demand and struggled to fill incoming orders. The addition of some eighty-five new manufacturers boosted the number of tractor makers more than two hundred. By prodigious exertion, U.S. tractor makers rolled out some 62,742 units in 1917.[5]

The tractor's potential for replacing horses and plowhands was more than just clever advertising. It was in fact plausible and was inviting to Europeans as well as Americans. In late 1917, the French government entered negotiations to purchase Universal tractors from the Moline Plow Company, and Moline soon entertained inquires from British interests as well. Even without foreign orders, Moline, like most United States' manufacturers, was straining its capacity while trying, simultaneously, to expand its facilities.[6] But orders poured in from home and abroad.

In terms of raw numbers, neither the output of Moline alone, nor of the industry as a whole seems remarkable at first glance. Yet, given the prevailing assembly methods, American production was a significant accomplishment. Moline's shop was modern by the standards of its time. The factory's organization attracted the attention of the *American Machinist* as a model of large-scale production and machining, using a process of "progressive assembly." The Moline shop, however, was a far cry from the giant assembly lines of the mass-production automobile builders. The automakers dwarfed even the largest tractor shops.[7]

The tractor industry could not satisfy the exploding demand for tractors that came with the war, but they were not alone. The railroads failed to allocate their rolling stock and had to be nationalized before rail traffic moved efficiently. When private firms could not provide large numbers of suitable aircraft engines, the government had to develop a standardized "Liberty" powerplant. Given the temper of the times, it is not surpising that there were also calls for government patronage of tractor manufacturing. An American engineer cited "the inability of companies to produce tractors fast enough and the quality of tractors that are being turned out," and therefore proposed that "a Liberty tractor should be designed to be manufactured by the government during the war." The proposed design would then have become common domain at the end of the conflict.[8]

The suggestion of government participation stirred up a storm of protest not only among entrepreneurs but also among engineers. The meeting of the Society of Automotive Engineers pounced upon the proposal with vehement hostility. The president of the Avery Company was incensed because he thought rumors of such suggestions hurt sales (although there is no extant evidence of this). Engineers at the meeting objected that toolmakers, draftsmen, and other skilled workers were too scarce to undertake such a project. Even the United States Department of Agriculture objected to the proposal through Arnold Yerkes, one of the bureau's leading engineers. Although the proposal died almost as quickly as it had been born, it illustrated the willingness of Americans in the period to consider alternatives to traditional laissez-faire ideology in national emergencies when such policies hampered production.[9]

In retrospect, federal entry into the tractor business would probably have been a boondoggle, because the war did not last long enough for any results to accrue from such an endeavor. Most Liberty tractors—like many Liberty aircraft engines—would have probably been consigned to the status of postwar surplus. The reaction to the proposal also indicates that the attitudes subsequently associated with the Coolidge years had already permeated the tractor industry.

Killing the Liberty proposal, however, did not eliminate government involvement in the tractor industry. Manufacturers who had opposed the Liberty tractor project still had to face the reality of government rationing of raw and semifinished materials. Shortages handicapped manufacturers sufficiently to reduce the number of tractors produced.[10] Yet shortages did not prevent new companies from entering the tractor-building business. Some of the new entrants were old firms already established in other lines, such as the Massey-Harris implement and harvester people. Massey-Harris attempted to copy the Parrett Company's successful tractors, introducing three models in 1918 and 1919. Like so many other entrants, Massey-Harris discovered that building tractors was not nearly as simple as it appeared. By 1923 the Canadian-American company had discontinued its first tractor effort.[11] Many others did not last as long.

Despite the best efforts of both old and new tractor factories, a shortage of tractors continued and made it imperative for the country to use every tractor as efficiently as possible. Farm periodicals exhorted farmers to keep their tractors working. Some magazines even advocated rigging up lights on the front of a tractor to extend plowing time into the night. As the war continued, state governments even began purchasing tractors in order to assure that each machine received maximum use and no owner hoarded his machine's potential.[12]

In the excitement of wartime, publications as diverse as the *American Fruit Grower* and *Horseless Age* promoted tractors as a national necessity. Civic organizations took up the cause. The Fort Worth Chamber of Commerce conducted a survey to determine the tractor needs of Texas. They concluded that there were a mere 4,144 units in the Lone Star State, some 5 percent of the number they felt were needed. The Cowtown chamber called for the sale of $50,000,000 worth of tractors to their state. Other writers chided the South for its backwardness in using tractors, denying that the smaller fields in the South were a legitimate reason for rejecting power machinery. Power advocates did not, however, offer to loan the poor smallholder or sharecropper in the South the requisite capital for the purchase of a tractor. Even as the war drew to a close, the tractor was touted as the agent for agricultural victory.[13]

As the guns cooled after the Armistice, there was time for reassessment of the tractor's role in the Great War. *Automotive Industries* computed wartime tractor production at 150,955. Many firms with little experience had entered the field. All faced shortages because of rationing, labor scarcity, and other factors. Yet despite wartime impediments to production, there were almost three times as many tractors *manufactured* during the war as had been *in use* at the time that the United States entered hostilities.[14]

The greatest single change in the tractor industry during the war was the introduction of true mass production. Although automotive-type engineering gradually influenced tractor designing before the First World War, it did not bring with it the feverish assembly lines that characterized the automobile industry. The tractor makers improved and streamlined their methods from time to time, but true mass production began only when an automaker plunged into tractor building.

For a number of years before the war, various rumors circulated that a well-known automaker was about to begin building tractors. Such rumors were creditable, in part because of the very nature of the tractor itself. Certainly the tractor was not an agricultural implement of the conventional sort. As persistent borrowing from automobile technology had indicated, in some ways the tractor was more similar to an automobile than to a plow or a binder. In 1915, the Universal Tractor Company advertised in *Horseless Age*, the trade journal of automobile dealers, appealing to car retailers to sell the Universal tractor. The advertisement claimed that auto dealers were winning the tractor trade from implement dealers.[15] Ironically, the Universal tractor itself soon became part of the implement industry, but the idea of car dealers selling tractors persisted.

Rumors of automakers tooling up for agricultural machinery took on real substance in 1918, when *Scientific American* reported that "the manufacturer of a very popular small car" was developing a tractor. The magazine described the tractor in an impartial, factual manner. The twenty-five-hundred pound tractor had no frame in the conventional sense, because the engine block and transmission case served as the basic structure. The new machine was kerosene fueled, had a fly-wheel magneto, a thermo-siphon cooling system, and a belt pulley.[16] Other reports of the tractor also leaked out. Edward Crossman foresaw major changes if a certain pacifist automaker did, in fact, introduce a small, cheap tractor. "If the long-promised tractor of the 'dove of peace' variety is as cheap and efficient as we're told it will be, the tractor will even clank merrily around the little farm of the two-horse farmer, unable now to afford a machine. A tractor for $250 will revolutionize American farming. Doubting the appearance of such a machine, consider the $360 automobile, with us to the number of 1,5000,000."[17]

The news leaks were precisely the type that Henry Ford engineered for maximum publicity. They worked well.

Henry Ford's lifelong interest in the tractor is well known, but he did not commit himself to commercial production until relatively late. As stated earlier, Ford wanted to build tractors even when he was a child. The automaker experimented with tractors as early as 1905 or 1906, and an experimental model from that period is extant in Ford's museum at Dearborn. Reynold Wik contends that Ford hoped to manufacture tractors as early as the opening of the Highland Plant and the birth of the Model T around 1908, but that the stockholders delayed his plans. Ford regularly attended tractor shows, meeting Edward Rumely at the Winnipeg show in 1910. Ford predicted a rosy future for gasoline tractors, a conclusion that Rumely must have shared. Ford finally decided to manufacture a gasoline tractor, but his experiments with a Model T tractor were not successful.[18]

But Ford did delay. He announced his intentions with maximum press coverage in the spring of 1915, predicting a price of $200.[19] Although the press was too awed by the eccentric industrialist to emphasize the fact, Ford's prediction was either a wild off-the-cuff boast or a calculated falsehood, because scrap metal the weight of a Fordson tractor would have been worth more than his predicted price, and later tractor prices never approached the figure, even when Ford was losing money on them. Nevertheless, Ford continued his bombastic announcements for some time, but no tractors were forthcoming. In January 1916, *Scientific American* carried an account of Ford's experiments, although the article reads suspiciously like a Ford press release. The first Fordson finally appeared on the market in 1917. Ford's dawdling was finally terminated by intense diplomatic pressure from the British government, which desperately needed tractors for the wartime food effort.[20] Once committed to produce Fordson tractors in England, Ford built them in the United States as well.

The Fordson tractor, when it finally went into production, was slightly distinctive from most other tractors of the day. Like the earlier Wallis tractor, it was frameless. This feature not only made for a clean design, but it also allowed the machine to be built in three separate segments that could be joined in final assembly. This unitized construction also allowed the Fordson to be built lighter and smaller than most other tractors on the market. The Fordson was also unusual in having a worm gear final drive in the differential case on the rear axle. It was feature of dubious benefit. No less dubious was Ford's use of a flywheel magneto, which was cheaper to produce than an impulse magneto but made starting far more difficult. Apparently, both worm gear and low-tension magneto were incorporated into the Fordson because of Ford's own unpredictable prejudices. Other unique features were the result of designing a tractor specifically for mass production.

By the time Ford's assembly line began to roll, the United States was at war. Ford announced that he would distribute his tractors only through state governments. It was a clever move, because it made the automaker appear to be a superpatriot. In fact, of course, it saved him the cost of building a distribution network. And when Ford's "$200" tractors were finally shipped to the various states, they carried a tag for a "spot cash price of $750 f.o.b." Ford's rhetoric exceeded his ability to deliver in at least one other area as well. He promised Oliver Chilled Plows with his tractors at a very attractive package price of $875. Unfortunately, Ford failed to consult or even inform the Oliver corporation before his announcement, which occasioned considerable consternation at the plowmaker's offices.[21]

Several states purchased Fordson tractors for various plans involving community use. Pennsylvania bought forty. Michigan, Ford's own home state, bought one thousand for resale to farmers who agreed to share then with neighbors. Such plans for government distribution were obviously departures from traditional laissez-faire theories, but were justified by the wartime emergency.[22]

Ford Motor Company's production was impressive. In March 1918, the company was finishing eighty units per day and was expanding toward a goal of three hundred units per day by December. By 1920 Ford boasted that he had sold one hundred thousand tractors. That number represented almost twice the number of tractors in use when the Fordson was unveiled in 1917. And, in fact, Fordson officials boasted in the 1920s that they had built more than half the tractors in the United States, and they were probably not exaggerating. Ford's engineers were deservedly famous in the automotive industry for their ability to fine-tune an assembly line, and when they applied their talents to building tractors, the automotive industry reported upon the procedures in detail. The implement makers were momentarily stunned.[23] Such production was breathtaking.

The flood of Fordsons out of Detroit overwhelmed the capacity of the wartime allocation system, and Ford began selling his tractors through Ford automobile dealers, many of whom were reluctant to sell and service tractors until Ford ruthlessly compelled them to do so. The decision to market tractors through car dealerships was a major factor in the Fordson's eventual demise, but Ford had few alternatives at the time and did not foresee the problems that would arise from the arrangement. Ultimately it proved advantageous for tractor companies to have a fairly integrated approach, one which offered a coordinated tractor and implement. But Ford had decided to leave the manufacture of implements to others and prohibited his dealers from carrying any farm tools except for a few approved items such as an Oliver No. 7 plow or a Roderick Lean Disk.[24] Most of Ford's competitors offered tractors as part of a "long-line" implement business. Such long-line manufacturers attempted to offer one or more models of every implement the that farmer might need.

At first the older implement and tractor manufacturers were ill equipped to compete with Ford. But as they recovered from the initial shock of the Fordson's fecundity, and as they saw other automakers preparing to exploit the wartime tractor boom, the old farm equipment companies began a frantic program of reassessment and retooling. A two-phase tractor war began. In the first, the automotive industry and the implement industry struggled to see which would control the building and sale of tractors. In the second phase, after the majority of the automakers withdrew from tractor making, Ford Motor Company challenged International Harvester, the champion of the farm equipment industry.

The opening rounds of the struggle between the automotive and tractor businesses as described in *Automotive Industries* clearly show the initial attitude of the automotive industry. "The opposition of many old-line tractor makers to the Fordson tractor has been very generally construed as not so much an attack against Henry Ford as rather a defensive act of those tractor manufacturers against the invasion of the old tractor circle of makers by the modern automobile and truck industry."[25]

The statement has a tone of condescension about it that was typical of much of the automotive industry, which entered the fray with smug confidence in their productive capability. Even the auto industry's opponents recognized that advantage and others that the automakers held. The auto industry had far greater access to capital and greater credibility with investors. The automobile men knew the value of standardization. And the automotive engineers were thought to be less preoccupied with petty engineering novelties and more concerned with "average results." Yet in accepting the challenge of the automotive engineers, and while aware of the car builder's advantages, an agricultural engineer cautioned that the automakers were entering a field that was new to them. He warned that the carmakers "will probably spend fortunes to learn what many of us have learned." It was an accurate prophesy.[26]

Ford was not the only automobile company to plunge into building tractors. The Chandler Motor Company also started making heavy tractors for the United States government, which furnished them to its allies. Maxwell introduced a sophisticated "auto engineered" design in early 1918. Giant General Motors bought the Samson Sieve Grip Tractor Company primarily to get manufacturing rights to a tractor. General Motors announced that their new tractor would be sold by a "tractor selling division of the corporation," and that it would be priced to compete with Fordson. Samson's advertising emphasized that it was a division of General Motors, "manufacturers of the Buick, Cadillac, Chevrolet, Oldsmobile and Oakland motor cars—all quality products. The Samson (Model M) is a *quality* tractor." In stressing quality, General Motors apparently contrasted its products with Ford's, whose name was associated with cheapness. In fact, the Model M was very similar to the Fordson.[27] Like Ford, General Motors advertised long in advance of its ability to deliver.

As automobile manufacturers began making tractors, they encouraged their dealers to retail the machines. *Horseless Age*, one of the major publications of the retail trade, assured its readers that automobile dealers had tremendous opportunities before them in tractor sales. More than that, tractor sales were touted as a patriotic duty to help forestall wartime shortages. *Automotive Industries* caried a bold headline proclaiming "Implement Dealers Losing Tractor Sales." The article below the headline claimed that most implement dealers were reluctant to carry tractors, but that new car dealers were willing to sell them. According to *Automotive Industries*, 60 percent of John Deere's dealers would not handle tractors, and of the remaining 40 percent, only a fraction carried proper stocks of spare parts. According to the magazine, the implement dealer's future was bleak because "the sentiment was general among automobile distributors and dealers that unless the implement dealer dominates in the selling of tractors and power machinery he will be wiped out."[28] But automakers and auto dealers both underestimated their opponents.

In October 1918, the War Industries Board curtailed steel deliveries to tractor and implement makers, limiting allotments to 75 percent of the previous year's tonnage. The newer entries into tractor making immediately cried foul:

> It is hinted by many of these newer tractor manufacturers that there is a very large representation of the old-time tractor interests on the War Industries Board and connected with this organization [i.e. the National Implement and Vehicle Association, the implement industry trade group], and that the ruling savors very strongly of being a protection measure in these old-line concerns, which have resented very much in the last two years the entrance of new blood into the tractor field and have also strongly resented

the entry of the auto manufacturer, as well as the influence of automobile design on tractor engineering.[29]

   The newer tractor makers offered no conclusive evidence to support their claim of skulduggery, and they certainly made no comments on the ironic coincidence of General Motors' sudden interest in tractors just as steel began to be rationed. But the newcomers did organize and succeeded in forcing the government to revise its allotments, purportedly the first successful challenge of wartime apportioning. Under the revised ration plan, the older manufacturers got 75 percent of their earlier use, whereas late entries got enough steel to have a "fair chance to develop." *Automotive Industries*, which characterized new producers like Henry Ford as the "small man," noted that many of the older builders had enough inventory on hand so that the 25 percent curtailment was no curtailment at all. The order also prohibited automobile-to-tractor conversion kits, which had proven almost useless anyway.[30]

   While the automakers were pressuring Washington to provide them with steel, they were also experimenting with new tractors. In 1919, Samson introduced a contraption called the "Iron Horse." The General Motors subsidiary's idea of an Iron Horse had four drive wheels instead of hooves. Its wheels were chain driven, a system that looked clumsy even in photographs. The monstrosity was steered with differential clutches similar to those on a crawler. To turn left, the left wheels were slowed or stopped and the right ones kept turning or even speeded up. Like a horse, the Iron Horse was "guided with reins or lines."[31]

   By October 1919, Samson was ready to unveil the prematurely heralded "Model M," but it was March 1922 before *Automotive Industries* finally got to examine the machine. The journal speculated that the tractor had been fairly well perfected. The engineer who wrote the article also speculated that the tractor would be expensive to manufacture.[32] In any case, by this time World War I was over, and rationing ended.

   With the end of steel rationing, the automobile manufacturers (except Ford) lost interest in tractors almost as rapidly as they had embraced them earlier. Later, *Fortune* reported that General Motors had lost $33,000,000 on the Samson tractor.[33] Only occasionally in subsequent years have American automakers dabbled in tractors—never seriously or on a large scale. In this respect, the U.S. is somewhat unusual. Almost all of the world's automobile manufacturers have tractor divisions—for example, England's British Leyland, France's Renault, Germany's Daimler-

Benz, Italy's Fiat, and Japan's Mitsubishi all build tractors. In the United States alone, the implement industry was strong enough to dominate tractor manufacturing and integrate it into the implement industry.

After the withdrawal of other automakers, Henry Ford's personal crusade to dominate tractor manufacturing continued unabated. For many employees of the Ford Motor Company, it must have seemed like an annoying eccentricity of the "old man." For International Harvester, Ford's continuing in the business meant a life-or-death struggle.

In 1919, tractors were Harvester's largest product. If Ford swamped the tractor market and International Harvester failed to recover a sizable majority of tractor sales, the old implement firm might wither away. In January 1922, Ford slashed prices by $230 to an all-time low of $395. International Harvester responded with "the most aggressive selling fight of its career." Cyrus H. McCormick, grandson of the inventor, who was later president of his family's empire, described the dramatic scene when the news of Ford's price slashing reached McCormick's management.

> That February morning is another of the many business hours I treasure in my memory. I had taken Mr. [Alexander] Legge, the Company's beloved and hard-boiled general manager on a visit to the new motor truck installation at Springfield works. As we were arguing some problem which then seemed important, the telephone rang—Chicago wished to speak to Mr. Legge. We could, of course, hear only his side of the conversation. There was much talk from the other end, and then an explosion from Alex: "What? What's that? How much? Two hundred and thirty dollars? Well, I'll be . . . What'll we do about it? Why damn it all—meet him of course. We're going to stay in the tractor business. Yes, but two hundred and thirty dollars. Both models—yes, both. And say, listen, make it good! We'll throw in a plow, as well."[34]

Legge and other Harvester executives then launched an intensive advertising campaign. They telegraphed sales information to dealers and mailed advertising materials. The company's branch offices wrote directly to thousands of farmers. As a result, sales boomed and losses skyrocketed. *Printers' Ink* estimated that Ford lost at least $300 per tractor, while IH lost an equivalent or greater sum. The cost to each company was staggering, and it took the victor years to recoup the losses. Yet neither combatant dared disengage, for at stake was the control of the tractor industry itself.[35] Like the frontier town in a cheap Western, the market was not big enough for both antagonists. McCormick himself later described the warriors as tersely as it could be related, "Ford was backed by the most popular commercial name of the time and by the uncounted millions earned for him his epoch-making car; and he was trying to capture a business with which he had no previous contact. International had on its side many years of training gained from contact with farmers, less capital by far, and utter inexperience with defeat."[36]

The six-year fight will stand as an epic in industrial competition, but in 1927 International finally surpassed Ford in the number of tractors sold to farmers. By 1928, Ford Motor Company discontinued building the Fordson in North America, and virtually withdrew from the tractor industry.[37] International Harvester and the implement industry won its desperate fight, but the victory came in the middle of a severe agricultural depression. It was, like most victories, the result of several strengths in the winner and several weaknesses in the loser.

Ford's mechanical surrogate in the battle with International was the Fordson tractor. At the time of its introduction, the Fordson was a remarkable machine. Henry Ford's refusal to update his tractor—similar to his freezing of the designs of the Model T and Model A—should not be permitted to overshadow the real contribution of the automaker's little gray machine.

In its brief lifetime, the Fordson accomplished some notable feats. It imposed its configuration upon so many tractors that the design came to be thought of as the conventional pattern for tractors. It introduced mass production into the industry for the first time, making tractors economically attractive to large numbers of farmers. And despite its ultimate failure, it accelerated the trend toward carefully designed "automotive type" engineering. Each of these accomplishments merits explanation.

Even before the advent of the Fordson, the tendency in tractor design was toward smaller tractors with multicylinder engines, enclosed, automotive-type transmissions, and general mechanical refinement. This trend, described earlier, would have undoubtedly continued even if the Fordson had never whined out of Detroit. But the Fordson did appear, and it carried with it the prestige of an idolized industrialist. The Fordson was mass produced and—at least at first—popular. It almost instantly outmoded less-polished designs that might otherwise have died a lingering death.[38] C. M. Eason, an engineer who had long advocated better-quality tractor designs, questioned whether "the general acceptance of the conventional tractor is due to the fact that this is inherently the best type of tractor" or whether the Fordson's overwhelming influence simply dominated rival designs.[39] The latter was certainly a factor, even if it was not the only influence. What Eason could not know in 1923 was that the competitive pressure generated by the Fordson had caused a mutation among tractors that would soon supplant the standard or conventional tractor.

The Fordson was the first mass-produced tractor, and all of its other attributes were really ancillaries to this fact. Mass production changed the tractor itself, it revolutionized the industry, and it made the tractor effectively available to the farmer for the first time. Even after the harrowing threat that the Fordson gave to his company, Cyrus H. McCormick still acknowledged the credit due to the Fordson. "It is questionable," he wrote, "if the business of making tractors would have become a large scale industry had it not been for Ford. . . . In 1918, the manufacturing methods employed by all tractor manufacturers were derived from implement and not automotive standards, and they were hardly up to date in terms of manufacturing progress." The Fordson changed that.

Mass production and the Ford-Harvester price war lowered the price of tractors to the point where a tractor cost "less than the price of a good team of horses."[40] But because horses were still necessary on many farms even after the purchase of a Fordson, the cheap price did not make tractors economically viable on all farms. A price of less than $400, however, made the Fordson attractive to millions of farmers who could not have seriously considered tractor power earlier.

Many of the veterans of the "Second Revolution in American Agriculture" are still alive. Any visitor who gently inquires will find that virtually all of them remember the Fordson. For many, the first proud memory of tractor ownership is indelibly stamped with the cursive trademark of Ford Motor Company. For them, that trademark is the symbol of a personal victory, an ambitious dream fulfilled. For others, "Ford" or "Fordson" is synonymous with the frustrations of a low-tension magneto, of a machine too small or too unstable to perform some urgent task that was vital years ago. But whatever their value judgments on the Fordson, few veterans remember it with indifference.

In June 1931, E. J. Baker, Jr., the sagacious and self-appointed chronicler of the farm implement industry, emphasized to readers of *Agricultural Engineering* that the Fordson and its competitors, the McCormick-Deering 10–20 and 15–30, were "designed as much for low cost production as for proper functioning." His analysis penetrated to the core of the character of the Fordson generation. They were intended to be cheap and utilitarian, and they generally succeeded more at the former than the latter. Cheapness was both their strength and their downfall.

Perhaps the kindest obituary for the Fordson was written long after the heat of rivalry had cooled. It was written by one who could pensively reflect upon a noble, fallen enemy. The Fordson, McCormick wrote, "would operate successfully in so many conditions that huge numbers were sold; but it failed in so many places that ultimately farmers would have no more of it. . . . The Fordson was a perfect theoretical answer to an imperfect practical problem."[41]

By introducing mass production, the Fordson brought down the price of the tractor to the point that a much larger number of farmers could try using tractors. But it did not issue in a perfectly adapted or even a mechanically perfected machine. Rather, it increased the capital requirements and market potential of the industry to a point that such improvements were imperative. And it intensified competition to the point that further innovation was virtually inevitable.

NOTES

1. "The Small Farm Tractor," *Scientific American* (April 3, 1915): 304.

2. Arthur L. Dahl, "Mobilizing the Farm Machinery," *Scientific American* (October 13, 1917): 274; Cash wages for hired labor were almost $1.1 billion in 1919, but only slightly more than a half-billion in 1909, Bureau of the Census, *Fourteenth Census of the United States* 6, Part 2, *Agriculture* (Washington: United States Department of Commerce, 1922), 4

3. Raymond Olney, "Power Farming Solves Crop Production Problems," *Power Farming* (May 1917): 9, 14; Olney, "Tractors to Solve the Food Problem," *Power Farming* (June 1917): 6, 38, 40; "An Army of Farm Tractor Operators Needed," *Power Farming* (June 1917) 8; C. M. Eason, "Tractors Increase Farm Resources," *Power Farming* (June 1917): 22; D. R. A. Drummond, "Timely Hints for Wartime Power Farming," *Power Farming* (July 1917): 7; Theodore H. Price. "Gasoline and Agriculture," *The Outlook* (June 27, 1917): 334–35; Dahl, "Mobilizing," 274.

4. "The Effect of the War on Power Farming," *Power Farming* (August 1917): 7–8, 20; E. Lloyd Watson, "Save the Corn Crop with a Tractor," *Power Farming* (November 1917): 22, 27.

5. Domestic sales for 1916 had been but 27,819, "Tractor Production Past and Present," *Automotive Industries* (January 16, 1919): 175; "A Threatened Implement Shortage," *Power Farming* (July 1917): 22, 24; Gray, *Development of the Agricultural Tractor*, 26.

6. *Minute Books* of the Moline Plow Company, November 11, 1917, as cited in Thomas, *Minneapolis-Moline*, 127–28.

7. M. E. Hoag, "Manufacturing a Farm Tractor," *The American Machinist* (December 19, 1918): 1135–37.

8. Strite, "Fundamentals of Tractor Design," 356.

9. "Much Opposition to Liberty Tractor," *Automotive Industries* (February 21, 1918): 422, 425.

10. "More Work from the Tractor," *Power Farming* (June 1918): 14.

11. Neufield, *A Global Corporation*, 23; Gray, *Development of the Agricultural Tractor*, 28, fig. 28.

12. "Keep the Farm Tractor at Work," *Power Farming* (October 1918): 34; Arnold P. Yerkes, "The Tractor's Influence on Crop Production," *Power Farming* (May 1918): 7–8. Yerkes was an engineer for the United States Department of Agriculture at the time.

13. "Tractor a Modern Necessity," *American Fruit Grower* (October 1918): 4; "Farm Tractor—A National Necessity," *Horseless Age* (April 1, 1918): 42–43; "Texas Has 4144 Tractors," *Automotive Industries* (November 28, 1918): 943; Paisley T. Hines, "Southern Farmers Find Tractors Profitable," *Power Farming* (April 1918): 9, 20.

14. "150,955 Tractors in 2 Years," *Automotive Industries* (November 14, 1918): 859; There were about fifty-one thousand tractors in use in 1917, *Historical Statistics*, 469.

15. Universal Tractor Manufacturing Company, "Automobile Dealers Are Winning Trade with Universals," [advertisement], *Horseless Age*, (April 14, 1915): 22.

16. "New Farm Tractor Burning Kerosene," *Scientific American* (January 19, 1918): 76.

17. Edward C. Crossman, "The Gasoline Horse in the West," *Scientific American* (January 5, 1918): 17.

18. Wik, *Grass-Roots,* 85.

19. Letter of the Mineapolis Steel and Machinery Company to Henry Ford, September 26, 1914, Henry Ford correspondence, as cited in Wik, *Steam Power on the American Farm*, 206.

20. "Ford Selects Oakwood Site for Tractor Plant," *Horseless Age* (June 23, 1915): 835; "Ford to Make Tires and Operate Steamship Line," *Horseless Age* (July 7, 1915): 5; "Light Weight Gas Tractor for the Farm," *Scientific American* (January 15, 1916): 80; Wayne Worthington, "The Engineer's History of the Farm Tractor II; World War I: Confusion, Development," *Implement & Tractor* (February 7, 1967): 33; Wik, *Grass-Roots*, 88–92.

21. "Plan for Distributing Fordson Tractors," *Automotive Industries* (April 4, 1918): 667–68; "$875 for Ford Tractor with Plow," *Automotive Industries* (March 28, 1918): 654; "Tractor Dealers Get Plow Sales: Oliver Gives Ohio Agency to Automotive Agency—Others May Follow," *Automotive Industries* (May 16, 1918): 971.

22. "Pennsylvania Buys 40 Tractors," *Automotive Industries* (February 28, 1918): 470; "Michigan Buys 1,000 Tractors," *Automotive Industries* (March, 14, 1918): 563.

23. J. Edward Schipper, "Ford Tractor Production Plan Unchanged in Growth," *Automotive Industries* (March 28, 1918): 621–24; Gray, *Development of the Agricultural Tractor,* 28; Wik, *Grass-Roots*, 94; "Manufacturing Worm Gear and Assembly Methods in Fordson Tractor Success," *Automotive Industries* (April 25, 1918): 810–14; Schipper, "Fordson Assembly Wholly on Progressive Plan," *Automotive Industries* (May 1, 1919): 960–66; Schipper, "Handling Parts

in the Shop and on the Assembly Floor," *Automotive Industries* (May 18, 1919): 1008–12; Schipper, "Machining Operations on the Backbone of the Fordson Tractor," *Automotive Industries* (April 11, 1918): 717–23.

24. "Standardized Fordson Equipment," *Automotive Industries* (May 16, 1918): 971.

25. "Tractor Makers Protest Curtailment," *Automotive Industries* (October 17, 1918): 657–59. 696.

26. Strite, "Fundamentals of Tractor Design," 356.

27. "Chandler to Make Tractors for Government," *Automotive Industries* (February 21, 1918): 425; "Maxwell Develops 3-Plow Enclosed Transmission Farm Tractor," *Automotive Industries* (February 7, 1918): 336–37; "New Samson Tractor at $650," *Automotive Industries* (November 28, 1918): 939; The Samson Tractor Company, "The Samson Tractor Company" [advertisement], *Power Farming* (December 1918): 28–29; Gray, *Development of the Agricultural Tractor*, 27, 29; "Mechanical Details of the $650 Samson Tractor," *Automotive Industries* (October 16, 1919): 772–73.

28. "Implement Dealers Losing Tractor Sales," *Automotive Industries* (October 17, 1918): 684, 696.

29. "Tractor Makers Protest," 658.

30. "Tractor Curtailment Order Modified," *Automotive Industries* (November 14, 1918): 849; "The Big Auto Tractor Attachment," *Automotive Industries* (March 6, 1919): 528–29; Worthington, "Engineer's History, II," 33.

31. "The Iron Horse Designed for General Farm Work," *Automotive Industries* (November 27, 1919): 1081; Gray, *Development of the Agricultural Tractor*, 30, fig. 29.

32. P. M. Heldt, "Cooling Capacity Increased in Samson Tractor," *Automotive Industries* (March 2, 1922): 502–5.

33. Worthington, "Engineer's History, II," 33; Gray, *Development of the Agricultural Tractor*, 33; "Allis Chalmers: America's Krupp," *Fortune* (May 1939): 55.

34. McCormick, *Century of the Reaper*, 163, 196–97; G. A. Nichols, "Harvester and Ford in Finish Fight for Tractor Market," *Printer's Ink* (March 30, 1922): 25.

35. Nichols, "Finish Fight," 25–28.

36. McCormick, *Century of the Reaper*, 197.

37. Wik, "Henry Ford's Tractors," 85.

38. In 1919 a partisan of automotive-type engineering wrote, "There is one factor which is retarding progress along sound engineering lines, and that is that many farmers do not appreciate good engineering. A farmer examining one of the best tractors exhibiting, remarked that there was too much fine machinery in the tractor. He recognized the quality of construction, but it actually repelled him. Some day he will probably learn that fine machinery is not synonymous with delicate machinery and that a machine carefully designed with respect to stress imposed on its parts is sure to give greater satisfaction that one bearing the marks of crudeness all over," in "New Models and Strong Representation of Parts Makers at K. C. Tractor Show," *Automotive Industries* (February 27, 1919): 494. By the

time of the Fordson's demise, engineers had learned that earlier designers had not anticipated the strains that would actually be placed on tractors in the field—strains that often exceeded the estimates that appeared on the drawing boards. The farmer's prejudice was at least partially justified. See also Howard Warren, "The Trend of Tractor Development," *Scientific American* (December 28, 1918): 516; Joseph Janasek, "Farm Tractor Design," *Automotive Industries* (June 12, 1919): 1265; and Crossman, "Gasoline Horse," 17. The dramatic change in engineering concepts can be seen clearly in the evolution of the Hard-Parr line from 1912 through 1922 in White Motor Corporation, *Progress . . . in Tractor Power from 1898.*

39. Eason, "The General-Purpose Farm Tractor," 600.

40. Worthington, "Engineer's History, II," 74.

41. McCormick, *Century of the Reaper*, 198–99.

4
Mass Production and Mass Experimentation

The Fordson ushered in a new era in tractor history by introducing mass production. Simultaneously, the Fordson touched off a bitter commercial rivalry that had lasting consequences. The preceding chapter described the commercial aspects of that rivalry, but technical innovation proved to be the decisive factor in the competition for the tractor market, and in the process it altered the nature of the tractor itself.

The feverish wrestling between Ford and International Harvester was an uneven match. But International, the underdog, ultimately out-smarted its financially stronger rival by exploiting the weakness of the Fordson and the strengths of the International Harvester organization.

The Fordson design incorporated several weaknesses that were com-mon in many tractors of the time. From the first, Ford's plowhorse was troubled with vertigo. "Unfortunately," wrote Wayne Worthington, a noted engineer, "the design of the Fordson flagrantly violated all principles of stability and many fatal accidents (rearward upsets) occurred." The Fordson itself was short, which deprived the front of the tractor of leverage to counteract the torque of the rear wheels. It had a fairly high hitch, which compounded the tendency to rear. Finally, the worm gear drive magnified the rearing motion if the driver hung a plow or lodged a wheel and did not manage to depress the clutch. Unless the operator reacted quickly, the worm gear continued to rotate around the suddenly stationary axle, and the tractor rotated backwards. Although such instability was by no means unique to them in that era, Fordsons capsized themselves so frequently that they earned a reputation as killers and became the subject for experiment station research.[1] And the Fordson had other weaknesses as well.

Early in the development of the Fordson, Henry Ford decided not to manufacture implements to accompany his tractor; it was a serious error in marketing strategy.[2] The rejection of implement manufacture deprived Ford of the opportunity to custom-tailor accessories to match the capability of the tractor. Although Ford did permit his dealers to carry a limited number of "approved implements," the line was never extensive and product identity was weak. Undoubtedly many farmers overloaded their Fordsons with implements purchased from local dealers carrying such lines as Moline or Deere; naturally the Fordson was often blamed when problems developed. By not building his own implements, Ford inadvertently brought the problem upon himself.

But Ford's decision not to make implements had a second serious consequence. It deprived him of feedback from the field. Henry Ford's unresponsiveness to consumer demand was proverbial, and there is no assurance that the arrogant Motor King would have responded any more to suggestions about tractors than he did to suggestions for the color of the Model T. But without implement salesmen, field representatives, and implement designers on the Ford staff, there was no chance of developing what was later to be called a "systems approach." Ford concentrated on a single operation and not the entire production process.

Another reason for Harvester's victory was that weaknesses in Ford's corporate structure competed against a commensurate strength in the Harvester organization. International Harvester's McCormick-Deering division made tractors and harvesting equipment and their Parlin and Orendorf ("P & O") division made tillage tools.[3] But divisions within the company were no barrier to communication, and distribution and sales staff served as reconnaissance personnel for all IH divisions. After the tractor war, the victorious industrial general wrote, "It [IH] had proved to the world that a farm tractor should be sold as a part of a farm equipment line and should not become the minor brother of the automobile."[4] That observation is unassailable in view of subsequent events.

International exploited its familiarity with the farm equipment industry to introduce innovations that met the needs of working farmers better than conventional tractors. One of these innovations, the row-crop or general-purpose tractor, revolutionized the tractor industry. Almost as significant was the introduction and mass production of the power take-off (PTO).

The PTO was designed to transmit power directly from the tractor to whatever implement was in use. In earlier days when horses provided almost all farm power, implements such as binders or mowers drew their power from a bullwheel, a large wheel with cleats or lugs that was forced to turn as the implement ran over the ground. It was an awkward system at best. When conditions were good, the bullwheel rolled and turned the rest of the machinery, but when the ground was soft or muddy, the bullwheel often slid along under motionless shafts and cogwheels. Yet the bullwheel continued well into the tractor era. Analytical minds recognized that such a system was ludicrous. One wrote that "Horses are obliged to transmit their power through the ground to the machinery they operate because of their inherent and unchangeable construction." Yet tractors had the advantage of a rotating engine—something seemingly ideal for powering accessories. That rotary movement was not used, however, and tractors "still do their work with re-designed horse-drawn implements, using as inefficient methods of transmitting their power to the machinery they pull as could be discovered."[5]

In searching for a competitive advantage over Ford, International saw an opportunity in replacing the bullwheel with a device that they designated a "power take-off." E. J. Baker, Jr., editor of *Farm Implement News* recounted the events in his delightful, inimitable, succinct style:

> The first power-take-off other than for lifting effects was designed by a Frenchman—Albert Gougis—in 1906 and connected between his experimental tractor and a McCormick bullwheel driven binder in that wet harvest. . . . M. Gougis was enabled to salvage a wheat crop that would have been lost to Boreas, the doves and the starlings.
>
> The report of Gougis' tractor and its tumbling rod shaft activating an otherwise stalled binder trickled back to the Wallut McCormick agency in Paris when Ed Johnson, v-p in charge of experimental work for IHC was scouting European engineering progress. So Ed hied himself to the Gougis headquarters and observed the first PTO-driven tractor binder operate.
>
> Ed had a photographic mind. He never forgot.

[Here Baker recounted the Fordson's success and its impact on International Harvester. He then continued:]

> The IHC sales department in their usual gentle manner told Ed Johnson he was faced with a situation and not an alibi, . . . the diminishing sales of the Titan 10–20's hurt.
>
> Ed . . . came up with the International 8–16 chain drive, whose transmission housing ended with a longitudinal shaft carrying a 1⅛" spline end. Ed had

raked his photographic mind and recalled the Gougis PTO. As a justification
for this power take-off shaft, Ed also cast as bread upon the waters a 10-foot
anti-friction bearing-equipped power binder solely dependent upon the 8–
16's PTO for activation. One had to buy both to banish the bullwheel.

Whether the 8–16 chain drive sold the power binder or vice versa, they
sold.

Thus did the experimental power take-off shaft emigrate from France and
enter into production in the USA. It was later metagrobolized [*sic*] as
package adaptations for the McCormick-Deering 10–20 (gear drive) and the
ancient and respected 15–30 which made history. . . . the PTO of these
models got from the binder snath to . . . transmission . . . in a sort of Rube
Goldberg manner whose justification was that it worked.[6]

Baker's account left out several pertinent facts. First, in order to
meet the Ford challenge, the PTOs were introduced with remarkable
speed. Both R. B. Gray and Wayne Worthington date the introduction of
the PTO in 1918,[7] but that particular date is difficult to justify. In 1931,
Arnold P. Yerkes, then with International Harvester Company, wrote to
W. L. Cavert with the cautious precision of one conscious that he was
recording events for posterity:

It is rather hard to say exactly when the first power take-off was actually
placed on the market. So far as we know, the first tractors designed and
built for the use of a power take-off were the McCormick-Deering 15–30's,
which were first marketed in 1922 . . . the International 8-[1]6 chain-drive
tractor, which had been on the market for a number of years prior to the
dates just mentioned, was provided with power take-off attachments as early
as 1916, although, as pointed out, no tractors designed from the first for a
power take-off were ever placed on the market until 1922.[8]

Because the real popularity of the PTO came with the introduction
of the 10–20 and 15–30, its commercial success should be dated after 1922
and reckoned as a part of the formula for the McCormick-Deering victory.

The introduction and success of the PTO were the results of team
action. After the idea was born in the mind of a French farmer, it immigrated to the United States and emerged as a competitive weapon through
the agency of Ed Johnson. But the PTO was transformed from a concept
to a mechanical reality by Bert R. Benjamin, the superintendent of the
McCormick Works' experimental division.[9]

The PTO attracted favorable comment almost from the start. In 1920,
when still an after-market accessory for the 8–16, the power take-off
impressed the president of a tiny rival of the International. An engineer

who reported on the new McCormick-Deering 15–30 for *Automotive Industries* praised the tractor, especially the novel power transmission feature. Farmers were equally impressed. The PTO soon became standard equipment on most tractors, but as different manufacturers adopted the concept, they varied the shape of the drive element and experimented with different speeds. Such variations made it difficult to manufacture interchangeable equipment, and eventually—due largely, no doubt, to International's domination of the market—a standardized speed and spline were specified for the industry. By the late 1920s a clockwise speed of 540 revolutions per minute and a 1-⅜-inch splined shaft were standard. This size and speed matched the McCormick-Deering specifications. Eventually, as tractors became more powerful, speed and size were increased to transmit more power.[10]

Of course not all improvements during the 1920's were due to the competition between Ford and IH. The introduction of the PTO was imaginative and improved the tractor's utility and appeal, but it was one of a great many technical improvements that emerged as tractors developed beyond the prototype stage. With the advent of mass production, the entire North American continent became a laboratory as more and more farmers had an opportunity to experiment with tractors. There were more and more opportunities to observe weaknesses and conjure up improvements. As a result, the first half-dozen years after the introduction of mass production form an era of rapid fine-tuning.

The trend toward better design continued unabated throughout the 1920s. Engineers enclosed more components to protect them from dust. They also used more antifriction bearings, more "unitized" construction, and more "automotive-type" engineering.[11]

Improved design helped improve reliability, but tractors still broke down and caused the farmer expensive and irritating delays. The manufacturers earnestly desired to improve reliability, but they faced both economic and technical problems in doing so.[12] For example, unfiltered air had devastating effects on tractor engines. Moline's Universal of the 1920s had a comparatively up-to-date engine—except for the absence of an air filter. Because of the effects of ingested dust, the Moline engine had a short life, a factor that may have contributed slightly to the tractor's demise. Other manufacturers recognized the problem of dusty intake air, but did not find immediate solutions. In desperation, International Harvester experimented with high-pressure steam engines and pondered the possibllity of abandoning internal combustion to avoid the problem of dust in the engine. Fortunately, before the company resorted to such drastic action, a variety of inventors came up with devices to mitigate the invasion of airborne particles.[13]

Air filters were small devices, yet their importance was quite large. They dramatically increased the service life of tractors and other motor-driven agricultural machinery. Journalists, engineers, and farmers all recognized the benefits of filtration, and the presence of an air filter became a prerequisite for tractor sales by the mid-twenties. The best method of filtering incoming air was disputed. There were centrifugal filters, oil-bath filters, water-bath filters, paper filters, and others, in which the air passed in sequence through two straining devices. But whatever the mode, the function was similar, and filters were essential for practical tractors.[14]

A practical tractor also had to be stable, and it had to deliver adequate power at the drawbar. Instability and lack of traction were closely related problems. Designers of medium-weight tractors such as the Fordson had less margin for error in their geometry than earlier, heavier tractors. In the 1920s researchers analyzed the dynamics of tractor draft and tractor stability, then experimented with a plethora of ideas. They examined the problems involved in mounting plows directly on the tractor and with hitching tractors to short-coupled plows. They recorded the results of experiments that attached loads to various points on the tractor and noted which combinations encouraged rearing. Experimenters in the twenties also evaluated different lugs in each of several wheel sizes in different types of soil. Such research allowed a gradual increase in a tractor's power-to-weight ratio, but did not produce any sudden breakthroughs.[15] When the dramatic increase in pulling power finally came, it was imported into the United States by a practical Scotch-Irish tinkerer. This tinkerer was already at work, but American tractor makers seem to have been unaware of Harry Ferguson or his work. Farmers had to content themselves with smaller, but no less real, improvements.

One of the minor, but most welcome improvements of the 1920s was the addition of an electrical system. As noted earlier, Moline electrified its Universal during the First World War. Other makers eventually offered generators and batteries as options at extra cost. Although electrical systems would not become common on tractors until after the depression, their value was appreciated as early as 1918.[16] The lag between the use of self-starters on automobiles and the use of starters on tractors may well be blamed in part on the abysmal prices of farm products in the twenties and thirties.

By the time Americans motored into the Roaring Twenties, the tractor had achieved a fair level of practicality, improved above the Fordson generation. The McCormick-Deering 10–20 and 15–30 were introduced in the early 1920s and were staple merchandise for their company for several years. In 1923, John Deere introduced the Model D, which earned the company a steady income for so many years that it probably set a record for production life—it was built for almost three decades. The Model D is fairly typical of the tractors of its generation, the generation that displaced the Fordson. Worthington's description captures the spirit of the machine:

> Its operation was noisy; the operator's position was low and he was subjected to much dust and dirt. Forward vision was poor. The exhaust was practically unmuffled and plagued the operator with fumes and smoke. The seat was a steel stamping supported on a rigid flat steel 'spring.'
>
> But the tractor was low in cost, durable and economical to operate, started readily [?], was easily accessible for repairs and thoroughly dependable. It introduced tractors into areas where tractors had heretofore failed to penetrate. . . .[17]

The designers of the Model D—and their colleagues in other companies—were able, for the first time, to draw upon the large-scale experience of thousands of on-farm tractors. To no small degree, that experience was conveyed to them by engineers at experiment stations and land grant colleges.[18] Relations between college faculties and experiment station personnel and the personnel hired by the manufacturers expanded as time passed.

The World War I tractor boom continued through 1920, but as the boom gradually cooled, weaker manufacturers were eliminated. That boom had attracted not only automakers, but also a huge assortment of would-be tractor makers. Some were relatively honest small firms with a large inventory of dreams and ideas, but with moderate competence and less capital. Other "tractor companies" manufactured stock and promises, but were esentially investment frauds. Together with fly-by-night tractor shops, these operations hurt numerous investors and farmers. They also damaged the credibility of the tractor industry as a whole.

As early as 1916, R. T. Mally described a fly-by-night operation that built a tractor that could not turn under a load. The company's ethics are clearly revealed in their subsequent decision to produce the tractor anyway. The firm obviously did not anticipate a legitimate, long-term trade. Fortunately for the farmer and for investors, the tractor failed to sell, but

Mally cautioned subscribers to *Power Farming* to select a tractor only from old, established firms with a good reputation.[19]

Other journals used cartoons to warn gullible farmers. For example, a 1917 cartoon in *Farm Implement News* pictured a con artist sitting at a desk in the office of the Skinum Tractor Company. Above his head was a poster that read "No tractors for sale—only stocks, bonds and territory." Beside the entrepreneur's chair was his suitcase—presumably packed and ready for a quick getaway. By 1920 there were one hundred companies actually making tractors of varying qualities, and according to one source "probably twice that many who are planning to begin in the near future."[20]

But the boom was about to bust. The postwar market did not absorb constantly growing numbers of tractors and could not support the countless tractor "factories." Tractor sales peaked in 1920 at two hundred thousand. The following year, despite the large stock carried over from the previous year, sales hardly passed twenty thousand—a mere 35 percent of the earlier record level of 1920.[21] The bubble had burst. The industry was devastated. Some well-established companies survived, but marginal operations and "stock jobs" did not. Much of the drop in sales may be attributed to disastrous crop prices, but the failure of many tractors—especially those of small manufacturers—reduced demand even farther. Disappointed farmers soon demanded more protection from unscrupulous companies.

Farmers had requested consumer protection even before the boom of 1918–20. The defective products and overly enthusiastic advertising of the overheated market intensified pressure for regulation. As early as 1915, Yerkes and Mowry had noted that horsepower ratings and tractor capacity were confused and inconsistent. To end the confusion the editor of *Power Farming* called for a general test for tractors.[22] But the industry was slow to respond to popular demands for more creditable ratings.

Gradually the demand began to focus on government, frequently on the Department of Agriculture:[23] *Power Farming* continued to editorialize for national testing, noting that the alternative was piecemeal legislation by the various states that would not be uniform and would in all probability "work a hardship on the tractor industry. . . ." Calls for such testing were becoming "more and more insistent," and the editor warned that tractor makers who opposed testing "laid themselves open to the accusation that they know their product would not fulfill the claims."[24]

Even though the tractor industry did not manage to agree upon a standardized testing procedure, there is little evidence of resistance to the idea of government testing. The industry's silent acquiescence has several

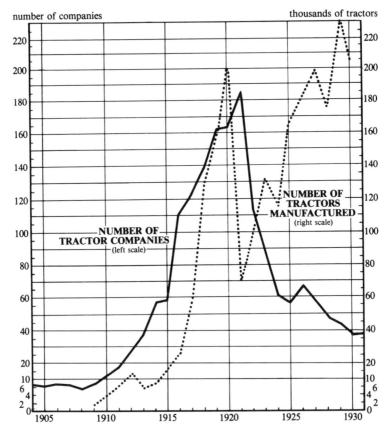

Figure 1. Tractor numbers.
Source: Archie Stone, *Farm Tractors* (New York: John Wiley & Sons, 1932), 2.

possible explanations. It is possible that the industry's leaders—like the great entrepreneurs studied by historian Robert Wiebe—sought regulation as an alternative to the confusion that persisted in their field. Or the leaders may have had more sinister motives like those imputed to the business community by Gabriel Kolko—a suspicion that the foxes would be appointed to guard the chicken coop, that the regulated would do the regulating.[25] Or, quite possibly, the various corporate policymakers concluded that some form of regulation and testing was politically unavoidable, and that opposition to it only aroused the antagonism of the farmers.[26] They may have remembered that many farmers were the sons of the strident Populists of the 1890s.

For whatever reasons, the industry did not immediately set standards for tractor tests, through either the American Society of Agricultural Enginerers (ASAE) or the Society of Automotive Engineers (SAE). Nor, on the other hand, did it oppose government ratings. In fact, representatives of the industry attended a conference in October 1919 in Chicago, at which national testing was called for. Undoubtedly, the manufacturers preferred to see a single national test rather than expensive and variable state tests. The conference, which had been called by the Secretary of Agriculture, included not only delegates from the tractor companies and the department, but also farmers, representatives of several agricultural colleges, and industry trade organizations. The official report to the Secretary of Agriculture specifically requested congressional appropriations for a proposed Bureau of Agricultural Engineering, which would, among other functions, test tractors.[27] In the Sixty-sixth Congress of 1920, Representative Sidney Anderson of Lanesboro, Minnesota, introduced legislation that embodied the committee's plans. He reintroduced it in the Sixty-seventh Congress, but the Republican Congresses of 1920 and 1921 allowed the bills to die before coming onto the floor.[28] Politicians who were callously indifferent to farm foreclosures were equally indifferent to funding tractor tests.

If federal legislators were indifferent to the needs of farmers after the First World War, some state legislators were not. In early 1919, Wilmot F. Crozier introduced a bill into the Nebraska legislature requiring all companies that sold tractors in the state to submit their machines for official testing. The bill also required them to maintain an adequate stock of spare parts. Crozier credited the idea for the law to an editorial in a farm magazine, but the representative himself had first-hand knowledge of the exaggerated claims and shoddy merchandise of some firms. On July 15, 1919, the law went into effect, and the University of Nebraska began testing tractors. Because the testing was expensive, other states abandoned plans for similar programs, and the Nebraska tests became a national and even international norm for tractor performance, with companies sometimes having tractors evaluated that would not be offered for sale in Nebraska. Eventually the law was modified so that the program was largely supported through testing fees.[29]

The tractors submitted in the first years of the Nebraska tests often had "surprisingly major defects." Testers found defective blocks, heads, valves, and other inferior parts. They also discovered that some tractors required excessive maintenance. Of the first 103 applications for testing, only sixty-eight appeared. The other thirty-five cancelled their applications. Only thirty-nine tractors passed after major changes. The mechanical reliability (or lack thereof) reflected in the tests was roughly equivalent to the ratio indicated in literery sources of the time.[30]

The Nebraska tests forced manufacturers to exercise restraint in advertising. The tests also encouraged the tractor makers to refine and improve their entire tractor lines. A commentator in the Rome-based *International Review of Agriculture* noted the improvement of tractors and the role of the University of Nebraska when he wrote. "If one considers the inevitable difficulties to be overcome in the application of motor force to field work it is remarkable what a high level has been reached in tractor construction in so short a time, in spite of various setbacks at the outset. This is largely due to the United States, where active research and the institution of now widely known Government tractor tests at Nebraska paved the way for other countries, though the United States still keeps the lead in the movement."[31] The Nebraska tractor tests, by their excellence and by the default of the federal government, became a vital international institution that continues today.

The inauguration of standardized rating and testing procedures encouraged tractor manufacturers to seek cooperative standards in other areas of tractor construction. The industry needed standards in numerous areas to insure that accessories and implements could be mated for maximum convenience and efficiency. The automobile industry had pioneered the standardization concept, and government rationing pushed the implement industry in that direction during the war. By 1919, belt speeds and drawbar hitch heights were specified, and, by common consent, codified by the American Society of Agricultural Engineers and the Society of Automotive Engineers. Other standards soon followed. Standardization was agonizingly slow, however, and the published data for the 1919 models indicated that much remained to be done.[32]

The spectacular boom in tractor sales during the war years extended for several months after the armistice, but it ended in an equally spectacular bust. In the euphoria of soaring sales, tractor advocates thought that they foresaw the rosiest of postwar worlds. There appeared to be every reason for optimism. In an article titled "America to Restock the World with Farm Machinery," *Scientific American* prophesied U. S. factories would face immense demands from "all the countries of the world [that] are today almost entirely stripped of their stocks of agricultural implements and machinery."[33] After reminding readers of the European casualty rates, the article's author reaffirmed his belief that the United States could supply the world with farm tools. And sales did continue high throughout 1919 and 1920. Farmers were assured that "the tractor industry is fast becoming one of the most stable in the country. Thousands of tractors are being sold to farmers who are buying their second machines."[34] In 1918, American farmers purchased 96,470 tractors. In 1919, the figure was up to 136,162; and in 1920 it was 162,998. Domestic sales accounted for the majority of the tractors manufactured, leaving only scraps for export.[35] But in 1921 European farmers were back in production, feverish wartime purchasing was over, and crop prices plummeted. American farm income slid to half the level of the previous year. Implement dealers who had sold ten tractors in 1920 sold three in 1921. Then, in January 1922, as a final blow to the beleaguered tractor companies, Ford began his price war with International Harvester. As a result, tractor prices bottomed out, and the manufacturers' ranks withered until only the sturdiest remained.[36] Of those remaining, some were mortally wounded and would not survive the depression of the thirties. Indeed, for many firms in the farm equipment industry, the depression had begun. The number of tractors sold did not reach the 1920 levels again until 1929, another peak year followed by a precipitous decline.

In 1921, in response to the decline in sales, the tractor industry slashed production. Very few tractors were built in 1922, because most companies carried over a heavy burden of unsold inventory. The mood of the industry in 1922 was gloomy. Trade publications reinforced and reflected the malaise. One wrote that "Manufacturers of farm machinery do not believe that there will be a return of highly profitable business before 1924. . . ." because raw materials were expensive and farm produce was cheap. The writer predicted that the worst was yet to come. But by the first of 1923, the market had recovered slightly, and the manufacturers who remained in the tractor business became mildly optimistic.[37]

The failure of the tractor market in 1921 and 1922 was a consequence in part of the narrow base for tractor sales. Tractor sales were possible only to relatively large-scale farmers with adequate capital or credit and located in an area where crops and farms were adaptable to tractor utilization. In 1920, during the height of the boom, Capper Farm Press, publishers of a respected agricultural paper, defined a "tractor belt" that encompassed the area where the most tractors were sold. The eastern boundary of this belt ran from Duluth to Minneapolis to St. Louis to eastern Oklahoma and Texas. The western boundary was the Rocky Mountains. This region, of course, included the wheat belt. It invaded a transition zone in the western part of the corn belt, but did not penetrate into the eastern corn belt or into the cotton belt. In the eastern corn belt and in the cotton belt row cultivation was necessary, and farms were smaller than the units in the Texas Panhandle or the plains of North Dakota. The geographic distribution of tractor sales in 1920 suggests two of its greatest shortcomings. It could not cultivate row crops, nor—because it replaced few horses—was it adaptable to small farms. The latter was largely because of the tractor's price in relation to the number of horses it displaced.[38]

In order to adapt to small row-crop farms, the tractor had to become cheap and maneuverable. Both qualities implied smallness, but if a tractor was too small, it had neither the power nor traction to be practical, as the marginal performance of the Fordson indicated. The dilemma was real and apparent, but solutions were difficult. The *Ohio Farmer* suggested a rental-purchase plan, but the idea never became popular. Although the tractor was smaller and less expensive than it had been before the war, its use was still limited to large holdings.[39] The advent of a practical small tractor lay in the future.

The problem of adapting the tractor to cultivating row crops was often confused with the replacing of horses with machine power, and several manufacturers tried to build a tractor that could simply be hitched in place of a horse. Indeed, the number of mechanical horse substitutes was exceeded only by the number of parts in some of the more complex models. Most of the horse substitutes were intended for use with existing horse-drawn implements, but the implements could not bear the added stress. And some tractors carried the idea of substitution to absurd lengths, such as the Samson Iron Horse, which was rein controlled. In addition to monstrosities like the Iron Horse, motor cultivators continued in limited production.[40] But tractors were not merely mechanical horses, and various attempts to manufacture an "Iron Horse" or a "Steel Mule" ultimately failed. In the straitened tractor market of 1921, there was little room for unconventional design or operation unless it was accompanied by undeniable advantages. None were.

Neither the dearth of tractor sales in 1921 nor the large number of farms too small for a tractor, however, should distract from the relatively rapid pace with which American farmers adopted the tractor—at least those farmers who could. Between January 1, 1918, and January 1, 1922, the number of tractors in use on American farms soared from eighty-five thousand to a third of a million. E. A. White estimated that farms with tractors increased from 3.6 percent of total farms in 1918 to 5 or 6 percent by 1922.[41] It was a large-scale change for so short a period.

The dramatic increase in the number of tractors on farms was often visible to local observers. Researchers from Cornell University discovered that tractors were proliferating in every county in New York, particularly in "level farming areas of western New York, the St. Lawrence, Mohawk and Hudson River valleys and on Long Island." *Power Farming* emphasized the importance of local experience with tractors when it editorialized in February 1919 in favor of local or county demonstrations. The American Society of Agricultural Engineers provided guidelines for just such demonstrations.[42] But the rules did not provide for the type of demonstration staged by International Harvester in 1923. After an area in southern Indiana was devastated by tornados at planting time, the Chicago company dispatched two trainloads of tractors to save the area's crops. The tractors saved the farmers' season and demonstrated the potential timeliness of tractor use. Undoubtedly they also saved some of the farms in the area which might otherwise have passed before the auctioneer.[43] It was a dramatic move, but less emotional events also allowed farmers personal contact with a tractor, replacing fear with familiarity.

The growing realization that tractors worked faster and longer than horses or mules was a strong selling point. Natural disasters, such as the one in Indiana, unseasonable weather, or an innumerable host of incidental delays could cause a farmer to fall behind schedule. Delaying beyond a seasonal deadline reduced yields or imperiled an entire crop. For the horse farmer, any attempt to hurry was a calculated risk, because overworking draft animals caused them permanent injury. Tractors were far less susceptible to strain. Gasoline horsepower did not require rest. And, unlike horses, tractors were sometimes equipped with lights and, with drivers working in shifts, could plow or plant virtually around the clock until completing the task. Thus tractors were a form of weather insurance. It was a well-recognized virtue.[44]

Many farmers complained that the quality of tractor work was inferior to that of horses. Defenders of tractors attributed some of the failures to farmers who neglected purchasing tools to complement their tractors, but in other cases, operators were simply too inexperienced to do a good job with their tractors. In such situations, it was the farmers' shortcomings that contributed to the failure of the tractor and may have slowed demand for tractors to some degree.[45]

The problem of inexperienced drivers was serious enough that the Department of Agriculture listed proper operator training as the first item in its "Suggestions for Reducing the Cost of Using Tractors." *Automotive Industries* urged dealers to send instruction books to farmers in the interval between taking the order for a tractor and delivering it. Numerous writers called for tractor schools or short courses, and some manufacturers actually underwrote the cost of such courses in areas where tractors sold well. But many tractor operators needed more instruction than they received. The level of advice offered in many magazines indicated that either the mechanical skills of the readers were quite rudimentary, or that they were insensitive to insultingly simple instructions. An agricultural engineer who offered advice in a popular farm magazine told his readers, "do not use plyers [*sic*] too freely and keep the pipe wrench off nuts and screws." Operators who owned their machines had fewer mechanical problems with their tractors than did hired hands, but even owners sometimes abused tractors because of inexperience.[46]

Not only were farmers inexperienced in applying tractors to farm tasks, but manufacturers were also equally neophytic. The necessary accessories for use with a tractor developed slowly. Not until 1920, for example, did a mechanical beet harvester clatter onto the market.[47]

To the beet farmer, the availability of such a tool might change the cost equation, making a tractor a profitable investment for the first time. Often this created a vicious cycle, because there was little demand for a specific tractor-powered implement until that particular crop began to be cultivated by tractors; at the same time, a particular crop could not be cared for with tractor power until the necessary tools were available.

As farmers gained experience with tractors, they discovered new cultural practices. For example, deeper plowing in conjunction with alfalfa improved soil fertility and tilth, a return probably not anticipated at the time that the original investment in a tractor was contemplated. But once the fortunate combination was discovered, it made tractors more attractive to the neighbors of the experimenter and increased the prospects for tractor sales in that crop area.[48]

Finally, in some jobs, the tractor was simply unprofitable. Although some farmers anticipated using their tractors for pulling wagons, such a use seldom proved profitable. One researcher found a whole neighborhood of six farmers hostile to the tractor because it had not proven satisfactory in hauling wagons, a purpose for which it was not intended.[49] The farmer who purchased a tractor intending to use it for work to which it was unsuited learned an expensive lesson. But before the tractor was widely proven, he had little alternative but experimentation.

The postwar years were a period of mass experimentation. Not until mass production and widespread distribution put tractors on thousands of different farms could the real capabilities of the machine be tested, and the myriads of unsolved problems be exposed by thousands of farmers. But the era also subjected the tractor to countless critics, tinkerers, and fresh minds. The farmer-technicians who purchased tractors were not reticent, and they offered millions of suggestions to tractor builders.

Yet, most tractor owners liked their machine despite its imperfections. Seventy-nine percent of Maryland owners evaluated their tractors as a success. In Kentucky, 71 percent said that their tractors were profitable. An agricultural engineer in Iowa reported that "most" farmers were satisfied with their tractors. Capper Farm Press promoted tractors "as the most important factor in the development and maintenance of profitable crop productions in the great grain and livestock belt of the Middle West." The University of Idaho concluded, "The tractor, when selected to suit the farm and intelligently and carefully operated, has been reported by owners in Idaho as a profitable investment." The tractor's acclaim was not unanimous, but it was almost universal. In fact, the introduction to one study said, "Probably the tractor business has suffered more from the over-enthusiastic salesmen than from non-believers in power farming."[50]

The status of engineering in the tractor business during the early twenties was well analyzed in several articles that were occasioned by the poor sales of the bust period. One said:

> Tractor engineering at this time can be said to present two major phases. One covers the detailed mechanical problems from fuel utilization and engine and transmission design to the development and traction members, and includes the refinement and perfection of established conventional tractors. The other major phase has as its objects the extensive of power application to all of the field operations of diversified farming and centers in the development of the general purpose type or types. Unquestionably, herein lies the greatest opportunity and the most important problem before the tractor industry, the solution of which offers rich rewards.[51]

Another commentator arrived at essentially the same conclusion, but added a few additional facts. Leonard Fletcher, writing in *Agricultural Engineering*, attributed the sluggish market to the low prices of farm products and the farmer's reluctance to buy when markets were down. But he also blamed the tractor industry itself for some of the slowdown. He accused his industry of poor service after the sale, inadequate designing, and "general disregard of the value of the 'satisfied customer'." He went on to criticize many companies for their "discontinuing of experimental and developing work . . . during the war period" when sales had been so good.[52]

"That the tractor industry is sick," wrote J. S. Clapper, "we must all admit." He predicted disaster for the industry "unless some changes are made by the manufacturers, and they very quickly. . . ." He criticized tractor makers for attempting to force farmers to use a "one purpose machine" when something more versatile was needed. Clapper suggested that "A tractor designed to meet all the conditions and requirements in the diversified farming sections will find five prospective purchasers where there is one for the one-purpose machine. It is only necessary to consult the government figures to show the annual acreage devoted to row crops every year in the different states, which must be cultivated from three to five times each season to convince anyone of the possible demand for the all purpose power plant on the farm."[53]

George W. Iverson, in *Agricultural Engineering*, was more eloquent. Dismayed by the manufacturers apparent unresponsiveness, the engineer wrote:

> The possible market for tractors, however, in the corn belt, has hardly been scratched, for study reveals that only about six per cent of the farms in these six states have tractors, while the other ninety-four per cent still depend on horses for power.
>
> The reason for this is very apparent to anyone who has made a study of the tractor situation. Unless the farmer has a large farm, where it is absolutely necessary to do the work faster than horses can do it, or if he has certain belt work considerations, whenever the subject of the purchase of a tractor is brought up, he will usually reply, "I have to have enough horses for cultivating my corn, and this is nearly enough to get all my work done." In other words, he cannot replace enough horses to make it an economical proposition.
>
> The logical solution, then is to design a tractor that will do cultivating as well as plowing, disking, dragging and other drawbar work.

A tractor for cultivating may seem simple to develop, but in actual practice, it was not.[54] Yet the need for a row-crop tractor was so obvious that the number of people calling for it began to sound like a chorus. A row-crop tractor, if built, could perform 77 percent of field operations. But a conventional tractor did only 38 percent of the work on row crops.[55] Even corn-belt farmers who owned tractors used them for limited purposes, usually just plowing. The situation was similar in the cotton belt.

Cotton, corn, and several other crops required cultivation in order to yield a respectable harvest. Cultivating returned several distinct benefits. It helped to control weeds in the field, of course, but it also loosened the surface of the earth and allowed water to penetrate the soil more readily. The soil that the cultivator disturbed was thrown at the base of the crop plants to prop them up and to help prevent lodging. Cultivation prevented the residue from earlier crops from collecting between the rows and denied insects a refuge. In irrigated areas, cultivation helped maintain the beds and furrows that guided water through the field.[56]

Because cultivating was difficult, designing a mechanical cultivator was a problem. The president of Toro Tractor Company described it:

> The most difficult operation in farming is the first and second cultivation of the tender plants and, unless the operator has an entirely unobstructed view of the rows and the machine has the necessary flexibility so that cultivating teeth or shovels will respond promptly to every move of the operator, good, clean cultivation is not possible without injury to the plants. Unless we can give the farmer a machine capable of doing equally as good cultivation, easier and more economical to operate, and which will perform the work faster with less effort on his part than can be done with horses, we have little argument to persuade him that he should motorize his farm.[57]

Most farmers believed that as long as they had to retain their horses or mules to cultivate, they might as well use them for plowing and planting as well. Row-crop farmers encountered a production bottleneck in the numerous cultivations necessary during the growing season. Conventional tractors were irrelevent to this phase of production.

The possibility of using a separate motor cultivator had been suggested earlier, and in fact, several companies produced such self-propelled cultivators. But economics worked against "tractivators." The purchase of a tractor alone was beyond the means of the small holder, and the additional cost of a motor cultivator made it far more expensive than horse farming.[58]

The solution to the problem of tractor sales lay in the development of a low-cost, all-purpose tractor—one that cultivated as well as performed the other work of a tractor. In early June 1922, E. A. White pleaded with designers to consider market research in the designing of tractors. He presented a compelling argument. White demonstrated that one major manufacturer sold more than 80 percent of its tractors to only 20 percent of the market. The remaining 80 percent of the market—average and smaller farms—were effectively excluded from the ranks of potential tractor buyers.[59]

One month later (July 1922), *Automotive Industries* published a market study by G. B. Gunlogson that had been done for the J. I. Case Threshing Machine Company. The study is a classic of technical writing; it is emphatic, succinct, and well researched. Gunlogson insisted that while the farmer and the state of technology were ready for horseless farming, the manufacturers were not. He charged that tractor makers were tinkering and fine tuning for a limited market, when a cheaper and more versatile tractor—one that could cultivate—would open up a whole new world to sales. No longer, he said, would the tractor market be restricted to the wheat belt and to large farms elsewhere. The average farmer—the one with 160 acres and only $1,400 in equipment—would also be able to purchase a tractor. In order to reach that market, according to Gunlogson, Case needed to commit the company to mass production and to employ extensive economies of scale. Yet Gunlogson believed that the results would be highly profitable. A tractor that was both versatile and cheap would sell in incredible numbers.[60] Apparently J. I. Case Threshing Machine Company turned a deaf ear to its own researcher. Case lagged behind International and Deere when the general purpose tractor was finally placed on the market.

Case was not alone in its distrust of row-crop tractors. The Universal failed to save the ailing Moline Plow Company, despite the tractor's real, if limited, success. The failure of earlier all-purpose designs seemed to many corporate directors like object lessons in company planning. And the technical problems were real. A. W. Scarret said in 1919, "I do not believe that a successful tractor will ever be a very good cultivator or vice versa because the operating conditions and requirements, as well as the power demands are [too] different." Opponents of trying to design all-purpose tractors also pointed to surveys such as one in California, which reported that less than one-half of the farmers surveyed wanted cultivating tractors.[61]

But people who opposed or ignored general purpose tractors overlooked a rising tide of sentiment. In 1919, the call for more versatile tractors had been limited to a few articles like an unsigned piece in *Automotive Industries*. In April 1923, O. E. Bradfute, president of the American Farm Bureau Federation, advocated a general purpose tractor in an address to a luncheon for tractor engineers at the Society of Automotive Engineers' meeting in Chicago. In June 1923, E. M. Eason wrote that, "Everyone, however, with the possible exception of Mr. Ford, is ready to admit that the conventional type of tractor has its limitations

. . . ," and that a new type was needed. By the spring of 1924, a survey of opinion among agricultural engineers at colleges and universities revealed that most foresaw and favored a general purpose tractor.[62]

As engineers thought about the problems of designing an all-purpose tractor, they began to set design parameters. George Iverson suggested a weight of 2,800 to 3,000 pounds and a drawbar rating of some six or seven horsepower. The same year, 1923, the *Journal* of the Society of Automotive Engineers reported "considerable progress" on the row-crop tractor during the sales slump of the early twenties. And O. B. Zimmerman read a short paper at the SAE tractor meeting in Chicago on April 19, 1923, in which he outlined some of the development work done on the general-purpose tractor by the International Harvester Company.[63] The following year the company released the first mass-produced row-crop tractor, although it was initially introduced in very limited numbers. With that row-crop tractor, the McCormick-Deering Tractor Works opened a new chapter in the history of the farm tractor.

The introduction of a successful general-purpose tractor marked the end of an era. The age of continental experimentation was over. It began in the confusion of the First World War, when prototype tractors first became mass-produced. That era saw diverse, experimental tractors developed into a conventional tractor configuration—one that was initially a commercial success. It saw that basic design polished until it reached the limits of its potential. But the "conventional" tractor was not sufficiently adapted to the farm environment to proliferate rapidly. And when a better-adapted machine evolved, the old convention was doomed like some nonadaptable animal confronted by a more virile species. Like some prehistoric creature, it was unmourned, at least by the farmer, because the conventional tractor had never completely fulfilled his hopes and had remained beyond the economic reach of all but the largest landholders in most communities. The new tractor promised more.

NOTES

1. A. H. Hoffman, "The Tendency of Tractors to Rise in Front: Causes and Remedies," *California Agricultural Experiment Station Circular* No. 276 (June 1923): 1–3.

2. "Standardized Fordson Equipment," 971.

3. Right up until acquisiton by Case (Tenneco) in 1985, many International plows had parts numbers beginning with the letters "PO. . . ."

4. Cyrus McCormick, *Century of the Reaper*, 198–99, 201. No tractor manufacturer has succeeded for more than a short time in the American market

without a long line of implements to accompany its tractor. Tenneco's decision to acquire International Harvester's farm equipment division was probably intended to reverse the company's disastrous earlier decision to drop the J. I. Case implement line and specialize in tractors.

5. Robert T. Pound, "Machine vs. Muscle," *Breeder's Gazette* (September 16, 1920): 512.

6. [E. J. Baker, Jr.], "Tractor PTO Speeds under Reconsideration," *Farm Implement News* (January 10, 1957): 4.

7. Gray, *Development of the Agricultural Tractor*, 28; Worthington, "Engineer's History of the Farm Tractor, II," 56. Worthington may have used Gray as a source.

8. As quoted in W. L. Cavert, "Sources of Power on Minnesota Farms," *Minnesota Agricultural Experiment Station Bulletin* No. 262 (February 1930): 50. See also L. B. Sperry, "Farm Power and the Post-War Tractor," *Society of Automotive Engineers—Transactions* 52 (November 1944): 504; Worthington, "Engineer's History, II," 46, 73–74.

9. " 'Daddy of the Farmall Tractor' Dies at Age 98," *Agricultural Engineering* 50 (November 1969): 649; LeLand Zink, "The Agricultural Power Take-Off," *Agricultural Engineering* 12 (June 1931): 209–10.

10. William C. Zelle, "What Form Will the Tractor Ultimately Take?" *Agricultural Engineering* 1 (October 1920): 35–41; Zink, "The Agricultural Power Take-Off," 209–10. Herbert Chase, "International Brings Out Advanced Design of Tractor," *Automotive Industries* (March 23, 1922): 653; G. W. McCuen, "Dividends from Your Tractor," *Ohio Farmer* (January 19, 1924): 9; Leland W. Zink, "Standardization of the Power Take-Off for Farm Tractors," *Agricultural Engineering* 11 (February, 1930): 75–79; F. N. G. Kranich, "The Power Take-Off for Tractors," *Agricultural Engineering* 6 (September 1925): 204–8, 216; L. J. Fletcher and C. C. Kinsman, "The Tractor on California Farms," *California Agricultural Experiment Station Bulletin* 415 (December 1926): 9.

11. For typical examples of more refined designs and the response of the industry, see "Tractor of Good Design and Construction," *Scientific American* (December 14, 1918): 482; P. M. Heldt, "Case 15–27 Hp Tractor," *Automotive Industries* (January 30, 1919): 256–61; "Avery 2-Plow Tractor has 6-Cylinder Engine," *Automotive Industries* (September 23, 1920): 604–5; "Building McCormick-Deering Tractors," *The American Machinist* (July 30, 1925): 183–86, (August 6, 1925): 223–28.

12. William Aitkenhead, "The Farm Tractor," *Indiana Agricultural Experiment Station Circular* No. 89 (January 1919): 3, 6–7, 18.

13. Worthington, "Engineer's History, II," 46, 73–74; Sperry, "Farm Power and the Post-War Tractor," 504.

14. Tractor Power Plant Improvements," *Scientific American* (November 16, 1918): 396; Warren, "Trend of Tractor Developments," 15; Aitkenhead, "Farm Tractor," 12; David Beecroft, "Tractor Problems That Are Awaiting Solution," *Automotive Industries* (March 13, 1919): 583, 601; "Requirements of Tractors for Use in Southern States," *Automotive Industries* (March 20, 1919): 662; "Dusty Fields," *Literary Digest* (August 30, 1919): 26; L. A. Reynoldson and H. R. Tolley,

"Choosing a Tractor for a Corn-Belt Farm," *Farmers' Bulletin* No. 1300 (Washington: United States Department of Agriculture, n.d.): 10; Fletcher and Kinsman, "Tractor on California Farms," 180.

15. Edward R. Hewitt, "Principles of Wheeled Farm Tractors," *Automotive Industries* (February 6, 1919): 312–15; A. W. Scarratt, "The Influence of Hitches and Drawbar Location on Tractor Design," *Automotive Industries* (June 12, 1919): 1334-35, 1359; H. Scott Hall and H. G. Burford, "The Agrimotor: Present Failings, Future Prospects," *Automobile Engineer* (November 1921): 387–89; R. U. Blasingame, "Relation of Lug Equipment to Traction." *Agricultural Engineering* 3 (May 1922): 79–81; O. W. Young, "Tractor Industry in 1922," *Journal of the Society of Automotive Engineers* 12 (February 1923): 188.

16. Howard Warren, "The Trend of Tractor Development," *Scientific American* (December 28, 1918): 534.

17. Wayne Worthington, "Engineer's Tractor History [III]: The 1920's: Eliminating and Consolidating," *Implement & Tractor* (February 21, 1967): 46, 73.

18. Chase, "Advanced Design," 651.

19. R. T. Mally, "Sidelights on the Tractor Business," *Power Farming* (October 1916): 14, 39.

20. Francis Z. Hazlett, "The Farm Tractor in 1920," *Scientific American* (December 18, 1920): 612–13.

21. Archie A. Stone, *Farm Tractors* (New York: John Wiley and Sons, 1932), 2.

22. Yerkes and Mowry, "Farm Experiences with the Tractor," 5–6; Raymond Olney, "How Much Will This Tractor Pull?" *Power Farming* (May 1916): 9, 50–52; Olney, "Standardization of Tractor Ratings," *Power Farming* (February 1917): 13–14; "Tractor Ratings," *Automotive Industries* (March 7, 1918): 513; C. M. Eason, "Efficiency of Farm Tractors: A Standard System of Testing Needed," *Scientific American* (July 29, 1916): 96–97; "A Test for Tractors," *Power Farming* (October 1918): 14; "Tractor Demonstrations," *Power Farming* (February 1919): 14.

23. "Authoritative Statement on Farm Tractor Progress and Education," *Literary Digest* (January 4, 1919): 46.

24. "Those Tractor Tests," *Power Farming* (April 1919): 16.

25. Robert Wiebe, *Businessmen and Reform* (Cambridge, Mass.: Harvard University Press, 1962); Gabriel Kolko, *The Triumph of Conservatism* (New York: Macmillan and Co., 1977).

26. For an alternative explanation, see David F. Noble, *America by Design: Science, Technology and the Rise of Corporate Capitalism* (New York: Alfred A. Knopf, 1977).

27. Office of the Secretary [of Agriculture]. "Proposed Farm Power Studies," *United States Department of Agriculture Circular* 149 (Washington: United States Department of Agriculture, March 1920): 3–8.

28. H.R. 11306, 66th Cong., 2nd sess. (1920); H.R. 234, 67th Cong., 2nd sess. (1921).

29. Wilmot F. Crozier, "Father of Nebraska's Tractor Law Explains It,"

Implement and Tractor Trade Journal (September 1919): 58, 70; E. E. Bracket, "The Nebraska Tractor Tests," *Agricultural Engineering* 12 (June 1931): 205, 206; "Nebraska Tractor Tests: Help or Hindrance," *Farm Implement News* (September 25, 1952): 30, 31, 78–80; Louis I. Leviticus, "Tractor Testing in the World," *Agricultural History* 54 (January 1980): 167–72.

30. O[scar] W. Sjorgren, "Why Standardize Tractor Ratings?" *Agricultural Engineering* 1 (November 1920): 67, 68: Sjorgren, "Tractor Testing in Nebraska," *Agricultural Engineering* 2 (February 1921): 34–37; Sjorgren, "Nebraska Test Analysis," *Journal of the Society of Automotive Engineers* 12 (June 1923): 587–94; "Can a Farm Be Worked with Tractors Alone?" *Rural New Yorker* (February 19, 1921): 267, 268; Carl E. Juengel, "Experience with a Tractor," *Rural New Yorker* (April 16, 1921): 587; Harry Cozens, "A Farm, A Farmer, and a Tractor," *Rural New Yorker* (June 3, 1922): 738.

31. "Agricultural Engineering: Recent Progress in Tractors," *International Review of Agriculture* 20 (September 1929): 359–65.

32. G. W. McCuen, "The Present Status of Tractor Farming," *Ohio Farmer* (January 11, 1919): 2–70; A. B. Welty, "Considerations Affecting Belt Speeds," *Agricultural Engineering* 3 (July 1922): 115–16; Zink, "Standardization of the Power Take-off," 75–79; Kranich, "PTO for Tractors," 204, 208, 216–17; "Detailed Technical Specifications for Gasoline Farm Tractors for 1919," *Automotive Industries* (January 16, 1919): 176–79.

33. "America to Restock the World with Farm Machinery," *Scientific American* (November 4 , 1916): 424–25.

34. McCuen, "Status," 2.

35. H. R. Tolley and L. M. Church, "The Manufacture and Sale of Farm Equipment in 1920," *Department Circular* 212 (Washington: United States Department of Agriculture, April 1922): 2.

36. Worthington, "Engineer's History, [III]," 46, 73–74.

37. David Beecroft, "Tractor Makers Assert They Can't Cut Their Prices Now," *Automotive Industries* (October 26, 1922): 804; Young, "Tractor Industry, 1922," 188.

38. Capper Farm Press, *The Tractor: Selling It as an Agricultural Implement and Fitting It to Midwest Crop Areas,* 4th ed.; (Topeka: Capper Farm Press, 1920): 9; Sherman E. Johnson, "Changes in American Farming," *Miscellaneous Publication,* No. 707 (Washington: Bureau of Agricultural Economics, United States Department of Agriculture, December 1949): 54; E. A. White, "Market Research Essential to Development of Tractor Design," *Automotive Industries* (June 8, 1923): 1211.

39. White, "Market Research," 1212; "What Farmers Say of Tractors," *The Ohio Farmer* (January 18, 1919): 14–82; Crossman, "Gasoline Horse," 14; "Small Tractors Increase Potential Market from 2% to 60% of Farms," *Automotive Industries* (January 16, 1919): 182.

40. J. M. Bird, "A Steel Mule that Drives Like a Horse," *Scientific American* (February 2, 1918): 109, 119; "Steering and Controlling Devices for the Four Wheeled Tractor," *Scientific American* (November 2, 1918): 358; "General Utility Tractor Controlled with Reins," *Scientific American* (August 17, 1918): 132; Gray, *Development of the Agricultural Tractor,* 30.

41. Bureau of the Census, *Historical Statistics*, Part 1, 496; White, "Market Research," 1210, 1211; Hazlett, "Farm Tractor 1920," 613.

42. G. W. Gilbert, "An Economic Study of Tractors on New York Farms," *New York Agricultural Experiment Station Bulletin* 506 (June 1930): 3; "Tractor Demonstrations," 14; "ASAE Drafts Tractor Demonstration Rules," *Power Farming* (May 1919): 57.

43. J. Edward Dies, "How Farm Tractors Saved the Spring Crop in Storm Area," *Power Farming* (May 1923): 5.

44. L. A. Reynoldson and H. R. Tolley, "What Tractors and Horses Do on Corn-Belt Farms," *Farmers' Bulletin*, No. 1295 (Washington: United States Department of Agriculture, January, 1923): 5; McCuen, "Dividends," 76; Capper Farm Press. *The Tractor*, 12–13.

45. P. T. Hines, "Give the Tractor a Chance to Make Good," *Power Farming* (January 1919): 9; Hines, "When You Buy a Tractor, Buy Tractor Equipment," *Progressive Farmer* (July 12, 1919): 1142; J. L. Justice, "Quality in Tractor Work," *Hoard's Dairyman* (April 22, 1921): 580.

46. L. A. Reynoldson and H. R. Tolley, "Cost of Using Tractors on Corn-Belt Farms," *Farmers' Bulletin*, No. 1297 (Washington: United States Department of Agriculture. 1922): 13; "The Farm Tractor Instruction Book: Send It in the Period between Purchase of Tractor and Its Delivery," *Automotive Industries* (February 21, 1918): 419; John T. Wright, "Why Power Farming Short Courses Are Needed," *Power Farming* (November 1918): 13, 35; L. J. Fletcher, "Tractor Service—Curative or Preventive—Which?" *Agricultural Engineering* 1 (December 1920): 71–72; "Many Tractor Schools," *Power Farming* (May 1919): 57; H. J. Metcalf, "The Farm Tractor in Iowa," *Hoard's Dairyman* (October 1919): 563. Admittedly, farm hands who know better may still misuse pliers and stilson wrenches under pressure to complete a critical field operation in a hurry. J. L. Justice, "Canvas Covers for Tractors," *Power Farming* (July 1920): 16; W. D. Nichols, "Tractor Experience in Kentucky, *Kentucky Agricultural Experiment Station Bulletin*, No. 222 (September 1919): 45–68.

47. Earle W. Gage, "Tractor Harvests Beet Crop," *Power Farming* (July 1920): 17.

48. W. F. Wilcox, "Tractor Alfalfa Combination Promises Big Returns," *Power Farming* (September 1920): 12–14.

49. R. R. Luman, "A Farmer's Views on Tractors," *Breeder's Gazette* (September 9, 1920): 466. Increasing numbers of tractors on farms were accompanied by increasing numbers of motor trucks, from 2,000 in 1911 to 25,000 in 1915 to 139,000 in 1920 and 459,000 in 1925. Automobiles increased at a similar rate, with 100,000 on farms in 1911, some 472,000 in 1915, up to 2,146,000 in 1920 and 3,283,000 in 1925. Automobiles—with or without trailers—were used by farmers for hauling, just as trucks were used. All three types of vehicles (tractors, trucks and automobiles) displaced horses. All three were expensive but complementary, and the adoption of one tended to encourage the adoption of the others if finances permitted.

50. Wirt, "Maryland Tractor Owners," 81; Nichols, "Tractor Experience in Kentucky," 47; Metcalf, "Tractors in Iowa," 545; Reynoldson and Tolley, "Tractors on Corn Belt Farm," 3; Capper Farm Press, *The Tractor*, 5; John C. Wooley,

"Power Farming in Idaho," *Idaho Agricultural Experiment Station Bulletin*, No. 111 (September 1918): 10.

51. Young, "Tractor Industry," 188.

52. L. J. Fletcher, "Factors Influencing Tractor Development," *Agricultural Engineering* 3 (November 1922): 179–82.

53. J. S. Clapper, "The 'All Purpose' Tractor on the Modern Farm," *Automotive Industries* (March 16, 1922): 622.

54. George W. Iverson, "Possibilities of the All-Purpose Tractor," *Agricultural Engineering* 3 (September 1922): 147.

55. F. A. Wirt, "The General-Purpose Farm Tractor," *Agricultural Engineering* 5 (May, 1924): 103; G. B. Gunlogson, "General-Purpose Tractor Needed for American Farm Market," *Automotive Industries* (July 6, 1922): 4.

56. E. Holekamp, W. J. Thomas, and K. R. Frost, "Cotton Cultivation with Tractors," *Arizona Agricultural Experiment Station Bulletin* 235 (March 1951): 4; Reynoldson and Tolley, "What Tractors Do," 8; "The Place of the Tractor in Cotton Belt Farming," *Progressive Farmer* (August 31, 1918): 962.

57. Clapper, " 'All-Purpose' Tractor," 622.

58. Lowell Carlson, "Remember the 'Tractivators?' " *Grain Producer's News* (October 1977): 4–8; Raymond Olney, "Signs of Progress in the Farm Tractor Field," *Power Farming* (October 1918): 10; P. M. Heldt, "Motor Cultivators at Kansas City," *Automotive Industries* (March 13, 1919): 580; "New Models and Strong Representation," 506.

59. White, "Market Research," 1210–13.

60. Gunlogson, "General Purpose," 4–7.

61. Scarratt, "Hitches and Drawbar Location," 1334, 1335, 1359; Fletcher and Kinsman, "Tractor on California Farms," 18.

62. "The Motorized Farm," *Automotive Industries* (March 20, 1919): 657; "Farmers Need Efficient Tools," *Journal of the Society of Automotive Engineers* 12 (May 1923): 501; Eason, "General Purpose Tractor," 600; Wirt, "General Purpose Tractor," 104.

63. Iverson, "All Purpose Tractor," 147; Young, "Tractor Industry," 188; "Tractor Defects Summarized," *Journal of the Society of Automotive Engineers* 12 (May 1923): 500.

The Fordson tractor was ideally suited to mass production. (Lubbock County Museum and Henry Ford Museum and Greenfield Village)

The Fordson in the field, pulling a disk originally designed for horses (hence, the seat). (Henry Ford Museum and Greenfield Village)

Like many new industries, the tractor industry experienced a boom period when expectations exceeded sales and provided opportunities for unscrupulous promoters. Cartoon originally printed in *Farm Implement News*, February 1, 1917. (*Implement & Tractor*, Overland Park, Kan.)

The John Deere Model D was probably the most successful wheatland-type tractor ever built, with a thirty year production run. (Deere & Company)

The Farmall ("Regular") opened row-crop farms to tractor use because it could cultivate a growing crop as well as plowing, planting, and harvesting. Although it only cultivated two rows, it was too expensive for use on farms of average or smaller size. Nevertheless, it was successful mechanically and economically. (Case-IH)

The GP, John Deere's first row-crop tractor, never proved popular, in part because of its three-row design. (Deere & Company)

Massey-Harris's first row-crop tractor was also called a GP. It was exceptionally well-designed, and some units remain in active use more than fifty years after they were built. Unfortunately, the four-wheel-drive design was expensive to produce, and its popularity was limited to areas where sand or mud made traction difficult. (Massey-Ferguson, Inc.)

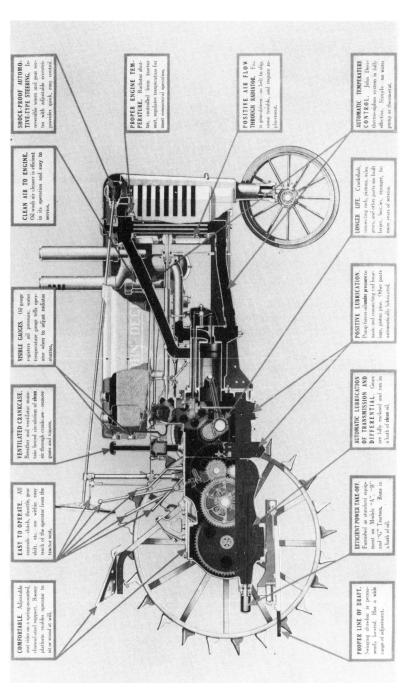

The John Deere Model A was an extremely popular tractor for many years; its two horizontal cylinders and minimal number of moving parts made it dependable and durable. The design was cheap to overhaul and very fuel efficient, although proponents of other brands mocked its distinctive "pop, pop" exhaust sound. (Deere & Company)

Harry Merrit (right) led Allis-Chalmers Corporation to a competitive position in the tractor industry by a combination of savy marketing and innovative engineering. The Allis-Chalmers WC (top) was the first tractor to be designed specifically to use rubber tires. The Allis-Chalmers B (bottom) was designed to be small and cheap enough for use on even average or smaller-than-average farms. It sold and performed well. (Deutz-Allis)

5
Of Cabbage Rows
and Tire Kings

The first farm tractors were cobbled together in blacksmith shops during the 1890s, but tractors did not reach a practical, mechanical maturity until the eve of the Second World War. As already described, in the period from the tractor's inception until the First World War, tractor makers experimented with basic design concepts. Then the Fordson brought mass production and intensified competition to the industry. That competition refined the tractor in innumerable minor ways, and the cumulative effect of those minor improvements was significant. But the tractors of the Fordson generation were ill-adapted to the majority of farms in the United States. Fordsons were of questionable value on farms growing corn, cotton, cabbages, or other row crops. And Fordsons were too large and too expensive for the thousands of farms that were smaller than average. Tractors were incapable of invading the majority of farms until they could cultivate growing crops and work economically within the constrictions of undersized farms.

The competition that the Fordson stirred up eventually provided the motivation for developing a row-crop tractor. Then the success of the row-crop tractor encouraged innovative engineers toward the ultimate down-sizing of the tractor.

The first mass-produced row-crop tractor changed farm production and the implement industry so profoundly that several agricultural historians have referred to the era it introduced as the second revolution in American agriculture. That description deliberately compared the scale of change to the initial mechanization of farming.[1] Yet seldom has a revolution had such a quiet and inauspicious debut. When the McCormick-Deering division of International Harvester rolled the first Farmall out of the factory door, they did so almost furtively. There were no brass bands, no advertising blitz, and not even a press conference. Indeed, implement periodicals and farm magazines ignored the occasion, if they were even aware of it.

Apparently, a sizable faction within the International Harvester organization was dubious about the Farmall project and did not want widespread unfavorable publicity in case the row-crop tractor failed. They did, however, arrange for extensive, anonymous, and obscure tests for the new machine.[2] But the Farmall worked, and Texas farmers who observed the tests were so enthusiastic that McCormick-Deering decided to go ahead and release the new tractor "for sale in Texas . . . until we could produce the required volume for greater sales."[3]

The Farmall's introduction was a triumph for its developers because the industry had not welcomed proposals for all-purpose tractors. One industry insider described the situation precisely. "No development in the industry was regarded with more distrust, and wholesale opposition than the suggested general-purpose tractor . . . . The opposition came more from farm implement manufacturers' home organizations than from the field, and those within the organizations certainly deserve credit for their relentless efforts to have this type of tractor released for experimental development. . . ."[4]

As Cyrus McCormick characterized it, credit for the Farmall must go to "collective rather than individual genius." The tractor was the product of a competent engineering staff working under cautiously innovative management.[5]

International's management might have been too cautious to push the experimental program in ordinary times, but "Fordson competition made it essential for the Harvester Company to do something drastic to meet Ford competition."[6] The new development project was a gamble.

The experimental unit at McCormick-Deering's tractor works built and evaluated various light tractors and motor cultivators for nearly a decade before the Farmall was introduced, but did not anticipate any immediate production of such machinery. In the process of their experimentation, the unit built some strange-looking devices, but they gained experience that ultimately proved useful. When the Fordson threatened the whole International Harvester empire, Bert B. Benjamin and his staff marshalled their accumulated knowledge and within a short time produced a remarkably adept row-crop tractor—the Farmall. In doing so, the inventors redesigned both the tractor and its implements, tailoring the machinery to fit the crop and farm practice rather than laying out the tractor on the basis of preconceived engineering standards. It was a radical change in the process of tractor design.[7]

The introduction of a general-purpose tractor was surprisingly long in coming. For several years, a growing chorus had demanded such a machine, but the demand largely fell on deaf ears. Proposals for a more versatile tractor first sounded during the sales slump of the early 1920s. Dozens of writers realized that the conventional tractor was inadequate for the average farmer. One said that progress in tractor engineering lay in two courses—mechanical improvement in existing types of tractors and "the development of the general purpose type or types."[8]

The major problem with the conventional tractor was that it could not cultivate growing crops. Yet United States farmers grew 149 million acres of row crops that required cultivation compared to only 119 million acres of uncultivated small grains. The row crops were estimated to be worth almost $4 billion, while small grains were worth only slightly more than $1.5 billion. Cultivation or intertillage was a major task on the nation's farms. A tractor that was too clumsy to cultivate was a useless expense during much of the growing season.[9]

Undoubtedly, in an age when most Americans had grown up on a farm, the tractor industry's executives could not have been ignorant of the importance of cultivation. And even if they had not known from first-hand experience, the periodicals of the age supplied the missing information. Finally, the executives had marketing studies available to them. One frustrated researcher forced such a report into print after it was ignored by the officials at J. I. Case Threshing Machine Company who had paid for it. Had Case stockholders—or those of any of the half-dozen largest tractor manufacturers—challenged their corporate officers, questioning the officials for allowing International to develop such a lead, the officers certainly could not have claimed ignorance. Yet habit, conventional wisdom, and indolent conservatism delayed most corporations for at least a half decade after the industry had acquired the technical expertise to build effective row-crop tractors.[10]

The only economically feasible solution for the problem of adapting machinery to a row-crop farm lay in the development of a tractor that could plow as well as a conventional tractor, but that could also cultivate. The Farmall was exactly such a machine.[11]

The Farmall tractor, when it was released for sale, appeared somewhat odd to people accustomed to the squat, fat, clumsy tractors that preceded it; but the Farmall and its imitators sold so well that it eventually changed the image of the tractor. There were two outstanding features of the new tractor. First, it was tall and narrow. It was tall in order to clear growing corn or cotton plants, and narrow so that the driver had maximum visibility of the rows that he was cultivating. The second noticeable feature of the Farmall and many of the imitators was a very narrow set of front wheels mounted in the center of the tractor under the front end. The tricycle arrangement allowed the tractor to turn in a very tight circle, but the combination of widely spaced, large-diameter rear wheels and small, tightly set front wheels looked odd, at least until people became accustomed to it. But the first generation of Farmalls maintained the traditional coloration—they were the same gunmetal gray that dominated the tractor industry.[12]

The little gray Farmalls were designed to plant, cultivate, and pull harvesting equipment. They had to perform these tasks in crops with row spacings varying from twenty-two inches (.55m.) to forty-eight inches (1.22m.), although a forty-two inch (1.07m.) row was most common. The forty-two inch figure was said to be derived from the anatomy of a mule. For cultivation, the little tractors were provided with attachment points for front- and side-mounted cultivators. To drive binders and harvesters, the tractors had a power take-off (PTO) shaft. An optional pulley was available for use with hammer mills and similar devices. The versatility that was designed into the Farmall was soon expanded, as farmers adapted the machine to do tasks that its designers had not expected.[13] As late as the thirties, engineers predicated new uses for the row-crop tractor as experiments by farmers revealed new capabilities hitherto unanticipated.[14]

Because of its adaptability and because of its ability to displace horses from the farm, the Farmall sold well. A few farmers were dubious, however, and hedged their bets by keeping their draft stock for a season or two after purchasing their first row-crop tractor.[15] But they were optimistic enough to purchase and try the new tractor, and few ever returned to horse farming. A contemporary reported that farmers were favorably disposed to the new tractors, suggesting that "the movement of general purpose tractors to farms will be restrained only by the farmer's financial inablility to purchase, and not by any lack of faith that [the] tractor will meet his requirements."[16] The Farmall worked well on the farm; it sold well at the dealership; it assembled well at the factory; and it paid dividends to the stockholders. The Farmall was a dramatic success.

The victory of the Farmall finished off the Fordson and prompted virtually all tractor manufacturers to develop a competitive product. On reviewing 1928, industry pundits observed that Ford had discontinued production in the United States but had continued to sell tractors that had accumulated in stock during 1927 as sales fell. These commentators pondered the impact of imported Fordsons upon the 1929 market.[17] They did not realize that the Fordson was dead. Finally, in the late thirties, the Ford factory in Cork, Ireland attempted to resurrect the defunct tractor by introducing a version of the Fordson that was crudely adapted to row-crop work. But the Fordson "All-Around" flopped.[18]

The Farmall's triumph over the Fordson, however, did not leave it without a competitor for very long. In 1927 John Deere attacked International's supremacy in the field with the John Deere "GP," a general purpose tractor. John Deere engineers equipped the GP with a lift to raise and lower implements with engine power instead of muscle power. The power lift quickly became a popular idea, although the John Deere GP did not. The GP was designed with a wide front end and was intended to work three rows instead of two, a concept that farmers rejected. Eventually John Deere replaced the GP with the four-row John Deere A, which had a tricycle-type format, and which was eminently successful.[19]

By 1935, the success of the Farmall and other row-crop tractors encouraged virtually every manufacturer to design and sell one or more general purpose tractors. Massey-Harris's first all-purpose tractor, like Deere's, was called a "GP."[20] Like the Deere GP, the Massey-Harris GP had a wide front end. Unlike other tractors of the time, the Massey-Harris GP was a four-wheel-drive model, with four equally sized wheels. The additional complexity and expense of the four-wheel-drive model was unnecessary for most farmers, but the tractor was popular in a few areas where the terrain was steep, sandy, or wet. In l936, Massey-Harris introduced their "Challenger," a refined tricycle-type tractor with a power lift. It sold relatively well. The same year, Oliver introduced a successful row-crop tractor, the six-cylinder "Model 70," with a high-compression engine. In 1937, Case discovered that its row-crop tractor, the "CC" was its best seller. Even Sears, Roebuck & Company entered the field with a Graham-Bradley tractor manufactured by the Graham-Paige automobile company. Sears offered David-Bradley implements to fit its tractor, but the Chicago mail-order firm did not thrive in the tractor business any more than General Motors had earlier.[21]

As most manufacturers began to offer row-crop tractors, there was a natural tendency for each tractor company to multiply its line. By 1937 John Deere offered twelve models in four power ranges. International supplied eleven models in row-crop, orchard, wheatland, or crawler models. As an additional competitive inducement, some makers started streamlining their tractors by covering the engines with sheet metal shrouds. Although this styling was purely cosmetic, it was thought to promote sales.[22] The competition among the various manufacturers refined the row-crop tractor quite rapidly.

Manufacturers also catered to the needs of larger farmers. The original Farmall was a two-row tractor. The F-20, F-30, Challenger, John Deere A and several others doubled the row-crop tractor's capacity so that it handled four rows. The size increase was part of a constantly accelerating horsepower race that began slowly but grew steadily. The largest tractors always sold to a small percentage of the total market—the portion composed of the largest farmers. But with constantly declining farm numbers and constantly increasing farm size, the market tended to shift toward larger tractors—even during a later period when manufacturers attempted to build tractors for small farms.

By 1940, the United States Department of Agriculture recognized the victory of the row-crop tractor. "Three-fourths of all tractors sold in the United States in 1937 were general purpose tractors," the Department reported, "and as the all-purpose type has dominated sales since 1935, it is probable that 50 percent of the tractors now on farms are of this type." That proportion steadily increased.[23]

When International Harvester introduced the Farmall, it did so hoping to boost company sales in competition with the Fordson, but the revolutionary design "brought a considerable spurt in tractor purchases," and helped the entire tractor industry.[24] In the period from 1925 to 1928, tractors on farms increased from 549,000 to 782,000, even as many farmers retired their older equipment in favor of newer. By 1932, there were more than a million tractors on farms; analysts estimated that one farmer in six owned a tractor.[25] The renewed prosperity for the industry was well represented by Deere and Company. John Deere was best known for plows, and was in fact the nation's largest plowmaker. Earlier in 1923, Deere executives considered abandoning tractor manufacturing entirely, but by 1936, some 40 percent of Deere's sales revenue came from tractors, of which the A and D models were most prominent.[26]

While the introduction of the row-crop tractor revived the implement industry, it had far more profound influences on American agriculture in general. Observers at the time often used variations of the word *revolutionary* to describe the impact of general purpose tractors on the nation's farming structure. Subsequent analysis has validated the appropriateness of that term. Baker, Borger and Landsberger, Wik, and Worthington all used the introduction of all-purpose tractors—the Farmall—as the watershed that divides the agricultural past from the present. An economist described a "revolution in cotton production" because of the row-crop tractor. Another attributed to the Farmall the outbreak of an "industrial revolution in agriculture." "I consider," wrote E. J. Baker, Jr., "the Farmall the greatest of the five great developments in power farming."[27] The tractor that revived the tractor industry revolutionized agriculture.

The effectiveness of the row-crop tractor was enhanced unmeasurably by three major refinements, the results of early competition for the general purpose market. All three innovations were soon adopted by most manufacturers.

The first major improvement upon the Farmall design was the introduction of the power lift by John Deere's GP. But Deere and Company had no monopoly on the power-lift concept, and the competitors rushed to add the device to their tractors.

The addition of power lifts was not a luxury, but a legitimate tool for increasing productivity. Raising and lowering tools could be tiring and tedious, "turning at the ends of the field presents quite a problem. The implements must be raised out of the ground, then a short turn must be made, and the implements must be lowered again." Before power lifts, such operations demanded tractor operators with powerful and tireless arms. However, when tractors with mechanical lifts came along, the operator merely stepped on a button or pulled a lever.[28] The amount of time that the power lift saved was significant. Works Progress Administration researchers estimated the average farmer saved about thirty minutes per day with a power lift, and that the mechanism produced an aggregate savings of one million man-hours annually nationwide.[29] For the farmer actually driving the tractor, the time was less noticeable than the welcome reduction in physical exertion, because raising implements out of the ground by brute strength was back-breaking work.

The second major innovation in tractor design, the adoption of rubber tires, also saved both time and human discomfort. The idea of using rubber tires on tractors was not new. As early as 1919 a manufacturer had offered rubber tires for road work, but retained steel for the field. Industrial tractors usually rolled on rubber, and various experimenters had tested rubber tractor tires unsuccessfully.[30]

The idea of low-pressure tractor tires apparently developed in the mind of Harry C. Merrit, an executive of the Allis-Chalmers tractor works who approached America's Tire King.

> The idea was broached to Mr. Harvey Firestone, who would have nothing to do with it—in fact, refused to make up a few sets for experimental purposes. But the story goes that once they had manufactured some big landing-gear tires for an airplane that crashed on take-off. The molds were brought forth, and without Harvey Firestone's knowledge, the tires were made. Apparently it took only a demonstration to cause Mr. Firestone to change his mind, for before long he was issuing publicity stories about his "rubberized" farm on which every piece of equipment that rolled had tires. And both Goodyear and Firestone began making tractor tires.[31]

Nor were Allis-Chalmers, Goodyear, and Firestone alone in their experiments. Tractor makers and tire manufacturers were both looking for any device to boost depression sales, and various professional societies and land-grant colleges were also experimenting. At their 1932 annual meeting, the American Society of Agricultural Engineers paid particular attention to rubber tires. Within the next two years more than twenty papers on the low-pressure tractor tire appeared in professional journals. The culmination came in a February 1934 editorial in *Agricultural Engineering*, "Awaiting the Tractor Designed for Rubber Tires."[32] The editor did not have long to wait. That same year, Allis-Chalmers introduced "WC," the first tractor designed from its inception for rubber tires.

Allis-Chalmers anticipated problems in pursuading farmers to make an initial test of pneumatic-tired equipment. To publicize rubber tires and to gain publicity generally, the company hired famous race car driver Barney Oldfield to race Allis-Chalmers tractors. For several seasons, various fair goers were treated to the improbable spectacle of tractor races. In the process, Oldfield established a world record farm tractor speed of 64.28 miles per hour, one that will presumably stand for lack of a challenge.[33]

While Barney Oldfield stormed the country in mile-a-minute tractors, agricultural engineers tested air tires in more practical research. Most experiment stations reported favorably on the newer tires. A typical report stated that rubber tires used less fuel, outpulled steel, were faster, and allowed the use of a higher gear. They also had less rolling resistance, were markedly more efficient in plowing, were more comfortable, and allowed the tractor to perform a greater variety of tasks.[34] Tractors with rubber tires also suffered less from vibration. All of these advantages were quickly exploited by manufacturers, although, interestingly enough, operator comfort—because of reduced vibration and dust—was low on the advertised list of advantages!

The benefits of rubber tires were so overwhelming that neither manufacturer nor farmer was able to resist the move to pneumatic tires for very long. "There is an almost complete swing to rubber tires. . . ." reported one observer at a tractor show, as he observed the shiny new merchandise on exhibit. He also reported that "the dealers are doing a brisk business in changing over steel-wheeled tractors already in use."[35]

A survey of users brought generally positive comments on tractors with rubber tires. "No man can ride a lug tractor in the heat and dirt and live very long," wrote a farmer. Another wrote that, "My wife says she would not drive any other but rubber-tires!" Hired hands preferred employers with rubber-tired tractors because "they do not shake the guts out of the engine or the driver."[36]

In a very short time, then, rubber tires dominated the new equipment market. The first rubber tires were sold in 1932. By 1935, with only a few manufacturers offering rubber, 14 percent of the tractors sold rolled on soft wheels. By 1939, the proportion had climbed to 83 percent, and the following year 90 percent of new tractors were sold with pneumatic tires.[37]

The use of rubber tires made the tractor more practical and more attractive. The "introduction of rubber tires . . . greatly facilitated the use of tractor power . . . and lowered the cost of tractor operation." The row-crop tractor benefited especially, and the pneumatic tires were a major factor in the rapid triumph of the Farmall-type over horses and standard-type tractors.[38]

The almost instant popularity of the new tires created a problem for the tire companies and tractor makers alike, who faced a haphazard proliferation of sizes and styles in tractor tires. Gradually the American Society of Agricultural Engineers and the Society of Automotive Engineers formulated standards to assure interchangeability and standardized sizes.[39] The societies' constant efforts at standardization have immeasurably aided tractor development but have generally passed unnoticed.

Pneumatic rubber tires and power lifts helped make the tractor more appealing to all farmers, but a third technical improvement in the 1930s

opened up a new tractor market: the introduction of the small tractor. In
a sense, the period from the invention of the tractor to the Second World
War was an intermittent process of down-sizing. Tractors had started out
as huge machines and had gradually shrunk in size and price. The introduction of four-row machinery was more of a concession to a special market
than an exception to the trend, because two-row units were more common
in most of the United States. Nevertheless, the majority of American farms
were still too small to be able to afford even a two-row tractor.

In 1932 International Harvester announced that it would build a
smaller Farmall, one of just ten horsepower. The company anticipated "a
sizable prospect list of small acreage bolders with big-farm ideas," because
more than half of the nation's farms were less than one hundred acres and
therefore too small for existing tractors.[40] Soon after International began
selling its "F-12" in 1934, Allis-Chalmers began selling an equivalent one-
plow tractor. Both tractors sold slowly, but gradually gained more customers. In 1937, Allis Chalmers's rubber-tired "WC" (a two-row tractor)
was the best selling of its eight models. The WC was priced at $785, which
was more than a small farmer could comfortably pay.[41]

Harry C. Merrit, one of Allis-Chalmers's vice-presidents and the
moving force behind rubber tires, studied the figures from an unspecified
U. S. Census (probably the 1930 census but possibly the Agricultural
census of 1925 or 1935). He found 6.8 million farms, only 1.2 million of
which had tractors. Most of the tractor farms were larger than one hundred
acres, while four million farms were smaller than one hundred acres.
Merrit went into the field to find out what sort of tractor a small farmer
could use. In "barnyard conversations" he devised a set of standards for a
new tractor. Late in 1937, Allis-Chalmers announced a "baby tractor," the
"B," which would sell for just $495. For the first time, the smallest farms
had an economically viable source of mechanical power.[42]

The introduction of the Allis-Chalmers B cut the market out from
under International and John Deere. Although Harvester had an excellent
reputation with farmers, "the price differential was too great." Allis-Chalmers's B played "hob with International's leadership in the field." The
McCormick-Deering works began to gear up to meet the challenge, designing a tractor "in the $500 class." To add to the competition, Henry
Ford returned to the tractor business with a little tractor in the same price
range.[43]

In 1939, International launched the Farmall "A" and Farmall "B,"
designed to meet any and all competition. Both models proved fairly

popular and extremely durable—many are still in use—but they did not
dominate the market. Business was booming for all of the small tractor
manufacturers, and remained both competitive and profitable until well
after the Second World War.[44]

Allis-Chalmers's role in the tractor industry far exceeds the company's size at the beginning of the era. In 1929, Allis-Chalmers commanded a miniscule 4 percent of the tractor market. Ten years later, in
1939, Allis-Chalmers was the third largest tractor manufacturer, behind
International Harvester and Deere. Part of the reason for that growth
were the tractors that Allis-Chalmers made in the 1930s.[45]

In 1928 Allis Chalmers bought the old Monarch Tractor Company.
A year later, they swallowed up the La Crosse Plow Company, and in
1939 acquired the venerable Advance-Rumely Corporation. Thus in three
years, the huge company added a long-line implement business to the
traditional heavy industrial activities. Monarch and Advance-Rumely gave
the company the experience and the facilities to build both light and heavy
tractors. Through La Crosse they acquired the requisite tillage tools to
accompany the power units.[46] None of the acquisitions appeared to have
been particularly well-managed before purchase. Allis-Chalmers's forging
of an effective implement company out of these diverse companies was
remarkable, but the rapidity of subsequent success was still more striking.

First, Allis-Chalmers stayed abreast of every significant technological
advance (until the arrival of the Ferguson system) and pioneered two of
the most significant innovations: rubber tires and one-row tractors. Second, Allis-Chalmers concentrated on producing an aesthetically pleasing
and distinctive tractor. Merrit repeatedly emphasized that his tractors
were to have, in his words, "sex appeal." That quality may be hard to
define when used with tractors, but sales figures support Merrit's appraisal. When Allis-Chalmers's tractors first emerged wearing "Persian
Orange" paint, other tractor makers thought them "vulgar." Farmers,
however, apparently preferred the color to the lackluster gray that coated
most brands. The bright color was eye-catching and identifiable. Allis-
Chalmers also sold its tractors at a lower price than the competition.
Presumably the lower price was possible in part because of cheaper design
and cheaper construction, but a major factor was Allis-Chalmers's willingness to accept a smaller rate of return in order to achieve larger volume.
During much of the period Allis-Chalmers received a 4 percent profit
while International made 6.7, Deere and Company, 18.1 percent.[47] Although basically managerial decisions, these policies were clearly reflected

in the physical nature of the Allis Chalmers tractors, and eventually by the whole industry.[48]

Allis-Chalmers's aggressive policies heated up the competition within the tractor industry, especially with International Harvester and Deere, the traditional industry leaders. But it also made tractors available for diminutive farms. By the eve of the Second World War, tractors were available for wheatland and row-crop farms, for large farms and small. In a perverse irony, the coming of the small tractors—such as the Allis-Chalmers Model B—represent the maturity of tractor design. The tractor industry had finally adapted its product to virtually every American farm.

NOTES

1. Rasmussen, "The Impact of Technological Change," 578–91.

2. International tested the Farmall in cotton fields in Texas around Corpus Christi and San Angelo, C. A. Bonnen and M. C. Magee, "Some Technological Changes in the High Plains Cotton Area of Texas," *Journal of Farm Economics* 20 (August 1938): 605; E. A. Hunger, "Forrestdale said 'Good-Bye' to Dobbin," *Power Farming* (June 1926): 12. Surprisingly, the Farmall faced some initial resistance from dealers in the corn belt, but this soon melted in the face of customer demand, [E. J. Baker, Jr.], "Five Transcendent Developments," *Farm Implement News* (March 10, 1957): 76.

3. L. B. Sperry, "Farm Power and the Post-War Tractor," 504. Sperry spent more than thirty-five years in International's tractor division, beginning in 1908, so presumably was a participant in these events. The gradual process by which International released the Farmall from experimental status to full production has caused the tractor to be dated differently by various chroniclers, ranging from 1923 to 1925; Worthington, "The Engineer's History, [II]," 33–56; Donald E. Borgman, Everette Hainline, and Melvin E. Long, *Fundamentals of Machine Operation: Tractors* (Moline, Ill.: John Deere Service Publications, 1974), 3; Arnold B. Skromme, "The Growth of ASAE and the Farm Equipment Industry, 1907–1970," *Agricultural Engineering* 51 (April 1970): 182; Bonnen and Magee, "Some Technological Changes," 605; Hunger, "Forrestdale," 12.

4. G. D. Jones, "General-Purpose Tractor Design," *Agricultural Engineering* 12 (March 1931): 91.

5. McCormick, *Century of the Reaper*, 209–11.

6. Baker, "Five Transcendent Developments," 76.

7. McCormick, *Century of the Reaper*, 209–11; Hunger, "Forrestdale," 12; [Baker] "Five Transcendent Developments," 76; Archie A. Stone, *Farm Tractors*, 3; Jones, "General Purpose Tractor," 91.

8. Young, "Tractor Industry in 1922," 188.

9. Gunlogson, "General Purpose Tractor Needed," 4–7; Holekamp, Thomas, and Frost, "Cotton Cultivation with Tractors," 4.

10. Gunlogson, "General Purpose Tractor Needed," 4. See also: White,

"Market Research Essential," 1210–13; Iverson, "Possibilities of the All Purpose Tractor," 147–49.

11. Carlson, "Remember the 'Tractivators'?" 4–8; Olney, "Signs of Progress," 10; Heldt, "Motor Cultivators at Kansas City," 580; "New Models and Strong Representation," 506.

12. The traditional Harvester Red on McCormick-Deering row-crop tractors came with the next generation, the F-20 and F-30. Because the second generation retained the Farmall name and appended a model number, it became necessary to somehow distinguish between the original Farmall and the newer Farmalls. Popular usage then nicknamed the original tractor the "Regular." The model numbers approximated the belt horsepower of the Farmalls.

13. For example, by 1930 experimenters were testing the tractor in potato fields, R. U. Blasingame and H. B. Josephson, "The General-Purpose Tractor in Potato Production in Pennsylvania," *Agricultural Engineering* 11 (February 1930): 58–60; and in nut production, J. M. Patterson, "Tractor vs. Mule Power in Nut Production," *American Nut Journal* (January 1930).

14. R. U. Blasingame,"Corn Production Studies with the General Purpose Tractor," *Agricultural Engineering* 12 (March 1931): 89–90; L. A. Reynoldson, et al. "Utilization and Cost of Power on Corn Belt Farms," *Technical Bulletin* No. 384 (Washington: United States Department of Agriculture, October 1933).

15. Charles P. Butler and D. C. Crawford, "The Use and Cost of Tractor Power on Small Farms in Anderson County, S. C.," *South Carolina Agricultural Experiment Station Bulletin* 368, (July 1947): 8; Sterling Jerden to Robert C. Williams, interview, Wolforth, Texas, 1978, cassette and transcript in Lubbock County Museum Archive.

16. Lee J. Ahart, "Corn Planting and Cultivation with the General-Purpose Tractor," *Agricultural Engineering* 11 (February 1930): 61; also see Theo Brown, "The Requirements and Design of Cultivation Equipment for the General Purpose Tractor," *Agricultural Engineering* 11 (February 1930): 63.

17. R. L. Cusick, "Tractor Industry Is Completing Record Breaking Year," *Automotive Industries* (December 8, 1928): 817–19.

18. "New Fordson Tri-Cycle-Type Tractor Passes Nebraska Test," *Automotive Industries* (August 27, 1938): 267–68.

19. Worthington, "Engineer's History, [III]," 47.

20. Heldt, "Varied Types of Farm Work Handled," 854.

21. "Two or Three Plow Rating for Massey," *Automotive Industries* (January 11, 1936): 49; E. P. Neufield, *A Global Corporation* 32–34; "Oliver Unit is 'Streamlined' " *Automotive Industries* (January 11, 1936) 48–49; Ralph W. Poulton, "The Farm Tractor on Parade," *Breeder's Gazette* (December 1937): 16–19; "The Graham-Bradley Farm Tractor Described," *Automotive Industries* (July 31, 1937): 154.

22. Poulton, "Tractor on Parade," 16–19; Wayne Worthington, "Engineer's Tractor History, IV: Depression and Recovery—Rubber Tires, Fuel, Ferguson," *Implement & Tractor* (March 1967): 64. Worthington's date is a little late. T. H. Koeber, "The Styling of Farm Machinery," *Agricultural Engineering* 26 (January 1945): 17–18.

23. R. S. Kifer, B. H. Hurt, and Albert A. Thornbrough, "The Influence of Technical Progress on Agricultural Production," *The Yearbook of Agriculture, 1940: Farmers in a Changing World* (Washington: United States Department of Agriculture, 1940): 513.

24. Johnson, "Changes in American Farming," 13, 15.

25. Donald D. Durost and Evelyn T. Black, "Changes in Farm Production and Efficiency," *Statistical Bulletin* No. 581 (Washington: United States Department of Agriculture, Economic Research Service, November 1977): 31; A. F. Waddel, "As Public Works Buying Slackens Returning Farm Prosperity Lifts Production of Adaptable New Models," *Automotive Industries* (December 28, 1935): 857.

26. Worthington, "Engineer's History, [III]," 46; "Farm Implement Demands Increase," *Literary Digest* (March 6, 1937): 40.

27. E. J. Baker, Jr., "A Quarter Century of Tractor Development," *Agricultural Engineering* 12 (June 1931): 206–7; Harold Barger and Hans H. Landsberg, *American Agriculture, 1899-1939: A Study of Output, Employment, and Productivity* (New York: National Bureau of Economic Research, Inc., 1942), 202; Wik, *Steam Power on the American Farm* 202–3; Worthington, "Engineer's History, [III]," 40; P. H. Stephens, "Mechanization of Cotton Farms," *Journal of Farm Economics* 13 (January 1931): 27; Carey McWilliams, "Farms into Factories: Our Agricultural Revolution," *Antioch Review* (Winter 1941): 413; [Baker], "Five Transcendent Developments," 36.

28. Heldt, "Varied Types," 856.

29. Eugene G. McKibben and R. Austin Griffin, "Changes in Farm Power and Equipment: Tractors, Trucks and Automobiles," *National Research Project Report* No. A-9 (Philadelphia: Works Progress Administration, December 1938): 16.

30. "A Rubber Tired Tractor," *Scientific American* (February 8, 1919): 122; J. W. Shields, "Pneumatic Tires for Agricultural Tractors," *Agricultural Engineering* 14 (February 1933): 39.

31. "Allis-Chalmers: 'America's Krupp,' " 150; George H. Nystrom, "The Development of Pneumatic Tired Tractors for Agriculture," *Proceedings of the World's Grain Exhibition and Conference* 1 (Regina, Saskatchewan: Canadian Society of Technical Agriculturists, July 24–August 5, 1933): 424–27; "Doughnut Tires Enter Farm Field," *Business Week* (October 12, 1932): 8.

32. Worthington, "Engineer's History, [IV]," 44; Skromme, "Growth of ASAE," 182.

33. Walter F. Peterson, "Barney Oldfield Turns a Plowhorse into a Racehorse," *Northwest Ohio Quarterly* 35 (Summer 1963): 122–28.

34. G. W. McCuen, "Ohio Tests of Rubber Tractor Tires," *Agricultural Engineering* (February 1933): 41-44; Warren S. Lockwood, "Rubber Tired Farm Tractors," *India Rubber World* (March 1, 1939): 43–45.

35. "Show New Tractors," *Business Week* (February 25, 1939): 41.

36. C. W. Smith, "A Study of Users' Experience with Rubber Tired Tractors," *Agricultural Engineering* 16 (February 1935): 45–52.

37. Barger and Landsberg, *American Agriculture*, 207, 208; McKibben and Griffen, "Changes," 13–15.

38. Johnson, "Changes," 15; Waddel, "Public Works," 857; Kifer et al., "Influence of Technical," 514.

39. Waddel, "Public Works," 857.

40. "Small Farms Will Have Small Tractor to Fit," *Business Week* (October 12, 1932): 8.

41. "Farm Tools Boom," *Business Week* (June 6, 1936): 33; "Farm Backlog is Rolling In," *Business Week* (May 5, 1934); Poulton, "Tractor on Parade," 16; "Allis-Chalmers: 'America's Krupp,' " 150.

42. "Allis-Chalmers: 'America's Krupp,' " 150.

43. "Keen Tractor Rivalry," *Business Week* (March 18, 1939): 34, 35; "New Ford Tractors," *Business Week* (June 24, 1939).

44. "The Tractors Are Running Hot," *Business Week* (July 15, 1939): 17; "Small Tractor Derby," *Business Week* (October 14, 1939): 42; "Farmall Model A Tractor with Adjustable Wheel Track," *Automotive Industries* (February 1, 1940): 119–20; "Mechanizing the Small Farm," *Popular Mechanics Magazine* (April 1940): 536–39; "Smaller Tractors," *Business Week* (October 20, 1945): 21–22; Howard E. Everett, "Big Expansion Ahead in Tractor Industry," *Automobile Industries* (July 1, 1947): 28.

45. "New Ford Tractor," 39; "Allis-Chalmers: 'America's Krupp,' " 150.

46. Federal Trade Commission, *Report of the Federal Trade Commission on Manufacture and Distribution of Farm Implements* (Washington: Federal Trade Commission, 1948): 45–49.

47. "Allis-Chalmers: 'America's Krupp,' " 53–54, 150.

48. Apparently Henry Ford and Harry Ferguson were the last to abandon the sacred gray color (after they had gone separate ways). John Deere apparently adopted their familiar green and yellow colors with the acquisition of Waterloo Boy, which put them in the tractor business initially. International Harvester tractors began to be painted red with the F-20, although some models continued to be gray for a few years. Massey-Harris "Challenger" was red with yellow trim, while Oliver/Hart-Parr had gone to "Safety Yellow" and then to the familiar green and white. Case used an orange and tan paint scheme, (then about five other color combinations before adopting International's red, white, and black in 1985). By the beginning of World War II, most tractors were brightly finished and presented an attractive sight in fields of dark green cotton or bright green corn.

Harry Ferguson (left) and Henry Ford in the happier days of their collaboration with the Ford tractor with the Ferguson system. (Henry Ford Museum and Greenfield Village)

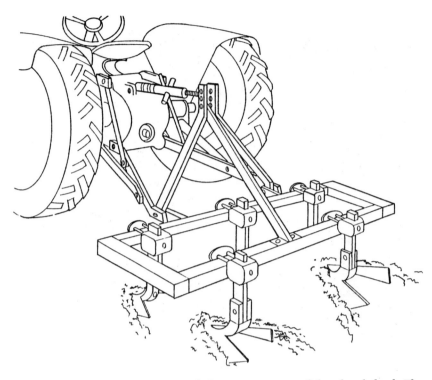

Traditional plow attachment caused the tractor to rear if the plow lodged. The toplink on Ferguson's three-point system blocked the rearing motion and transferred it to the tires, making the tractor act as though it were heavier.

The need for more pulling power and greater traction lead to many experiments with tandem tractors, such as this one at Iowa State University. Tandem tractors were difficult to synchronize, and some were hard to steer. Nevertheless, they led the way to the big four-wheel-drive models that followed. (Iowa State University)

John Deere's decision to retire its old two-cylinder designs with more modern engines was one of the best kept secrets in industrial history. Here, William Hewitt introduces the 3010. Hewitt—and tractors such as the 4020—led Deere to capture a major share of the market from the 1960s through the early 80s. (Deere & Company)

Versatile Farm Equipment Company's model 1150 is typical of the huge tractors that dominated large-scale farming in the early 1980s. (Versatile Farm Equipment Company, Winnipeg)

The Versatile 256 (top) may be the most versatile tractor ever built. It was designed to be bi-directional, with a seat that pivots to face either end of the tractor. Many were equipped with three-point hitches and PTOs on both ends. By placing the tractor cab forward and pushing a cultivator, the farmer could achieve unparalleled accuracy in cultivating. At other times (bottom), one implement could be used in front and another at the rear of the machine. The 256 was designed to be easily serviced; it did not need to be broken into several pieces for repair. (Versatile Farm Equipment Company, Winnipeg)

6
Refining the Already
Workable Tractor

The Allis-Chalmers B was the final step in adapting the tractor to American farms. The age of tractor development was over. The tractor worked. But functional adequacy was merely the first step in the machine's development. It was crucial: until the machine worked acceptably, there was little or no competitive motivation for perfecting and polishing—for the minor improvements that made the difference between crudeness and sophistication. Although there was steady evolution toward larger sizes, the major trend in the development of the tractor from 1940 to 1980 was simply refinement.

Refinement—rather than price change—was the product of competition in the tractor market. In fact, the first improvement caught the industry by surprise when the Allis-Chalmers B and the Farmall A were challenged by a competitor from an unexpected quarter. In 1939, a publicity campaign bearing the unmistakable imprint of Henry Ford came rolling out of Detroit. The automaker was reinvading the tractor market. In the last week in June 1939, Ford summoned the press to his Fairlane estate, where he demonstrated a new tractor and lavished praise upon its co-designer, Harry Ferguson.[1]

The relationship between Ford and Ferguson is an intriguing one. Harry Ferguson began his inventive career with a homemade airplane, one of the first in Northern Ireland. Following some unpleasant landings, Ferguson changed his career and began repairing and racing automobiles. When the British government discovered the Fordson's tendency to overturn, Ferguson was ordered to cure the problem. He soon developed a "duplex hitch" plow that ingeniously eliminated the Fordson's rearing by transferring the tractor's upward thrust back down to the plow. It was an engineering principle of immense significance for the future, and the invention led to Harry Ferguson's first meeting with Henry Ford. That initial interview was an impasse at best.[2]

Ferguson cured the problem of longitudinal instability in a matter of weeks while American engineers continued to struggle with the matter for years. The British engineer then became fascinated with the interrelationship of transferring the thrust from the plow to the rear wheels with the associated problem of depth and draft control. In February 1925 and June 1926, he applied for patents for a new draft control concept.[3]

It took several years to perfect the system. The first Ferguson-designed system was built by the David Brown Company, an offshoot of an old and respected English machinery company that had not previously worked with tractors. David Brown eventually became a major tractor company after several years manufacturing the Ferguson-designed David Brown tractor that was introduced in 1936. It was mechanically successful, but sold slowly at first, and Ferguson lost interest in the David Brown Company before sales improved.[4]

While Ferguson developed a new hitching system in England, Ford lost out in the American tractor market. But Ford's preoccupation with tractors had persisted, and he had continued experimenting. At a remarkably propitious moment, Ferguson arranged to demonstrate his system to Ford. In October 1938, Ferguson plowed some of Ford's Fairlane estate, and Ford compared the performance of this Ferguson-Brown tractor with an Allis-Chalmers B and a Fordson. The feisty little British tractor outperformed both. Ferguson produced a small, spring-powered model tractor and explained the principles of the Ferguson system to Ford. Following a short discussion of the social impact of the proposed tractor, the two men negotiated an informal agreement and sketched out a general plan to manufacture the tractor. They sealed the agreement with a handshake.[5]

The "Fairlane handshake" sealed one of the largest oral agreements in history. Under this informal compact Ferguson was to have charge of engineering and sales, while Ford had the responsibility for financing and manufacturing. The two eccentric geniuses began a stormy partnership that eventually ended in an unparelleled lawsuit. But before the divorce, the union brought forth a product that was a credit to both men.[6]

The Ford-Ferguson collaboration resulted in a tiny tractor called "the Ford tractor with the Ferguson system." The small tractor outplowed machines that weighed far more, and it did so because of Harry Ferguson's brilliant method of mounting implements on the tractor. Ferguson placed two arms on pivots under the rear axle and mounted a single strut on the back of the tractor. The upper strut sloped up from the tractor to the top of a triangle mounted on the implement. The lower arms connected to the lower corners of the triangle. It was the geometry of this triangle that gave the system the term "three point hitch." By means of a hydraulic valve, the upper link also sensed the implement's resistance and raised or lowered the plow for a constant draft. The arrangement of pivot points provided the tractor with a downward force on the rear wheels as draft requirements increased—thus the greater the load on the plow, the greater the "weight" and the traction on the rear wheels. It was this unique weight-transfer feature that allowed the Ford-Ferguson to plow effectively at such a light weight.

However, aside from the Ferguson system, the little tractor was unimpressive. It had two front wheels set on the same tread as the rear wheels. The tractor had a small, four-cylinder engine, many components of which were drawn from Ford or Mercury automobile parts bins. The axle and differential were interchangeable with those of some Ford trucks.[7] The Ford-Ferguson rolled off of the assembly line at typical Ford speed.

The new Ford tractor did not sweep the market the way the Fordson had, but it nevertheless enjoyed steadily increasing sales. Because it was small and light, much like the smallest International and Allis-Chalmers tractors, many people perceived the Ford-Ferguson as belonging to that class. Yet Ford and Ferguson promoted it as being capable of working as much land as heavier two-row tractors. And while the Ford-Ferguson was priced more than $100 higher than Farmall's A or Allis-Chalmers's B, Ferguson claimed that, at $600, the tractor was 20 percent cheaper than "any tractor of comparable work capacity." Because of the Ferguson system, the tractor performed as much work as tractors nine hundred pounds heavier.[8] In addition, the Ford-Ferguson, with its mounted tools and hydraulic lift, maneuvered in tight quarters where even its smallest competitors could not operate.[9]

In 1942, after two full years in production, Ford climbed to second or third place in tractor production, with some 20 percent of the market. By comparison IH, the industry leader had 40 percent. The Ferguson-Sherman firm that distributed the Ford-Ferguson tractors collected $25 million in annual sales and by the time the war was well started, there were more than one hundred thousand Ford-Fergusons in the field.[10]

The gradual growth of Ford-Ferguson sales may well have been due in part to what appeared to be exaggerated claims for the little gray tractors. Farmers discovered only slowly that the Ford-Ferguson performed as claimed. "On the average," said Ferguson, "it takes the farmer two years to believe it."[11] The reason for such outsized performance was, of course, the Ferguson system. That hydraulic system was also incredibly versatile, and farmers found dozens of uses for it other than the original purpose.[12]

After observing the success of the new tractor, Ferguson planned a million tractors annually, a figure four times the size of the industry's record output. But Ferguson did not know of the plans that lurked in the hearts of the Ford family. The Fords hired a cost accountant to evaluate the performance of the Ford-Ferguson tractor in company account books. The investigator, Ernest R. Beech, claimed that the increasingly successful Ford-Ferguson tractor had lost the Ford Motor Company some $25 million, a creditable assertion only if one remembers Henry Ford's careless bookkeeping. Upon turning in an answer that pleased the Ford family, Beech was promoted to the position of executive vice president of Ford Motor Company. Using the alleged loss as a pretext, Beech terminated the distributing agreement with the Ferguson-Sherman Company and turned distribution rights over to a new entity, the Dearborn Motors Company. Later testimony revealed that Beech had been lured away from his previous remunerative job by stock in Dearborn Motors—stock that would have been worthless unless the Ford family and Beech planned from the start to ambush Ferguson. By July 1947, Dearborn Motors Corporation had launched a massive campaign to capture the Ford-Ferguson market for a new Ford tractor that employed the Ferguson system, but that neither recognized Ferguson's contribution nor paid him royalties.[13]

The Ford Corporation apparently intended to ignore Ferguson's patent rights and, by utilizing the limitless resources of Ford's legal department, delay and postpone any court action until Ford countersuits had browbeaten Ferguson into accepting the company's theft. But the stubborn little Scots-Irish inventor refused either to be cowed or to back down. The subsequent legal battle became one of the largest, most protracted, and most complex ever waged, with literally millions of pages of testimony and depositions.

When the interminable legal wrangling finally ended in an out-of-court settlement, Ferguson received $9.25 million and Ford's agreement to cease making some parts covered by Ferguson's patents. Ferguson had incurred $3.5 million in legal costs. Ferguson won in principle, but the Ford Corporation's stalling saved the Detroit company untold milliions in royalties that otherwise were due Ferguson.[14] For the tractor industry, it meant that two vigorous competitors were now selling tractors with a standard dimension three-point lift and hydraulic draft control. It also meant that other companies that wished to use Ferguson's brilliant mechanism—or one essentially like it—found little legal impediment in doing so, because the suit weakened both Ford's and Ferguson's claims to exclusive rights.

While Ferguson's legal counsel besieged Ford's immovable army of lawyers, Ferguson attempted to organize a company to manufacture the Ferguson tractor and to gather the necessary tools and facilities. It was, by any sane analysis, an impossible task. Yet Ferguson tractors soon began to appear across the nation. Externally, they were similar to the Ford-Ferguson, but were powered by a Continental "Red Seal" engine and contained sufficient refinements that many farmers and mechanics felt that they were superior to either Ford-Fergusons or the new Ford "8-N." Ferguson was definitely—if not securely—in the tractor manufacturing business.

By 1953, Harry Ferguson was aging and suffering from increasingly frequent sessions of depression, and he was looking for a different way to manage the Ferguson Company. In August, 1953, the Harry Ferguson Companies and Massey-Harris Limited merged, an initially stormy marriage, but one that eventually produced the largest implement company in the world. Although the company's parts numbers today retain an MHF prefix, the Massey-Harris-Ferguson Limited designation proved too long. Because the Canadian family that had furnished the corporate middle name had long since dropped out of the firm, the corporation soon became "Massey-Ferguson." Ironically, Ferguson himself eventually withdrew from the company that bore his name—a company that he could influence but not dominate.[15]

The old man who retired from Massey-Ferguson left the industry an invaluable legacy. The Ferguson system was an excellent example of "Beauty in Engineering." As defined by Harry Ferguson himself, "Beauty in Engineering" was "that which performs perfectly the function for which it was designed and has no superfluous parts."[16] The system solved several problems simultaneously. By transferring the downward thrust of the plow onto the back wheels of the tractor, the Ferguson system gave a light tractor the traction of a heavy one. And the upper link sensed the plow's resistance, automatically raising or lowering the plow as needed. Thus, a much lighter tractor was able to do a superior job of plowing. In addition, because the implement was tractor mounted, the operator could raise it, back the tractor into a tight spot, lower the implement and pull forward, an added bit of versatility far beyond the capability of drag-type equipment of the time. The three-point lift was also used to do a variety of chores not part of the original concept. A farmer with a little imagination and a welder could use the Ferguson system as the basis for a detachable forklift, a small boom-type hoist, a post puller, or countless other devices.

E. J. Baker, the editor of *Implement & Tractor*, once wondered why the three-point system was developed by Ferguson, who was not formally educated to any extent, and who had not served any time in a college of engineering. When the quarrel with Ford Motor Company came, each side hired scores of engineers to show why the system worked. But an Ulster mechanic invented it. Perhaps Baker implied a criticism of schools of engineering, but he certainly paid fitting tribute to the irrepressible genius of Harry Ferguson.

The Ferguson system, or a similar hydraulically controlled, three-point system, became virtually mandatory on almost all tractors. But recognition of the advantages of the system came slowly. The first tractor to employ the technique other than Ford or Ferguson was the Oliver "Super 55" introduced in early 1953. Others followed just before the end of the year—except for International Harvester. For some reason, the Chicago firm obstinately refused to acknowledge any benefit in the three-point system. About ten years earlier, in 1945, Harvester introduced a crude power lift to compete with Ferguson. It did not have draft control and was never popular. Then in 1953, to buttress sagging sales, Farmall introduced the "Fast Hitch" and an adapter that could accommodate three-point implements,[17] but still rejected the Ferguson system as such. Sales remained unimpressive. An astute observer of the implement scene reported:

> Rumors from distant points tell about pilgrimages by thousands of Harvester dealers to Chicago to witness the unveiling of an entirely new line of implements developed in recent years by the Leading Producer as elements of a new three-point hitch system for its newer tractors. . . . Apparently every farm tractor producer in the U. S. A. as in the United Kingdom now employs the three-point hitch system. Even the reluctant have been converted, not to mention some downright stubborn cussers! . . . It's been thirty years since the idea was conceived, and it was nearly as good then as

it is now. It has taken three decades of skull weathering to break through
the cementitious crust of prejudice and make the idea common practice.
Make your own philosophic comments.[18]

But the editor had underestimated the durability of Chicago's "cementitious" skulls. A hot letter from an International Harvester partisan soon
informed the editor that the new IH hitch was not at all similar to Ferguson's. The editor then acknowledged that the objection was correct—
the hitches were different—and he cooly implied that the Harvester hitch
was probably inferior. Whether their executives had "cementitious crusts"
or not, International persisted in rejecting the three-point system for five
years, until 1958, when sales losses simply became intolerable.[19] Such was
typical of that which eventually led International to the abdication of the
title of "Leading Producer."

There is a natural question concerning International's resistance to
the three-point trend. The most plausible hypothesis notes that historically
Ford was Harvester's bitterest rival. The three-point system began on a
Ford tractor, therefore was anathema to loyal McCormick-Deering engineers. It is also possible that with a lion's share of the market, International
simply ignored what was happening around the industry until too late.

Whatever the reason for International's resistance, the company was
not unique in failing to recognize the value of the three-point hitch. The
American Society of Agricultural Engineers was equally laggard. Nevertheless, by 1970 there were three sets of international standards on three-
point hitches, and the devices were widely recognized as one of the
greatest technical improvements in the history of the tractor.[20]

The draft-controlled three-point hitch was about the last major feature to be universally adopted on farm tractors. Thus, by the opening days
of the Second World War, almost every component of the modern tractor
had been developed and placed in production. Although not all refinements were found in any single tractor at that time, the industry was
technologically mature.[21] Perhaps not coincidentally, a huge market developed for tractors.

In 1940, the Census of Agriculture found slightly more than 1.5
million tractors on American farms. By 1949, in spite of wartime restrictions, that number had doubled.[22] Part of the reason for the rapid mechanization lies in the perfecting of tractor machinery so that it was more
adaptable. Part of the explanation must also include the relatively cheaper
prices compared to earlier times. But the major reasons for increased

demand for tractors were physical and economic: the end of drouth and
of the depression. Of these two impediments a contemporary wrote: "It
was the breaking of these . . . that caused the flood of production in the
war years—in the same way that a simultaneous breaking of dams on
several tributaries will cause a river to reach a flood stage from water that
was accumulated from a normal flow at the source."[23] Rains returned to
the Dust Bowl, wartime demanded raised food prices, and for the first
time, farmers who had long dreamed of a tractor could afford to buy one.

But demands for farm equipment in periods of war must compete
with other demands. On July 12, 1941, several months before Pearl Har-
bor, manufacturers began allocating farm equipment. Equipment production was up 20 percent over the 1940 rate, but demand still exceeded
supply. A sizable share of sales went to small farms not previously
mechanized.[24]

By the middle of 1942, wartime shortages began to pinch the industry. Japanese conquests in Asia cut off supplies of natural rubber, and
synthetic substitutes had not yet been perfected. As a result, the government ordered implement makers to return to steel wheels. It was an order
that automatically cut production. Tractors with copious sales were put on
crash reengineering programs so that they could be modified to steel
wheels. Slower selling or less profitable lines were simply dropped. International Harvester, for example, abandoned its A and B models with
their small markup.[25]

While manufacturers struggled with shortages and government reg-
ulations, many farmers had a new-found prosperity, aspirations of tractor
ownership, and a patriotic desire to increase production to feed and clothe
America and her allies. When confronted with "endless instances of reg-
ulatory dumbness" that frustrated both patriotism and profit, they lashed
out at the rationing agencies. They cited concrete instances of bureaucratic
foul-ups. And the farmers' voices were heard. *Business Week* reported that
"Every congressman from a dirt-farm district could comprehend these
complaints—and did."[26] Farmers' complaints became even more forceful
in the early summer of 1943, when floods delayed planting. Farm equipment manufacturers and deans of agricultural colleges predicted food
shortages for 1945. The government then increased the number of agricultural implements that were permitted, but did not allocate the steel to
make the new quota.[27]

Wartime controls caused endless controversies. In an attempt to
reserve larger, well-organized plants for war use, the government tried to

consolidate farm implement lines to fewer types and to concentrate production in smaller shops. This may be the reason that Ford-Ferguson got
a large share of the quota for 1944. But the concentration program was
criticized because the small, short-line firms did not have distribution
networks.[28] No doubt regulators and regulated alike were glad to see
wartime controls eliminated at the war's end.

Patterns of shortages and regulation persisted throughout the war,
but despite irritating problems, farm equipment manufacturers turned
out a flood of equipment. If 1941 is taken as a base year, the index of
tractors on farms was 111 for 1942, 123 for 1943, 130 for 1944, and 141 for
1945. In spite of scarcities, manufacturers produced more than a million
tractors during the war.[29]

Soon after the war ended, well-fed critics pounced upon the priority
given farm machinery production, claiming that the farmers' tools did little
to end the war. One such critic pointed out that "2,000 tractors require
as much steel as a naval destroyer," yet tractors were used "only about
500 hours [apiece] annually during 1940 and 1941."[30] The critic obviously
figured that each tractor should have been used more, and fewer tractors
built. While the economic logic of the observation is unimpeachable, the
critic failed to realize that farmers must perform their tasks seasonally. On
the High Plains, for example, cotton planted in late June yields far less
than a crop planted in May, and everyone knows that corn does not grow
in January.

Wartime rationing drew criticism from the opposite quarter as well.
By 1946, there were eloquent and detailed denunciations of the government's failure to get machinery to the farmer during the war and condemnations of the breakdown of reconversion efforts after the war's end.[31]

Apparently wartime planning efforts pleased virtually no one. Farmers cited innumerable instances of bureaucratic bumbling, while others
called attention to wasteful uses of precious resources during the national
emergency. In all probability, both sides were often correct. But those
who castigated the various allocation agencies were able to voice their
complaints on a full stomach. Farmers, with declining numbers of draft
stock and declining amounts of available labor, aimed at food production
goals that far exceeded record crops of the past. Often they were forced
to use aging equipment or mismatched implements. But they produced
crops of vast proportions and absorbed every available new machine.

When wartime restrictions ended, the farm equipment industry
anticipated a period of booming sales. Although farmers had desired trac-

tors in the thirties, they had been unable to afford them because of depression-ridden farm prices. During the war, farmers had earned high prices for their produce, but they were often unable to make the desired purchases because of shortages. The industry estimated that, by the end of the war, farmers had accumulated some $14 billion, much of that would be spent on equipment. In addition, the war had reduced the rate at which farmers retired outdated equipment, as many of the implements and tractors in use were overdue for replacement. Many farmers who had managed to obtain a new tractor or some new equipment during the war were still imcompletely supplied, because much of the other equipment they needed was unavailable.[32]

Even if the economy sagged after the war, tractor production had to be maintained at fairly high levels. According to one expert, "More than a million farm workers who were in the various military services or employed in War industries are not returning to agricultural employment. Farmers cannot compete with . . . industrial wages. Work animals are no longer available. Hence there are no longer substitutes for tractors."[33]

As a result, the leading tractor makers expanded their facilities and their production. Allis-Chalmers doubled their prewar capability. Case expanded all its production lines by at least 50 percent through the purchase of two new plants. Deere opened a new plant in Dubuque and expanded the old Waterloo works. International projected a production half again as large as prewar levels. Massey-Harris and Minneapolis-Moline each aimed at doubling their output. Oliver anticipated a multiphase program, with a 25 percent expansion in the first phase alone. Seldom has an entire industry stepped up production so much in so short a time, and expanding sales justified industry optimism.[34]

One reason for the expanding sales of tractors in the postwar period was the fact that the tractor had finally started to displace horses and mules on a large scale, even on smaller farms. Only a year after the war ended, for example, an observer noted that "three-fifths of the land planted to cotton in the United States was broken with tractor-drawn implements, as against half that percentage seven years earlier."[35] The industry correctly anticipated that, once begun, the trend toward horseless farming would continue. The change was so rapid that by 1962, "the Statistical Reporting Service . . . discontinued reporting the number of horses and mules on farms. They were no longer of significance."[36] The tractor had finally replaced the horse.

The ultimate displacement of draft animals was made possible by the use of row-crop tractors and by the continued development of tools to take advantage of the all-purpose tractor's versatility. The Ferguson system and its imitators increased the potential utility of the tractor before the conventional row-crop tractor had been completely exploited. Then World War II interrupted the development of accessory implements for both the all-purpose tractor and its new type of power lift. But at the end of the war, a frantic race began to develop and to exploit the tractor's remaining potential.

Both short-line and long-line manufacturers entered the race—the latter often by buying up the former after it had perfected and tested a new device on the market. Manufacturers soon offered farmers PTO-driven post-hole diggers that were raised and lowered by a three-point lift. Loaders for mounting on the front of a tractor were not new, but in the postwar market they sold as never before. With the advent of chemical agriculture, farmers needed spray booms, pumps, and tanks to mount on their tractors. To some observers, it seemed like a gadget-happy spree. But most of the tools increased the tractor's capacity for doing useful farm work and increased the productivity of the farmer.[37]

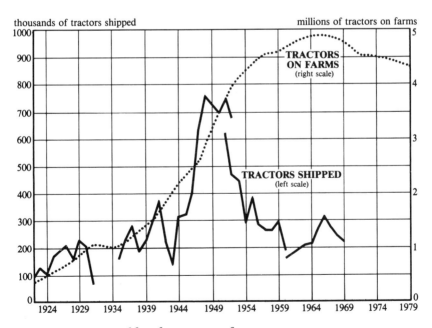

Figure 2. Tractors sold and tractors on farms.

Sources. Current Industrial Reports/Facts for Industry, 1953-70; Durost and Black, "Changes in Farm Production," 31.

The postwar tractor boom did not slacken much until the 1960s, but tractor numbers peaked in 1965. After that the number of tractors on farms gradually decreased so that there were about 7 percent fewer tractors in 1977 than eight years earlier. From 1950 to 1953, manufacturers shipped more than four hundred thousand tractors annually. From 1956 to 1960, the annual rate was closer to two hundred thousand.[38] By this time, however, the number of tractors on American farms had reached a saturation point. Increasing numbers were no longer needed.

While the number of tractors in the United States began to recede, their horsepower did not; the average size of postwar tractors constantly increased.[39] The increasing horsepower of tractors touched virtually every make and model. International increased the power of their classic M by some 21 percent and renamed it the "Super M." Allis-Chalmers introduced a turbocharged diesel tractor, the first wheel-type tractor to use such a device. As tractors became larger, other changes had to be made. More powerful tractors required more electricity to operate, thus most tractors in the 1960s came equipped with alternators instead of old-style generators. The old standard three-point hitch was too light for the increasingly larger tractors; larger, stronger, three-point systems had to be developed. The old standard was maintained for small tractors but renamed as a "Category I hitch," while the engineering societies issued specifications for "beefier" Category II and Category III hitches. The standard PTO was likewise too small for bigger tractors. By the late 1950s, new standards had been promulgated for a one thousand rpm PTO, which was more compatible with bigger engines and heavier loads.[40]

Perhaps the increasing horsepower of tractors was a greater potential trauma for Deere and Company than for any other manufacturer, but the firm ultimately turned the potential crisis into a green-and-yellow bonanza. For years John Deere tractors persistently maintained several features that most of the remainder of the industry had long since abandoned, such as the hand-operated clutch. But the Deere's greatest anachronism was its two-cylinder engine.

Deere and Company believed very strongly in the two-cylinder engine. They had persisted in using it for some three decades after other tractor manufacturers had gone to four- and six-cylinder power plants. The company emphasized the merits of the design, including the fact that its two cylinders had far fewer parts to wear out than the more complex engines of its competitors. The distinctive design required large flywheels and produced a unique exhaust noise. Defenders and detractors of the

Deere design both referred to the machines as "Poppin' Johnnys." Many farmers were fanatically loyal to the eccentric arrangement, and even critics had to concede that the green-and-yellow tractors were remarkably efficient and durable.

But there were limits to the amount of power that could be extracted from just two cylinders, and as larger horsepower became a competitive issue, John Deere engineers saw that change was inevitable. After building more than 1.5 million two-cylinder tractors, they were forced to abandon the old engineering feature that had been such a strong selling point.[41]

The engineering prospect was staggering because the Deere executives decided upon a clean sweep. The entire line of tractors was redesigned, starting with a "clean drawing board." The project employed more than four hundred people and required a huge new facility. It took some six years and $50 million, but amazingly, no word of the change leaked out. It was the "Best kept industrial secret in the business." Had word gotten out, sales of the older models would have suffered. At the beginning of the 1960s, John Deere sprang its new line on its dealers and began an unprecedented publicity campaign. In a sense, the company had to undo some forty-six years of advertising.[42] Johnnys no longer popped.

John Deere dealers and salesmen reacted differently to the announcement of the new line. Some felt that the change was long overdue and were relieved to shed the image of peculiarity that separated them from the rest of the industry. They felt that the change opened the way to customers who shied away from Deere before. Others reacted quite negatively at first. They were not convinced that the change was necessary, and they feared losing the loyal customers who had made Deere the second largest tractor maker. Yet both shared the surprise, even shock, of the suddenness with which the new models came.[43]

The new John Deere tractors were apparently well timed, and the company's aggressive sales campaign was quite effective. Under the leadership of William Hewitt, John Deere gradually nudged the napping International Harvester Company aside and became, by a large margin, the largest manufacturer of tractors in the United States.[44]

While John Deere raced the other large manufacturers in an attempt to dominate the market for average tractors, new, small companies sensed an opportunity in custom-building extra-large tractors. Although all of the major manufacturers gradually offered larger and larger tractors, the largest sizes were a specialty market that was too small for regular factory production. By the late sixties, there were numerous specialty companies that concentrated on the monster market—companies like Versatile, Steiger, and Big Bud. Their tractors were primarily useful in the western portion of the wheat belt. A typical example of the huge machines was described in 1978. It had 747 horsepower and weighed 95,000 pounds empty or 130,000 pounds with ballast. Options included a closed-circuit television to monitor the plow and a refrigerator to hold the operator's lunch. The Big Bud company boasted that even larger machines were on the drawing boards.[45]

Tractors seemed to reach optimum efficiency at about one hundred horsepower since larger sizes encountered problems with wheel slippage and soil compaction. But a significant demand existed for tractors of more than one hundred horsepower. The solution to the dilemma came in the form of four-wheel-drive.

The idea of four-wheel-drive tractors was not new. Some experimenters attempted to build four-wheel-drive tractors in the earliest days. Massey-Harris's first general-purpose tractor, for example, was a mechanically successful four-wheel-drive design that failed only because it was marginally superior to two-wheel drive on most farms and was more expensive to build.[46] The Massey-Harris GP was popular, primarily on farms with difficult conditions such as some areas of West Texas where the fields were too sandy for other tractors, or on soggy bottom lands in the Midwest. But marginal farming areas did not provide enough market to support a steady production of all-wheel drive tractors in the 1930s.

By the 1950s, larger tractors were encountering problems with traction and soil compaction on many large farms with average soil conditions. Both innovative individual farmers and farm equipment researchers then began experimenting with connecting two tractors together in tandem to get twice as much traction and draft without increasing labor costs.[47] It was an innovative concept, but the problems of synchronizing two engines and integrating two sets of controls were exceedingly difficult. Gradually the experimenters began to look instead at a single engine and single set of controls connected to four drive elements.

Experiments showed that the pulling power of four-wheel drive tractors was appreciably greater for a given horsepower than conventional tractors of the same size. The all-wheel drive pulled 20 to 50 percent more than a similar two-wheel-drive tractor. Because four-wheel-drive tractors had far less wheel slippage, they required less ballast, which meant less soil compaction. But the four-wheel-drive tractors had one big disadvantage: price. The mechanism that conveyed power to the front wheels was complex and expensive.[48] Yet gradually all of the major manufacturers developed and marketed four-wheel-drive tractors. These sold well at first in the areas dominated by huge farms: the wheat regions and the central California valley. The success of the four-wheel-drive tractors in these areas tended to push crawler tractors out of the last small market that they claimed in agriculture.

At first, four-wheel-drive tractors did not make large inroads in row-crop areas.[49] Throughout the sixties and early seventies, four-wheel-drive tractors were generally confined to a specialty status in most row-crop areas. But in 1979, International Harvester introduced two new four-wheel-drive tractors (the "3388" and "3588"). There was no foolproof way of predicting the future of the new introductions, but they were purportedly so successful initially that International was forced to shut down production of the popular 1486 in order to meet demands for the new row-crop, four-wheel-drive ("2+2") tractors. Undoubtedly, International hoped that the new machines would recoup lost markets and return them to a position of dominance similar to that secured by the first Farmalls. That hope did not materialize.

The fuel crisis of the seventies and subsequent developments in the industry did push most manufacturers into marketing more machines with four-wheel-drive or power-assisted front wheels that could help the back drivers through slick spots. By the mid-eighties, the majority of experts expected the two-wheel-drive tractor to continue losing ground to its competitors with traction.[50]

The ultimate success of the four-wheel-drive tractors would depend on several factors: the successful adaptation to row-crop work, fuel efficiency, fuel availability, and cost. The initial cost of the four-wheel-drive tractor had to be within reach, and the farmer must have sufficient income to retire his old equipment.

The period from 1980 through much of the Reagan administration was an unmitigated disaster surpassed only by the Great Depression in farm foreclosures and other indicators of hard times. But with less than 3 percent of the American population on the farm, the farm problem was an almost invisible issue in the 1984 elections. But the problem was not invisible to the tractor and implement industry.

During the eighties hundreds of tractor dealerships failed, many of which had been in business for decades and were as well managed as comparable ventures outside the industry. Virtually every agricultural community witnessed untimely business deaths. The manufacturers were not much healthier than their dealers. Tractor sales plummeted. In 1983, the tractor market had shrunk by 60 percent from the 1979 level. John Deere, the biggest name in tractors, posted losses of $28.5 million in the first quarter of 1983 alone and was forced to lay off 40 percent of its hourly workers and 15 percent of its salaried employees worldwide. International Harvester, the second largest domestic manufacturer, tetered on the edge of bankruptcy for months. Massey-Fergusson, the world's second largest farm equipment maker, discontinued manufacturing two-wheel-drive tractors in the United States and avoided bankruptcy only by a voluntary reorganization agreement with its creditors at the last moment. White Farm Equipment Company of Canada went into bankruptcy.[51] The tractor/ farm equipment divisions of Allis-Chalmers, Ford, and Tenneco (Case) appeared to many commentators to be intolerable drains on their respective diversified parent companies.

With such dismal conditions prevailing, it is no wonder that the entire atmosphere in the industry became gloomy and fatalistic. John McGinty, research vice president for First Boston Corporation, told a marketing and management conference that "you're in a no-growth industry in a slow economic situation with worldwide industry overcapacity. You're entering a disinflation period in which you won't be able to raise prices to cover costs. . . ."[52]

Kathryn Harrigan of the Columbia University Business School suggested that tractor manufacturing was an "endgame industry," one that could anticipate little but stagnation or decline. When she asked her audience of farm equipment people if they concurred with her assessment, the majority answered "yes."[53] Few people in the industry could offer much proof to the contrary. By the closing weeks of 1984, the dire predicament of the tractor and implement industry was even more serious and had attracted the attention of daily newspapers. A story in the *New York Times News Service* speculated that several of the industry's oldest names might disappear, names like Case, Massey-Ferguson, Allis-Chalmers, or even International Harvester. The story also predicted that "marriages" were likely in the industry as well as deaths. The same week, Tenneco announced a tentative agreement with International Harvester to purchase the majority of the farm equipment interests of the Chicago firm, leaving it with little more than the truck division. Undoubtedly Tenneco sought primarily the "longline" implement business without which its Case tractors were far less salable. The elimination of either Case's or International's tractor-making factories would have little effect on the overproduction capacity of the industry, however, for any one of the major manufacturers in North America could supply the entire needs of the continent without any production from the other firms—and either of the largest could do so operating at partial capacity. No one foresaw prosperity for the industry anywhere in sight.[54]

The gloom and pessimism in the industry perhaps accounted for its willingness to "roll over and play dead" in front of increased foreign competition. The manufacturers had showed little inclination to challenge imported tractors when they first became common during the booming sixties and the prosperous seventies, nor did they do so in the early eighties despite excess manufacturing capacity for large tractors that probably approached 400 percent. If any company even discussed the possibility of converting some of its excess large tractor facilities into the production of smaller units, no whisper of it reached the industry papers or financial press.

American manufacturers have consistently concentrated on larger and larger tractors and abdicated the small tractor market. By 1960, the United States manufactured few tractors of less than fifty horsepower, and because most foreign nations protected their small farms, huge American tractors sold poorly outside North America.[55] Indeed, even within the United States tired old veteran Fords and Fergusons sold in the sixties and seventies for more than they had when new. There was obviously a vacuum in the domestic market.

In the sixties, foreign tractors began infiltrating the American market. American implement makers responded much like the automakers had reacted to Volkswagens and Hondas in the automotive domain. At first the automakers denied that there was a problem, claiming that there was not a significant market for small cars in the United States. When it became obvious that there was indeed such a market, the car companies decided that they were unable to compete in it, a self-fulfilling prophesy confirmed by half-hearted early efforts with Corvairs and Falcons. Only after the energy crisis of 1974, when their continued survival was at stake, did the vehicle people put forth an intense effort to become competitive. By that time they had wasted a number of valuable years and given their foreign competitors a huge lead.

The tractor market diverges somewhat from the automotive analogy in several aspects. In the early days of tractor imports, market demand was reduced by the fact that there were a seemingly endless supply of old, small units—John Deere Bs, Farmall Cubs, Ford 8Ns, and Ferguson TO-

20s. But the migration to suburbia placed heavy demand on such supplies as existed, and prices edged up while spare parts became harder to locate. The veteran machines also lacked some of the convenient modern refinements.

When the market for new, small tractors opened up, it did so quite rapidly. Long, Kubota, Yanmar, Mitsubishi, and others came rushing in between 1974 and 1984 with numerous dealers and rapidly growing sales. Domestic manufacturers reacted by entering into marketing agreements to distribute foreign-made products. Some American firms either purchased their overseas suppliers or used existing overseas branches to build small tractors, but many merely marketed someone else's machinery.

Allis-Chalmers and White, for example, imported Fiat tractors painted in the familiar Persian orange and silver, respectively. Both companies used their own names and trademarks on their Italian imports. Massey-Ferguson, of course, had overseas factories of its own that specialized in small tractors, so that all that was necessary was the shipment of the tractors from one Massey-Ferguson branch to another. International Harvester offered a Japanese import bearing the same trademark as Mazda automobiles, and, although they were painted Harvester red and sported the familiar IH logo, they also imported sizable numbers of Mitsubishi tractors. In slightly larger sizes, International tractors were built by the firm's own European plants. By 1980 every major long-line company in North America offered imported small tractors bearing its company colors. Gradually, foreign tractors, like foreign cars, began to differentiate into separate market segments with units from Japan distinct from those from Europe. Japanese imports specialized in the under-thirty-horsepower range (although they were not restricted to it), while European makers dominated the thirty-to-fifty-horsepower range. Perhaps because of the specialization by size, American trade officials smugly dropped tractors of less than forty horsepower from their reporting program.[56]

Foreign tractor makers did not remain content with the segment that they inherited by default. In 1981, Hesston Farm Equipment— formerly a short-line company—began marketing Fiat tractors including large, four-wheel-drive models. Other overseas manufacturers, too, looked enviously at a bigger share of the American market. In 1985, when Allis-Chalmers executives concluded that the prospects for agricultural implements were terminal, the company sold its farm equipment division to the Deutz corporation of West Germany, whose penetration of the American market had hitherto been rather slight. Simultaneously, more

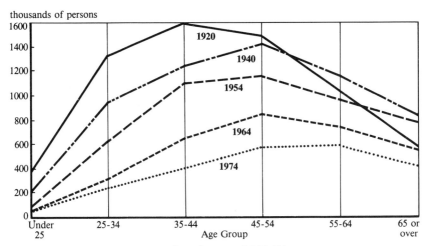

Figure 3. Farm operator age distribution, 1920-74.

Source. Economics, Statistics and Cooperative Service, "Status of the Family Farm: Second Annual report to the Congress," *Agricultural Economics Report* No. 434 (Washington: National Economics Division, United States Department of Agriculture, September 1979), 7.

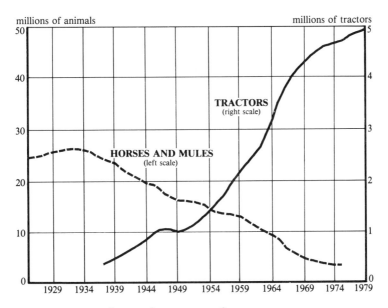

Figure 4. Horses, mules, and tractors on farms.

Sources. Historical Statistics I: 457; Durost and Black, "Changes in Farm Production," 31.

and more imported tractors bore their own marks and bypassed any royalties to American manufacturers. And the foreign tractor lines began expanding to include larger tractors. In 1983 well over half of the tractors sold in the United States were manufactured elsewhere. In 1984, Japan's Kubota claimed to be the third largest tractor vendor in the United States, with more than one thousand dealers and with tractors as large as 85 hp.[57] Like many American industries, cowed tractor makers appeared to assume they could not compete with imports and resigned themselves to their demise without a fight. There was no evidence that any major American manufacturer seriously investigated the possibility of making small tractors in this country or sought innovative technology to make such production possible.[58] Apparently, the Americans consoled themselves with the thought that it would take Asian manufacturers several years to work up to large-scale tractors, the market segment where domestic profits centered. Such industrial cowardice was in ironic contrast to the high profile government foreign policy popular at the time in areas other than international trade. Yet the tractor industry had seen hard times before, and the possibility existed that a dynamic leader would emerge in one of the companies in the way that Alexander Legge, Harry Merritt, Harry Ferguson, and William Hewitt emerged in their respective firms in earlier crises.

The mechanical development of tractors in North America after the Second World War was largely devoid of bold, innovative changes. The changes that did take place were a matter of small incremental improvements. Few of these improvements were remarkable in and of themselves, but cumulatively they made tractors more useful, safer, and above all else, more comfortable. An engineer described the process well, "Whenever a new machine is invented, nearly all the initial effort is directed toward developing the machine to the point where it will do the job for which it was intended. After this has been established to a satisfactory degree, efforts are then extended toward improving secondary features so as to offer the most attractive product possible to the customer. One of these so-called secondary features . . . is 'operator comfort'. . . ."[59]

Without a doubt, one of the biggest improvements in operator comfort was the installation of tractor cabs. Cabs on tractors were uncommon until the late sixties, but they were not new. Many of the steam traction engines had locomotive-type cabs, and that feature was carried over into many of the earliest tractors. Indeed, most of the tractors before 1915 had some type of cab roof. But when manufacturers shrank their products to the size of the Fordson or the McCormick-Deering 10–20, they abandoned the cab. Farmers could purchase a flimsy canvas awning as an option, but not a cab.

In 1939 Minneapolis-Moline built a tractor for publicity purposes. They styled it like an automobile, including an automobile-like cabin or enclosure. The dream tractor had a radio, a heater, and a cigarette lighter. Much to Moline's surprise, the tractor attracted potential purchasers, and the company soon placed a similar model on the market, dubbing it the "Comfortractor." Oliver and Montgomery-Ward's Graham-Bradley followed suit with the deluxe cab models of their own.[60] Apparently the luxury tractors were too novel, too expensive, or were not available long enough to become popular; therefore, most wartime and postwar tractors lacked cabs.

In the mid 1950s, automobile manufacturers began offering air-conditioned cars, and within half a decade such luxuries became common in automobiles. About the time that air conditioners became common in automobiles, farm equipment retailers began to offer cabs for their tractors. The cabs were frequently unavailable from the manufacturers, so retailers or farmers turned to custom manufacturers. Custom-made cabs were often crude and loose-fitting and were seldom air-conditioned, but they were welcome alternatives to sitting out in the open, exposed to hot sun or to freezing mist. Soon the manufacturers began to offer cabs as factory options, and by 1965 they were fairly common.[61]

With cabs came a multitude of small improvements that made tractors more comfortable. Power steering, long common in automobiles, finally came to tractors, where it was even more badly needed. Padded seats replaced the old steel stampings. Heaters became common. In 1964 Allis-Chalmers grouped all the tractor's controls to the driver's side, where they were more convenient and less of a hazard than the traditional location between the operator's feet. It was a move that other makers eventually copied. All of these small changes had a huge cumulative impact. With the final introduction of air-conditioning and pressurized cabs, the farmer moved into a new environment. No longer was his workplace miserable during much of the year. One long-time observer of the industry described cabs and other refinements as virtual necessities. "They increase operator efficiency and productivity," he said, "while reducing hazards to health, comfort and safety. Often they enabled the elderly farmer or the farmer in poor-health to continue farming."[62]

The engineers' concern for operator comfort was paralleled by a growing concern for operator safety, that developed quite rapidly in the late sixties and early seventies. The reasons for the concern were probably as complex as American society itself, but several contributing factors are easily identified.

A greater public concern for safety was among the major motivations for safer tractors. This broad social concern is readily seen in the consumer movement and its impact on the automobile industry, but its implications were clear to tractor makers as well. The era witnessed the introduction of seat belts in American automobiles, safety caps on medicine bottles, million-dollar liability suits, and corporate executives assigned exclusively to safety matters. Although it is impossible to quantify the impact of this broad social consciousness upon the tractor industry, tractor makers must have been influenced by it, and farmers were certainly more safety conscious than they had been earlier.

A second factor in the mounting concern for safety was the mechanical maturity of the tractor itself. So long as engineers had been straining to develop a tractor that performed effectively, they had little time to devote to anything else. Once the tractor was sufficiently developed to do its job effectively, then safety emerged as a top priority. Careful examination of the industry's periodicals revealed a steady increase in articles and public service advertisements promoting safety, an ever-increasing theme after the Second World War.

A third factor possibly contributing to the industry's concern for safety was the nature of the tractor business itself. The tractor and implement business was far smaller than many American industries. With the possible exception of Chicago, most of the tractor factories were in small to medium-sized cities in relatively rural regions. By proximity, and frequently by background, the implement companies' employees were close to rural life. To a sizable proportion of these personnel, safety was more than an abstraction—it was the story of how Uncle Harry lost his left arm or how a friendly neighbor was killed when his tractor overturned.

The implement and tractor industry was well aware of the hazardous nature of power farming equipment and of the need for improvement. In 1967, when Wayne Worthington, a retired John Deere engineer, wrote an informal history of the tractor, his last chapter was devoted to tractor safety.[63] He noted the need for the industry to install roll bars on tractors—but he also observed the numerous improvements that had already been made.

In 1971, the Department of Transportation was ordered to investigate the farm equipment industry in order to determine whether or not the government should mandate compulsory standards, as was being done in the automobile industry. After investigating the status of the industry, the Department recommended that the industry be allowed for the present to set its own, voluntary standards. It was a remarkable vote of confidence.[64]

Subsequent activities have largely justified the government's decision. Tractors did not become perfectly safe—no piece of machinery ever will be—but nearly every manufacturer worked hard to reduce the hazards.

One of the most dangerous aspects of tractors until recently was their noise level. An overwhelming proportion of tractor drivers showed measurable hearing loss as a result of exposure to excessive noise. In 1972–73 the manufacturers launched an all-out war on noise. International, John Deere, and Massey-Ferguson developed cabs, mufflers and insulation to reduce the noise level below 85 decibels.[65] Allis Chalmers and the other manufacturers took similar steps.

Noise reduction was not, of course, the only measure needed to improve tractor safety. It was, however, one of the most obvious because of the impact on the operator, and because of the large amount of reen-gineering needed. Sound conditioning was joined by "roll-over protective structures" (ROPS), seat belts, shielded shafts, and numerous other improvements in an ongoing safety program. The average farmer or farm hand was probably unaware of the benefits of the safety program, but his health and safety were unquestionably protected from at least some of the liabilities of an earlier age.

Between the introduction of the Ferguson system and the introduction of safety devices, the tractor gradually evolved into a much larger, much more refined machine. Power lifts, cabs, air-conditioning, and noise reduction were accompanied by growth to larger sizes and—in some cases—the addition of four-wheel-drive capability. Most of these changes were encouraged by the competitive nature of the tractor industry. Yet the domestic segment of that industry increasingly concentrated upon the medium-to-large segment of the market, leaving the largest and smallest segments to foreign or short-line companies. The result was the development of a remarkable variety of tractors, from a tiny twelve-horsepower Kubota to gigantic Big Bud tractors with hundreds of horsepower. Yet the most refined tractors remained those fitted to the average American farm.

Throughout the period, the tractor retained its primary purpose—pulling implements through farm soil. And the basic configuration of the tractor changed little. Throughout the forty years following the introduction of the B, the tractor remained the same in essence even as it changed in size and convenience.

NOTES

1. "Ford's Tractor," *Newsweek* (May 8, 1939): 53, 44; Colin Fraser, *Tractor Pioneer: The Life of Harry Ferguson* (Athens: Ohio University Press, 1973), 116–17; "Historic Furrow," *Time* (July 3, 1939): 45, 50.

2. Faser, *Ferguson*, 48–56.

3. See Skromme's comments on McKibben's 1927 papers in "Growth of ASAE," 182.

4. This was more than a year before the classic studies of tractor geometry by E. G. McKibben in the United States. Skromme, "Growth of ASAE," 182.

5. Mr. Ford's Only Partner," *Fortune* (January 1942): 66–67, 153–57.

6. Fraser, *Ferguson*, 101–19.

7. "Tractors Running Hot," 17; "Ford Makes a New Tractor and Implements," *Automotive Industries* (July 15, 1939): 66–67; Joseph Geschelin, "Following Ford Tractors Down the Line," *Automotive Industries* (July 1, 1940): 4–11, 43–44.

8. "Ford's Only Partner," 156.

9. " 'Offset' Tractor Allows a Clear View of Row," *Popular Mechanics* (November 1939): 703.

10. "Ford's Only Partner," 67.

11. "Ford's Only Partner," 156.

12. F. Leland Elam, "Hydraulics—Hard Working Farm Hand," *Popular Mechanics* (June 1954): 134–37, 218, 220.

13. "Tractors: Ferguson's Fight," *Newsweek* (May 19, 1947): 76; "New Field Plowed," *Time* (July 21, 1947): 88; "Ford Tractors Move to Showrooms," *Business Week* (July 12, 1947): 28; Ironically, Ford eventually purchased Sherman, "Ford to Buy Assets, Plants of Sherman Products, Inc.," *Implement & Tractor* (May 28, 1970): 18.

14. "Ford Pays Off," *Time* (April 21, 1952): 97,98; "Ford Settlement," *Newsweek* (April 24, 1952): 92; Fraser, *Ferguson*, 183–204; Neufeld, *A Global Corporation*, 94–104.

15. "Massey-Harris-Ferguson Announcement," *Farm Implement News* (September 10, 1953): 154; Fraser, *Ferguson*, 225–40; Neufeld, *Global Corporation*, 130–47.

16. Fraser, *Ferguson*, 45.

17. "Three-Point Tractor Hitch," *Agricultural Engineering*, 34 (January 1953): 44; "Smaller Tractors," 22; "Parade of Progress," *Farm Implement News* (August 10, 1953): 66, 67, 116–17.

18. "This Must Make It Unanimous," *Farm Implement News* (July 10, 1953): 59.

19. R. H. Atteberry [letter to the editor], "IH Hitch Not the Ferguson," *Farm Implement News* (August 10, 1953): 14, 124; Louis L. Tigner, "Six Cylinders

and a New 60 HP Tractor Highlight IH's 1959 Challenge," *Implement & Tractor* (August 23, 1958): 70–73.

20. Skromme, "Growth of ASAE," 182.

21. For a description of postwar mechanization, see Sam B. Hilliard, "The Dynamics of Power: Recent Trends in Mechanization of the American Farm," *Technology and Culture* 13 (January 1972): 1–24. Some of the innovations that Hilliard mentions (such as multiple hitching) are neither recent nor widespread.

22. Durost and Black, "Changes in Farm Production," 31.

23. Johnson, "Changes in American Farming", 3.

24. Wayne D. Rasmussen, "Impact of Technological Change," 579; "Farm Tool Rush," *Business Week* (July 12, 1941): 26.

25. "Implement Pinch," *Business Week* (August 29, 1942): 17, 18.

26. "Farmers Get Aid," *Business Week* (April 24, 1943): 28–30.

27. "Food Prospects Grow Worse," *Business Week* (May 29, 1943): 15; "Implements Freed," *Business Week* (October 7, 1944): 20.

28. "Farmers Get Aid," 29; "Tractors for '44," *Business Week* (November 13, 1943): 19, 20.

29. Durost and Black, "Changes in Farm Production," 31.

30. Bela Gold, *Wartime Economic Planning in Agriculture* (New York: Columbia University Press, 1949), 225–29.

31. Ladd Haystead, "Machines That Weren't There," *Fortune* (June 1946): 195–96, 198.

32. Everett, "Big Expansion," 28–29; Butler and Crawford, "Use and Cost of Tractor Power," 8; H. L. Patterson, "A Statistical Analysis of Farm Mechanization in Canada," *Agricultural Institute Review* 2 (March 1947): 88.

33. Everett, "Big Expansion," 28.

34. Joseph Geschelin, "Oliver's Modernized Facilities for Producing Three Tractor Models," *Automotive Industries* (March 1, 1949): 34–36, 52; Donald Peddie, "Production Control as Applied in a Farm Tractor Plant," *The Iron Age* (January 29, 1948): 56–61; Everett, "Big Expansion," 54, 62.

35. Reuben W. Hecht and Glen T. Barton, "Gains in Productivity of Farm Labor," *Technical Bulletin* No. 1020 (Washington: United States Department of Agriculture, December 1950): 24.

36. Johnson, "Changes," 59; Sperry, "Farm Power and the Post War Tractor," 501; Butler and Crawford, "Use and Cost of Tractor Power," 3; quote from Rasmussen, "Impact of Technological Change," 578.

37. Ladd Haystead, "Can Farmers Afford Their New Tools?" *Fortune* (September 1946): 177, 179–80, 183. The process by which wheatland-type tractors were replaced was not completed until well after the war, but the wheatland types were discarded faster than were row-crop tractors, "Life of the Farm Tractor," *Farm Implement News* (July 10, 1951): 111.

38. Durost and Black, "Changes in Farm Production," 31; "The Bank Eyes Changes in the Farm Equipment Market," *Implement & Tractor* (February 20, 1960): 106.

39. Mark Zimmerman, "The Farm Tractor," *Implement & Tractor* (November 21, 1964): 28–31; Zimmerman, "Profile: Today's Heavyweight Tractors," *Im-*

plement & Tractor (February 21, 1965): 18–20; "Dealers Delivered More Horsepower in 1966," *Implement & Tractor* (November 21, 1967): 30–35; "Lost Retail Sales: The Horsepower Went Up," *Implement & Tractor* (August 7, 1967): 30.

40. "IH Brings Out New Tractor Models," *Farm Implement News*, (March 25, 1952); "How Does a Turbocharger Work?" *Implement & Tractor* (July 15, 1962): 20; Melvin E. Long, "Supercharging the Diesel Engine," *Implement & Tractor* (February 21, 1965): 26–28; Mark Zimmerman, "Why Alternators?" *Implement & Tractor* (February 7, 1964): 50, 51; Melvin C. Long, "All About Tractor Hitches," *Implement & Tractor* (January 21, 1964): 23–25, 54; James Basselmon, "New 1,000-rpm Power Take-off Standard Approved for Farm Tractors," *Agricultural Engineering* 39 (February 1958): 86–87.

41. George W. Wormly, "Brand New Line of Tractors," *Farm Journal* (October 1960): 44.

42. Merlin Hansen, "Engineering a New Line of Tractors," *Agricultural Engineering* 42 (November 1961): 602, 604; George Seferovich, "Deere's Engineered New Line of Tractors," *Implement & Tractor* (September 17, 1960): 66–69.

43. Interview with Gene Scarborough, former John Deere salesman, Muleshoe, Texas, October 1979; interview with Terry Parr, former John Deere blockman, Shallowater, Texas, February 1980.

44. Deere certainly did not become the lowest priced, however. In the late seventies, I was shopping for a tractor and priced all of the major makes before ultimately purchasing a used machine. All the makes were equally equipped, but new tractor prices ranged from $5,500 for an Allis-Chalmers to $10,500 for a John Deere. The other manufacturers were spread uniformly between the price extremes. Some of the variation in price was doubtless because of the circumstances of the various local dealers, but much of the difference was a reflection of corporate price differences.

45. "The New Tractors: Giants of the Earth," *Agricultural Engineering* 59 (July 1978): 38–44.

46. "Two or Three Plow Rating," 49; Neufeld, *Global Corporation*, 32.

47. "New One-Man Hook-Ups," *Farm Journal* (July 1956): 37; Wesley F. Buchele and E. V. Collins, "Development of the Tandem Tractor," *Agricultural Engineering* 39 (April 1958): 232–34, 236.

48. Frank Buckingham, "4-Wheel Drive," *Implement & Tractor* (March 21, l963): 46–49; H. K. Dommel and K. W. Race, "Design and Performance Characteristics of Four-Wheel-Drive Tractors," *Agricultural Engineering* 45 (August 1964): 424–27, 429. Tractors designed to utilize four-wheel-drive generally have all four wheels the same size. Many companies, however, offer auxiliary drive trains to power the front wheels on conventional tractors. These generally have front wheels somewhat smaller than the rear wheels.

49. Buckingham, "4-wheel Drive," 46.

50. Rex L. Clark, "Tractor Performance in Two- and Four-Wheel-Drive," *Transactions of the American Society of Agricultural Engineers* 27 (January/ February 1984): 8–11; "Future Tractors: The Size and Shape of Things to Come," *Implement & Tractor* (January 1983): 12, 13.

51. "The Drought in Farm Equipment Isn't Over Yet," *Business Week* (April 23, 1984): 36; Jill Betner and Lisa Gass, "Planting Deep and Wide at John Deere" *Forbes* (March 14, 1983): 119–22; "Get Through to the Good Times," *Forbes* (March 14, 1983): 123–26; Carliss Y. Baldwin and Scott Mason, "The Resolution of Claims in Financial Distress in the Case of Massey-Ferguson," *Journal of Finance* 36 (May 1983): 505–16; Jennifer Wells, "Jilted," *Canadian Business* (May 1984): 73–76.

52. "The Seventies Are Over," *Implement & Tractor* (July 1983): 30.

53. "Are We an Endgame Industry?" *Implement & Tractor* (March 1983): 14.

54. Steven Greenhouse, "Farm Equipment Sales Still Hurting," *Lubbock Avalanche Journal* (December 7, 1984): D-11; Thomas Petzinger, Jr., and Betsy Morris, "Tenneco to Buy Farm-Gear Unit From Harvester," *Wall Street Journal*: (November 27, 1984): 2; Bill Richards, "Allis-Chalmers Could Be First Big Loser as Harvester Leaves Farm Gear Business," *Wall Street Journal* (December 7, 1984): 2.

55. George H. Seferovich. "Tractors: The Surge in Imports," *Implement & Tractor* (May 28, 1960): 28–30.

56. Seferovich, "Tractors," 28–30; "Oliver 500 Tractors Made by David Brown," *Implement & Tractor* (March 5, 1960): 30 (David Brown was later purchased by Tenneco and integrated with their Case subsidiary); Bill Storm, "How Frick Co. Is Distributing England's Nuffield Tractor," *Implement & Tractor* (December 2l, l964): 14–15; "Imports of Farm Equipment by Product 1975–1976," *Implement & Tractor* (November 7, 1977): 102; "Tractors: Where the Horsepower Went in 1977," *Implement & Tractor* (April 21, 1978): 26–27; Bill Fogarty, "Tractor Imports, Tractor Exports," *Implement & Tractor* (March 21, 1978): 20–22; "Future Tractors," 12, 13.

57. "Mervyn H. Manning, "Future Technology and Foreign Competition," *Agricultural Engineering* 65 (March, 1984): 13; "Deutz Buys Allis-Chalmers", *Progressive Farmer Soybeans [Midmonth Supplement]* (May 1985): 21; "New Star Rises in Far East," *Progressive Farmer* (May 1984): A-4.

58. "Future Tractors," 12, 13; Manning, "Future Technology", 13.

59. Harlan W. VanGerpen, "Evaluating Tractor Seating Comfort." *Agricultural Engineering* 37 (October 1956): 673.

60. "Tractors Are Running Hot," 18; "Show New Tractors," 41.

61. Melvin E. Long, "Cabs for Tractors and Combines," *Implement & Tractor* (August 21, 1965): 34–37.

62. Long, "Cabs for Tractors," 34; C. S. Morrison and R. E. Harrington, "Tractor Seating for Operator Comfort," *Agricultural Engineering* 43 (November 1962): 632–35, 650–52; J. M. Mather and K. C. Adams, "New 5-Plow 'One-Ninety' Tractor by Allis-Chalmers," *Agricultural Engineering* 45 (December 1964): 677–78; R. J. Ronayne, "Oliver Introduces Three New Tractors," *Agricultural Engineering* 45 (December 1964): 666–67, 676.

63. Wayne Worthington, "Engineer's Tractor History, VII: Manufacturers, Customers and Safety," *Implement & Tractor* (April 21, 1967): 16, 22.

64. R. H. Hahn, "Federal Safety Standards for Tractors," *Agricultural Engineering* 52 (March 1971): 108.

65. "News on Noise in Chicago," *Agricultural Engineering* 53 (July 1972): 12; Marianna Pratt, "A 'Sound Idea' from Deere," *Agricultural Engineering* 53 (September 1972): 23; R. W. King and J. L. Jessup, "[Massey-Ferguson] Introduces the New Line of Tractors at ASAE Meeting," *Agricultural Engineering* 54 (January 1973): 24.

II

The Impact of the Tractor on America

7
Witches' Promises

When the idea of the tractor was first discussed, it is improbable that anyone could have anticipated more than a fraction of the machine's eventual impact. Perhaps the best procedure for investigating the impact of the tractor is to examine people's expectations for it, how it filled or failed those expectations, and what the unexpected consequences of the tractor were.

The single most appealing feature of the tractor to the average farmer was the machine's ability to reduce his workload. Even as early as 1910, tractor advocates saw it as means of emancipating farmers from drudgery. In celebrating the anticipated demise of "the man with the hoe," an early tractor booster calculated that the average farmer who turned an acre of ground trudged some eight and one-fourth miles. If the same farmer plowed a section, he walked 5,280 miles.[1]

A decade later, in 1920, tractors were far more common and far less theoretical. They did reduce drudgery. A farmer's wife described the change. Speaking of her neighbor, she wrote, "Her husband's and my husband's parents gave their bodies to the making of that big farm. She and her husband do not have to do that. [Because of tractors and other machinery,] when they are forty, their steps will not drag and their shoulders round into a weary droop. The machines are saving them from that."[2] Farmers continued to buy tractors in an attempt to avoid back-breaking toil. It was a marvelous change for the farmer. The tractor transformed him from being the "source of the power" to being "the director of the power."[3]

Closely related to the goal of reducing physical effort was the farmer's desire to reduce his workday, giving him more free time. Although this was sometimes an elusive quest, some farmers achieved additional leisure time because of the tractor. Other potential purchasers then entertained similar expectations, and regarded them as plausible reasons for purchasing a tractor. One early tractor farmer said that since buying a tractor he and his employees were able to quit shortly after five and not "have to spend another forty minutes to two hours taking care of six to ten head of horses." During World War II, the War Production Board estimated that the tractor saved the farmer 250 man-hours per year in caring for animals. Such a prospect was a compelling argument for purchasing a tractor, and a constant chorus repeated a refrain urging tractors and leisure time.[4] Certainly few tractor purchasers expected to spend any more time farming with a tractor than they had with horses.

Time and effort were not the only savings that the tractor had to offer in order to be successful, for its use had little appeal unless it also promised the farmer money. Almost from the time the first tractor was put together, there were arguments about its economic feasibility. Tractor advocates constructed hypothetical budgets as early as 1908 in order to prove that tractors were good investments, and econometric historians as late as 1980 built similar—if more sophisticated—conjectural cost estimates. While such exercises are entertaining, and even instructive, farming is too complex, too diverse, too varied, and too subject to random circumstances for precise modeling.[5]

From 1916 to the late thirties, carefully conducted college extension studies showed little difference in profitability between horses and tractors. But gradually the question of tractor profitability ceased to be an issue and dropped from experiment station notice.[6]

The real test of tractor profitability came in the fields and on the pages of farmers' ledgerbooks; from 1918 on, an ever-growing majority of farmers reported that tractors were profitable. Reports from tractor owners obviously were neither scientific nor utterly objective, but they were the result of practical experiences. The use of tractors promised profit.[7]

Financial profit is closely associated with social standing, and for many farmers the tractor was also a status symbol. In an age when electric lights and indoor plumbing were frequently the prerogative of sophisticated urbanities, a high technology machine like a tractor reassured the farmer of his modernity and proclaimed that he was no ignorant rube. Even opponents of the tractor sensed that it promised increased prestige.

"In the first place, if you own a tractor," wrote a critical farmer, "your neighbors and the people in town will consider you a progressive and up-to-date farmer."[8]

The use of the tractor seemed to promise the farmer numerous rewards that were largely realized. Yet, like the witches' promises to Macbeth, the fulfillment of those promises did not result in precisely what fallible humanity had expected. Much of the price of the adoption of the tractor was concealed at the time of the bargain, and the contract had to be paid in dear coinage indeed.

The initial price of a tractor was paid in United States currency. In exceptionally good years, few farmers resisted the temptation to update their equipment. In a sense, a new tractor was a type of insurance against future breakdowns. It was an investment that might be used later for collateral if necessary. A new tractor could also be used to level out some of the ups and downs of income in order to reduce the size of the tax man's painful bite. But most years were not so rosy that the farmer purchased a new tractor with cash. And when a farmer bought a new Farmall on credit, he lost much financial flexibility. The bank demanded payment regardless of the wild fluctuations in the price of cotton or corn. The instability of the farmer's income made him extremely vulnerable.[9] When conditions were particularly bad, farmers were forced to stop purchasing tractors or any other major capital-intensive items.

But much of the time low crop prices and the high cost of machinery forced most farmers to borrow money to purchase up-to-date equipment. That indebtedness intensified their vulnerability to the downside of cyclical crop prices. As a result, farmers were often unable to meet their loan obligations in hard times, and bank foreclosures were anything but rare. Sometimes the former owners were retained as tenants; sometimes they were "tractored out." On rare occasions, the former owners managed to recoup their losses and regain their farms. But few commercial farms operated long without mortgage encumbrance. Mechanization and expansion were mutually complementary trends, and both required capital. The larger scale of the resulting operation promised more rewards, but it also placed the farmer's entire equity in jeopardy.[10] A Canadian farmer, while purchasing a 1970 tractor, said that he now commanded "more field power, more working comfort and convenience and more debt" than ever before in his life.[11]

The same farm wife who lauded the tractor for reducing her husband's physical work also recognized that it had a negative effect. "And yet," she wrote, "If the machines are saving the bodies of today's wheat grower and his wife, they are landing them squarely in a predicament that the former generation of growers did not have to face . . . men buy machinery. . . . But in a certain real sense, it [machinery], and not they, is the master of their joint destiny".[12]

One student of mechanization and society declared bluntly, "Keeping up payments on farm machinery has taken years off the lives of a good many farmers."[13] The tractor had promised leisure, but the "saved" time often had to be reinvested in an attempt to pay off mortgages. Although some farmers managed to find more time for recreation and personal development, far too many fit the pattern described by an economic historian who wrote, "It is a notable fact that retired farmers are, as a rule, not adept in the enjoyment of leisure after a lifetime of hard work. Too often, instead of killing time, they kill themselves."[14] After a lifetime of compulsory labor, farmers found it impossible to relax.

The drudgery that the tractor eliminated was replaced, at least in part, by increased danger of accidental injury. In describing the impact of tractors and other farm implements, one engineer wrote, "We've reduced man's physical burdens with machines, but we've added to his mental work. . . . When we complicate his life by adding to his mental work load, demanding that he make more decisions to operate machines, he may make mistakes that lead to serious accidents."[15]

Farmers were no longer restrained by the stamina of their team. Horses could not work endless hours, but machines could. It was easy to forget that man was not a tireless machine. In 1919, in the press of war, farmers were encouraged to put electric lights on their tractors to extend their workday. Little was written about fatigue and the limits of human endurance. A more recent advertisement promoted comfort improvements on a leading brand of tractor as a way of aiding the farmer in tolerating an even longer workday.[16] In neither instance was the longer workday questioned relative to its accident potential.

In 1930, an economist who studied tractors concluded that accidents were no more common with tractors than with horses. He studied some 240 tractor operators on 175 farms, but found only nine accidents, and "Most of these injuries were of a minor nature."[17] But that study compared accidents with horses to tractor-related accidents. Later researchers arrived at less complacent conclusions. By 1945 agricultural engineers discovered that agriculture had a fatality rate twice that of manufacturing. Only construction, mining, and a few other high-risk industries were more dangerous. By 1960, farm accidents were killing 2,400 people per year, with more than one thousand of these related to tractors. Tractors rolled over and fatally crushed some five hundred people per year.[18] The tractor was in fact hazardous to the farmer's health, even though by the sixties engineers had began to eliminate some of the most obvious dangers.

The major impetus for accelerated research came after 1957, when insurance companies financed roll-over protection research, and after 1971, when the United States Department of Transportation set a five-year deadline for industry standards on roll-over protective structures. The same year, the American Society of Agricultural Engineers embarked on a ten-year safety campaign. Gradually the benefits of improved tractors will reach the farmer, but because tractors are quite durable, it will take a long time for every farm tractor to be replaced with the newer, safer models.[19]

Even with the best of safety engineering, however, tractors—like automobiles—continued to demand a toll from those who were impatient, tired, or careless. If a safety device was slightly inconvenient, it was likely to be removed and discarded, leaving an unshielded danger.[20] An engineer who intended to save limbs and lives had to design his tractor with human nature in mind, because the farmer who actually operated the equipment was not necessarily a perfectly alert, perfectly coordinated youth. Rather, he was often, "A weary, sweating man at the end of his long day . . . a man who is probably taking an antihistimine for hay fever and a tricyclic depressant to help him face another session with his bank manager . . . a man who has been jolted about for twelve hours and whose hearing is reduced by the continuous roar of his machine . . . a man whose eyes are red from dust and who has been receiving a small but continuous quota of carbon monoxide."[21] The engineer whose company ordered him to design a foolproof machine for such an operator faced a major task. But the understanding of the operator's predicament is vital to explaining why earlier safety studies attributed half of farm machinery accidents to "carelessness."[22]

Not all of the damage done to farmers by tractors came in sudden and spectacular accidents like tractor upsets. Many injuries were gradual, cumulative and long-term. In two particular areas, vibration and noise, tractors did significant but slow injury to farmers.

Tractors develop countless vibrations, ranging from the high-pitched whine of a hydraulic pump to the slow, wracking oscillations of a machine crossing furrows. Farmers complained of the damage done by such vibration from the very first. Serious engineering studies in the late fifties and early sixties concluded that, "rough riding may result in gross damage to the spine, which leads to pain and discomfort in the back."[23]

Equally damaging was the cumulative effect of noise. Repeated tests of farmers who had driven tractors for five to ten years showed significant damage to their inner ears. Like the problem with accidents, the solution required both engineering and psychology. Farmers often listened to their tractors to determine how heavily they were loaded, and so rejected ear plugs or shields. The solution lay in better muffling and advertising to transform quietness from a sales liability—because quiet tractors did not sound *powerful*—to an asset. The addition of cabs also helped to quiet and soundproof tractors.[24]

All such improvements paid large dividends in operator comfort and health. The farmer in 1980 in an air-filtered, air-conditioned, roll-over-protected tractor was safer than his grandfather was behind a kicking mule. Whether the same could not be said for the Fordson jockey or the operator of early row-crop tractors is open to question.

In addition to offering a lighter workload to the farmer, the use of the tractor seemed to promise a bigger income. It did for a fortunate few.

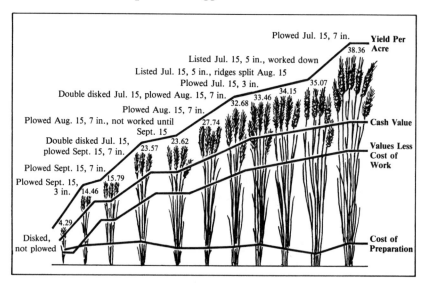

Figure 5. Effect of timeliness on crop production.

Source. Capper Farm Press, *The Tractor: Selling It as an Agricultural Implement and Fitting It to Midwest Crop Areas,* 4th ed. (Topeka: Capper Farm Press, 1920), 12.

But the arrival of a tractor on the farm not only changed the physical effort the farmer expended and the nature of the dangers to which he was exposed, but it also changed his entire manner of operating. During the depression, an astute observer wrote: "The managerial problem of agriculture is probably the most acute one which has arisen as a result of the mechanization movement . . . by no means . . . can we simply put power machinery into our farm organization as it had developed in the horse age."[25] The tractor industrialized the farm, and the successful farmer needed the same skills as a successful industrial manager.

A successful farmer in the tractor age had to use capital in a skillful manner. Tractors and other equipment drove up the capital requirements for farming, and only the man with access to capital succeeded. Access to capital meant that farmers had to prove to bankers that they were businesslike and good credit risks. In the process, the farmer was compelled to keep better records than ever before. No longer could he keep a running tally on the barn door. Bankers required "scientific management," and if the farmer objected, the banker simply withheld his loan. No wonder an economist declared that the "farmer's role as a financier is fast gaining ground on his role as a skillful husbandman."[26] The farmer was no longer a farmer—he was a businessman who grew commodities such as food and fiber. Farming, as a way of life, was dead.[27]

Thus farmers who survived the industrialization of agriculture had different characteristics than the traditional American farmer. The stereotype had been honest and hardworking, but something of a plodding dullard. Like all stereotypes, that was probably an exaggerated caricature. The new farmer had to be a mechanic, a business analyst, and a biologist. His new attributes were "as difficult to acquire as are the technical requirements of an administrator in big business."[28] The tractor, the automobile, and other new machinery decreased the farmer's need for brute strength and stubborn persistence. One person noted that mechanization, "Like every other major invention, . . . has furthered social differentiation, and has increased the relative advantage of ability and education and the possession of capital. It puts a premium on foresight, initiative, mechanical aptitude and ability to deal with men, and imposes a corresponding handicap on those who lack these qualities. Old-fashioned, standardized farming is ceasing to be a refuge for the routineer."[29] No longer could the farmer think at the two-miles-per-hour mentality of a walking mule. The farmer himself was changed by the tractor—or at least, the personality profile of the successful farmer changed.

As an industrialist, the farmer was forced to specialize. Before the

First World War there were few tractors on farms. Those few farms that used tractors still grew about the same variety of produce as their horse-drawn neighbors. Most farms produced from a half-dozen to nine different products. Most produced some oats.[30] There were regional exceptions, of course. In the South, cotton was the staple cash crop, although corn occupied more acres. Wheat dominated the Plains. Even in those regions, however, the farmstead frequently had a garden, and supported some pigs, chickens, and milk cows. But by the thirties, farm specialization and farm tractor numbers were both growing. Both trends continued down through the mid-sixties[31] and were intensified by the arrival of chemical farming. And while some areas maintained or even expanded a diversified production, the general trend was toward specialization. The more diversified a farm was, the more specialized equipment it required; the more equipment it required, the more capital or credit it needed. Even though diversification provided a measure of security against the vagaries of volatile commodity prices, many farmers were forced to concentrate on one crop that promised the greatest return on investment in the short run.

The tractor brought other problems to the new businessman-farmer, problems unknown in his grandfather's day. Managing skilled labor and avoiding overcapitalization, for example, were both related to the adoption of tractors. Farmers tried to get by with as few hired tractor drivers as possible. Hired hands did not care for the tractor as carefully as an owner would, and skilled tractor drivers were hard to find and relatively expensive. To complicate the process, potential hired hands sometimes balked if the farmer's tractors were not the latest and most comfortable.[32] Such difficulties were similar to the problems facing the manager of a small manufacturing plant.

But the manager of a small plant did not normally operate the equipment in that plant. The farmer did. So not only did the farmer face pressure from his employees to buy a new tractor, but he was also personally tempted. As a result, the farmer generally had a huge proportion of his assets tied up in machinery. Because the nature of the operation was highly seasonal, much of the equipment sat idle for eleven months, while interest on his overhead continued to mount. Managers in few other industries could last against such unfavorable economics.[33] Yet many farmers did survive.

Farmers who survived not only had to use capital wisely, but they also had to be innovative. An Ohio rural sociologist described such innovative farmers as "adoption leaders." They adopted "new-fangled" methods of using equipment long before the average farmer, and reaped the economic benefits of improved technology. "This means," he said, "that farmers who adopt an improvement that actually reduces cost always gains in the early period of its adoption. The farmers who do not make the change are not affected by the improvement until or unless prices of farm products are reduced."[34] The readiness to innovate gave this type of farmer a distinct economic edge in the longer period. Such "adoption leaders" were easily identifiable. They tended to be better educated—or at least had more formal education. They tended to participate more in social activities, civic clubs, farm organizations, and church activities. The adoption leader was likely to be a young, second-generation family farmer. The larger his operation, the faster he was apt to innovate. His income increased along with his rate of innovation. He was prone to keep better-than-average records. He had distinctive sources of information, patterns of credit use, and a distinctive view of the future. In short, the adoption leader was clearly identifiable by a characteristic social profile.[35]

Finally, if the tractor forced the farmer to be more innovative than before, it also forced him to rely more on off-farm inputs in his production process. In fact, many of the hours "saved" in the production process were, in fact, merely moved off-farm. For example, in the days of draft horses, the farmer furnished much of his own fuel. After the adoption of tractors, the labor and capital that supplied farm fuel were located in towns and oil fields miles from the farmer's door. Although the additional crops that the farmer raised in place of hay and oats more than offset the cost of the fuel, it was still not cheap. As one writer observed as recently as 1976, "About one-third to one-half the cost of owning and operating a tractor is the cost of fuel. If we paid as much for a calorie of gasoline as we paid for a calorie of corn, the cost of operating farm machinery might cause them to be abandoned."[36] And, worst of all, outside purchases—such as fuel— were beyond the farmer's control, making him dependent on others.

Soon after tractor makers began mass production, farmers began agitating for crop-based fuels, primarily fuel alcohol or an alcohol-gasoline blend. Farmers hoped that by producing fuel alcohol, they could raise the disastrously low price of farm commodities and gain some control over their fuel supply. Agitation increased in the thirties, and both politicians and engineers exhibited some interest in the concept. But the petroleum industry suffered from a glut of crude oil and furiously opposed any implementation of a fuel-alcohol program.[37] The combination of cheap petroleum prices and the oil industry's political influence blocked experimentation on a commercially viable scale. Although there were sporadic articles on farm-based fuels, interest dwindled until 1973, when petroleum suppliers were unable to meet America's addiction to petrofuels. The intermittent fuel shortages of the 1970s revived interest in fuels made from farm crops.[38] Some optimistic farmers hoped that they might be able to distil their own fuel alcohol or produce their own vegetable-based diesel fuels right on the farm.

Some farmers—although by no means all—found that the tractor reduced their independence by forcing them to rely upon off-farm mechanics. In the early days of tractor production, owners were given little training in caring for new machines, and unnecessary repairs were common. Farmers in 1922 had little experience with tractors, and they probably were as inept at repairs as they were careless in operation. But by 1931, Minnesota agricultural agents reported that more than half of the tractors in their survey were repaired exclusively by on-farm labor. And four-fifths of the farms did 50 percent or more of their own repairs. Still, according to a survey, almost half of Minnesota farmers had almost half of their mechanical work done by off-farm mechanics.[39]

If the tractor promised the farmer less work, more money, and more prestige, it hardly offered less to his family. In fact, the reduction in drudgery applied to the average farm family fully as much as to the lord of the demesne—and perhaps even more. An advocate of mechanization wrote, "the problem of labor displacement . . . is primarily one of displacing the farmer's wife and children from the fields to the home and the school."[40] While that was true of all family labor, another writer was a bit more emphatic, "If the child of the industrialist is freed from toil to complete a wholesome period of bodily growth and socially desirable training both for his vocation and citizenship, it is equally important that the country child should have comparable conditions of life."[41]

No wonder there is a clear implication in much of the discussion of tractors that the farmer's son held a special interest in mechanization. In fact, one of the great claims put forward by tractor boosters was that the tractor would provide a positive answer to the question of "How do you keep 'em down on the farm?" The end of drudgery, the fascination of intricate, powerful machinery, and the sense of accomplishment that the tractor allowed—all these things were said to tie the would-be prodigal to the mechanized farm.[42] Some of the prose was maudlin, but tractor advocates apparently believed that tractors would retain youth on the farm.

Naturally, opponents denied that tractors had any ability to hold boys on the farm. One antitractor individual listed three facetious reasons for buying a tractor. His second one was "if you buy a tractor you can keep the boy on the farm one year longer. He will stay with you the year the tractor is new, but will leave the next year."[43] If the critic was correct, it was an expensive maneuver for so temporary a gain.

Perhaps the tractor did keep some young men on their fathers' farms. Although the reduction in physical fatigue must have been a factor, another influence may well have colored the apparent holding power of the tractor. The farmer who could afford a tractor was more likely to have enough work to make use of his son or sons than did a smaller, poorer farmer. Also, the farmer who could afford a tractor was more likely to have a farm large enough to hold some promise of a remunerative patrimony for potential heirs. The tractorless tenant had nothing comparable to offer his sons. For whatever reasons perhaps sons did stay on tractor farms slightly more often than on other farms.[44]

Nor were the farmer and his male progeny alone in hearing alluring pledges from the tractor. Wives and daughters also had hopes for the machine. In 1933, amid the voices questioning the role of the tractor in the worldwide depression, one speaker hailed the tractor for providing "almost a complete liberation of women in the field."[45] And to a great many women, liberation from hard manual labor in the field must have been a much more immediate victory than the right to vote.

Women's displacement by tractors did not necessarily mean that they were elevated to a status equal to that of their mates, but merely that they could now do chores at home rather than chop cotton or drive a team. A woman's status was often not too different from that of a tractor or a mule. She was sometimes considered to be little more than property that a wise owner treated with care. A farmer with the improbable name of "Push Potty" told a reporter that wives and tractors were similar. "You can oil her [your tractor] and give her new rings and keep her tuned up, but if you don't treat her right she wears out fast. Just like a woman. Take my neighbor up the road. He beats his wife and he beats his tractor. Slams her in reverse, swings her around corners at top speeds, loads her down and always has her running wide open—his tractor that is. He gets a new Machine every four or five years and is always having trouble. Me, I expect to keep one wife and one tractor a good many years yet."[46]

Not all women viewed displacement from the field as liberation. For some women, driving a tractor was preferable to housework, and they became as much farmers as their fathers or husbands.[47] The tractor helped to overcome the physical disabilities—primarily the lack of brute strength—that hampered a woman's entry into farming. Although women had occasionally become farmers before the tractor arrived, tractors made it easier for a woman to compete in agriculture by reducing the level of physical exertion.[48] As early as 1917, a "quiet, modest little old lady" had farmed successfully with a tractor. Her success was applauded as "a fine example of what a woman, backed by her good business sense and a firm determination to succeed, can accomplish."[49] Another farmer may have revealed more about his family constellation than about tractors when he responded to a questionnaire about rubber tires by saying, "My wife says she would not drive any other than rubber tires."[50]

The world wars opened up jobs for women on the farm just as they did for women in urban industry. No songs celebrated the female tractor driver the way "Rosie the Riveter" glorified factory workers, but women's agricultural contribution was essential and publicized.[51] In March 1918, one journal assured its readers that "One girl can do the work of several men with the help of a tractor."[52] In both wars, women did the work of many men, and at least some remained in the driver's seat after the war.

The tractor's conquest of physical barriers to women farming was not enough, however. The tractor did not promise to change the sexual stereotypes of the age and had no means of doing so. Relatively few women have come to prominent positions as farm operators. In 1970 the Bureau of the Census found 1,281,000 male farmers and farm managers, but only 62,000 female farmers and farm managers. The bureau's report indicated that only 4.6 percent of American farm operators were female.[53] Although the actual number of women farmers probably exceeded the reported number by a considerable margin, because of a cultural bias that always listed a partnership in the husband's name rather than the wife's, the number was still small. By the late seventies, however, social values appeared to be changing as increasing numbers of coeds enrolled in agriculture courses. The tractor remained indifferent to the sex of its operator.

The use of the tractor had seemed to promise something to nearly everyone on the farm. The fulfillment of those promises was not always exactly what had been anticipated. Work reduction was sometimes made actually available only at an excessive monetary sacrifice, and potential leisure was often offset by physical danger. Reduced physical exertion was frequently counterbalanced by greater financial worries. While few farmers would choose to return to premechanization days, the tractor's benefits to the individual farmer were not free.

The tractor's promise to the farm family was fulfilled in a much more straightforward manner, but not without hidden costs. But the costs paid by the farm family were roughly comparable in nature to those paid by the society as a whole, although perhaps the farm family paid a bit more.

NOTES

1. Rumely, "Man with the Hoe," 1324.

2. Avis D. Carlson, "The Wheat Farmer's Dilemma," *Harper's Magazine* (July 1931): 210–11; Archer P. Whallon, "Farming with Tractors the Cheaper Way," *California Citrograph* (January 1920): 79.

3. Jackson V. McElveen, "Family Farms in a Changing Economy," *Agricultural Information Bulletin* No. 171 (Washington: United States Department of Agriculture, March 1957): 60; Leonard J. Fletcher, "The Real Effects of Mechanization on Wheat Production," *Proceedings of the World's Grain Exhibition and Conference* 1 (Regina, Saskatchewan: Canadian Society of Technical Agriculturalists, July 24 to August 5, 1933): 362. The reduction in the laboriousness of farming was a frequent topic for articles. Some received odd responses. A manufacturer wrote one farm publication claiming that he had once been a farmer, "and there is no more drudgery on the farm than in the factory." The editor noted drily that the manufacturer "does not say why he left the farm," "Horse vs. Tractor," *Market Growers Journal* (September 1, 1926): 39.

4. E. A. Hunger, "Forestdale Said 'Good-Bye'," 6; "Tractor Most Reliable," *Power Farming* (July 1926): 3; James A. McAleer, "Farm Machinery and Equipment Policies of the War Production Board and Predecessor Agencies," *Historical Reports on War Administration: War Production Board Special Study* No. 13 [mimeographed], (November 10, 1944): 1, as quoted in Gold, *Wartime Economic Planning*, 203.

5. Perkins, "Farmer's Tireless Horse," 458; Robert E. Ankli, "Horses vs. Tractors in the Corn Belt," *Agricultural History* 54 (January 1980): 134–248. Perkins's article is an early, fairly simple cost estimate. Ankli's work is highly complex. Ankli notes that the results depend to a considerable extent upon the classifications and presuppositions of the study. For example, horses may be treated as a fixed cost or as a variable cost, a procedure that influences the results. He assumes five cuttings of alfalfa, when the actual number could easily be less.

6. Rumely, "Man with the Hoe," 1325; Rutenik, "Efficiency of the Farm Tractor," 5; "Tractor Saves Half Expenses," *Orange Judd Farmer* (February 17, 1917): 20; "Power Costs," *Power Farming* (February 1921): 10; J. L. Justice, "Comparing Horse and Tractor Costs," *Hoard's Dairyman* (September 2, 1921): 160, 184; M. R. Cooper and J. O. Williams, "Cost of Using Horses on Corn-belt Farms," *Farmers' Bulletin* No. 298 (Washington: United States Department of Agriculture, 1922): 1; Neil M. Clark, "The American Farmer Wakes Up," *World's Work* (November 1926): 52; Fletcher and Kinsman, "The Tractor on California Farms," 3; Waddel, "As Public Works Buying Slackens," 853; Butler and Crawford, "Tractor Power on Small Farms in Anderson County, South Carolina," 20; C. Leroy Quance, "Capital," *The Overproduction Trap in U. S. Agriculture*, ed.,

Glenn L. Johnson and C. Leroy Quance (Baltimore: Resources for the Future, Inc., 1972), 96; Venkareddy Chennareddy, "Labor," *Overproduction Trap*, 113–36.

7. John R. Eustis, "On the Trail of the Tractor," *The Independent* (September 21, 1918): 389; F. A. Wirt, "Experiences of Maryland Tractor Owners," *Maryland Agricultural Society Report* 3 (1918): 81; Wooley, "Power Farming in Idaho," 10; Arnold P. Yerkes and L. M. Church, "Tractor Experiences in Illinois," *Farmers' Bulletin* 963 (Washington: United States Department of Agriculture, June 1918): 5; Nichols, "Tractor Experience in Kentucky," 47; Tolley and Church, "Tractors on Southern Farms," 8, 9; R. D. Barden, "Ohio Fruit Growers Prove Tractors Pay," *Power Farming* (October 1925): 5, 19; F. L. Morison, "The Tractor on Ohio Farms," *Ohio Agricultural Experiment Station Bulletin* No. 383 (May 1925): 24; Arthur A. Collins, "General Purpose Farm Equipment in Iowa," *Agricultural Engineering* (November 1931): 417; W. R. Humphries and L. M. Church, "A Farm Machinery Survey of Selected Districts in Pennsylvania," *Pennsylvania Agricultural Experiment Station Bulletin* 237 (March 1929): 7; H. B. Josephson and R. U. Blasingame, "Farm Power and Labor," *Pennsylvania Agricultural Experiment Station Bulletin* 238 (April 1929): 19–20; Stephens, "Mechanization," 29–30.

8. Hazlett, "The Farm Tractor in 1920," 612.

9. Troy J. Cauley, *Agriculture in an Industrial Economy: The Agrarian Crisis* (New York: Bookman Associates, 1956), 26; Kenneth L. Bachman and Ronald W. Jones, "Sizes of Farms in the United States," *Technical Bulletin* No. 1019 (Washington: United States Department of Agriculture, July 1950): 171–72.

10. Walter John Marx, *Mechanization and Culture: The Social and Cultural Implications of Mechanized Society* (St. Louis: B. Herder Book Co., 1941), 56–57; F. J. Skogvold, "Farm Loans and Farm Management by the Equitable Life Assurance Society of the United States," *Agricultural History* 30 (July 1956): 115; McWilliams, "Farms into Factories," 424; Bachman and Jones, "Sizes of Farms," 2; Bill Fogarty, "What Banks Think About Financing Farm Equipment," *Implement & Tractor* (August 23, 1958): 38–40.

11. Grant McEwan, *Power for Prairie Plows* (Saskatoon, Saskatchewan: The Midwestern Producer, 1971): 104.

12. Carlson, "Wheat Farmer's Dilemma," 210–11.

13. Walter John Marx, "Farm Machines and the Good Society," *The Commonweal* (December 24, 1948): 173; Marx, *Mechanization and Culture*, 80–81.

14. A. N. Johnson, "The Impact of Farm Machinery on the Farm Economy," *Agricultural History* 24 (January 1950): 58.

15. Page L. Bellinger, "Man-Machine Compatibility," *Agricultural Engineering* (January 1969): 17.

16. Archie A. Stone, "Putting Tractors on the Night Shift," *Power Farming* (May 1919): 26, 28; "Heavy-Duty Power, Easy-Duty Comfort," [advertisement], *The Furrow* (November-December 1978): 6–7; "Sound-Gard Body Gives You Staying Power to Handle Big Tractor Power," [advertisement], *The Furrow* (July-August 1979): 6–7.

17. Gilbert, "Tractors on New York Farms," 69.

18. C. L. Hamilton, "Agriculture's Safety Challenge," *Agricultural Engineering* 26 (April 1945): 145–46; Merlin Hansen, "Reducing Tractor Fatalities," *Agricultural Engineering* 47 (September 1966): 472–74.

19. "Making Tractors Roll-Over Safe," *Farm Implement News* (February 25, 1957): 53; Charles S. Floyd, "Cab Makers Confer on DOT Manifesto," *Implement & Tractor* (June 21, 1971): 12–14; Howard Pyle, "Setting ASAE Goals for Agricultural Safety," *Agricultural Engineering* 52 (January 1971): 15–16; Richard G. Pfister, "Do Tractors Last Too Long?" *Agricultural Engineering* 54 (May 1973): 12–13; Morrison and Harrington, "Tractor Seating for Operator Comfort," 632–35, 650–52; Melvin E. Long, "New Emphasis on Operator Comfort, Convenience," *Implement & Tractor* (May 21, 1965): 24–26; W. M. Van Syoc and N. F. Lemmon, "The ASAE Quick-Attaching Three-Point Hitch Coupler Standard," *Agricultural Engineering* 48 (February 1967): 80.

20. Carlton L. Zink, "Safety in Farm Equipment: The Manufacturer's Concern," *Agricultural Engineering* (February 1968): 74–75.

21. Edward Llewellyn Thomas, "The Subtle Pollutants," *Agricultural Engineering* 51 (March 1970): 127.

22. Hamilton, "Agriculture's Safety Challenge," 146.

23. Richard J. Hornick, "Effects of Tractor Vibration," *Agricultural Engineering* 42 (December 1961): 674.

24. John B. Gregg, "Noise Injuries to Farmers," *Agricultural Engineering* 53 (March 1972): 12–15; James K. Jensen, "Are Tractors Noisy?" *Agricultural Engineering* 47 (October 1966): 534; G. W. Steinbrugge, Gary K. Schmer, and Ned Maier, "Measuring Tractor Noise at the Nebraska Tractor Testing Laboratory," *Agricultural Engineering* 51 (March 1970): 142; Charles S. Floyd, "Dust, Noise, Cold, and Heat Are Out, Cabs Are In," *Implement & Tractor* (June 21, 1971): 15–17.

25. E. G. Nourse, "Some Economic and Social Accompaniments of the Mechanization of Agriculture," *The American Economic Review Supplement* 20 (March 1930): 128; William L. Bowers, "Country-Life Reform, 1900–1920: A Neglected Aspect of Progressive Era History," *Agricultural History* 45 (July 1971): 217; H. P. Roberts, "What It Costs to Run the Tractor," *Progressive Farmer* (July 12, 1919): 1142; G. Douglas Jones, "Tractor Power in Relation to Agriculture," *Proceedings of the World's Grain Exhibition and Conference* 1 (Regina, Saskatchewan: Canadian Society of Technical Agriculturists, July 24 to August 5, 1933):419–23.

26. Nourse, "Economic and Social Accompaniments," 124.

27. Jones, "Tractor Power," 419–23; Wayne Worthington, "Engineer's Farm Tractor History, V, Post War Standards Progress and the Beginning of the Businessman Farmer," *Implement & Tractor* (March 21, 1967): 34–37.

28. William L. Cavert, "The Technological Revolution in Agriculture, 1910–1955," *Agricultural History* 30 (January 1956): 20.

29. H. W. Peck, "The Influence of Agricultural Machinery and the Automobile on Farming Operations," *The Quarterly Journal of Economics* 41 (May 1927): 543.

30. Yerkes and Church, "Farm Tractors in the Corn Belt," 2; Arnold P.

Yerkes and L. M. Church, "The Gas Tractor in Eastern Farming," *Farmer's Bulletin* 1004 (1918): 4.

31. C. G. Pearse, "Power on the Farm," *Proceedings of the World's Grain Exhibition and Conference*, 1 (Regina, Saskatchewan: Canadian Society of Technical Agriculturalists, July 24 to August 5, 1933): 410; McWilliams, "Farms into Factories," 410; Cavert, "Technological Revolution," 24.

32. Yerkes and Church, "Tractor Experiences in Illinois," 24–25; A. J. Schwantes and G. A. Pond, "The Farm Tractor in Minnesota," *Minnesota Agricultural Experiment Station Bulletin* 280 (September 1931): 57; A. N. Johnson, "Impact of Farm Machinery," 59; McWilliams, "Farms into Factories," 407.

33. Marx, "Farms, Machines and the Good Society," 273; Walter Goldschmidt, *As You Sow* (New York: Universe Books, 1978), 32–33.

34. Everett M. Rogers, "How Farmers Make Decisions," *Implement & Tractor* (July 26, 1958): 26–27, 80–81; Johnson, "Changes," 67.

35. Bill Fogarty, "Spotting the Adoption Leader," *Implement & Tractor* (July 26, 1958): 28–29, 73.

36. Michael Perelman, "Efficiency in Agriculture, the Economics of Energy," *Radical Agriculture*, ed., Richard Merrill (New York: New York University Press, 1976), 81.

37. For a good description of the fight between the farmers and the oil men during the depression, see August W. Giebelhaus, "Farming for Fuel: The Alcohol Fuel Movement of the 1930's," *Agricultural History* 54 (January 1980): 173–84.

38. "Farmers Need Efficient Tractors," 501; R. B. Gray "Performance Tests of Alcohol-Gasoline Fuel Blends," *Agricultural Engineering* 14 (July 1933): 185; Gray, "Alcohol-Gasoline Blends as Engine Fuels," *Agricultural Engineering* 15 (March 1934): 106–8; E. L. Barger, "Power Alcohol in Tractors and Farm Engines," *Agricultural Engineering* 27 (February 1941): 65-67, 78; Cooper, Barton and Brodell, "Progress of Farm Mechanization," 27; Thomas A. McClure and D. Alan Scantland, "Energy: New Crop Sources," *Agricultural Engineering* 58 (September 1977): 17–20.

39. G. M. Gillette, "Tractor Service Has Been Neglected—It Must Be Improved," *Automotive Industries* (May 11, 1922): 1016, 1017; Schwantes and Pond, "The Farm Tractor in Minnesota," 56–57, 66.

40. J. Allen Tower, "Cotton Changes in Alabama, 1879–1946," *Economic Geography* 26 (January 1950): 21.

41. Nourse, "Economic and Social Accompaniments of Mechanization," 125.

42. Raymond Olney, "Power Farming and the Farm Boy Problem," *Power Farming* (February 1917): 8; Olney, "The Tractor and the Boys, *Power Farming* (May 1919): 7.

43. Hazlett, "The Farm Tractor in 1920," 612.

44. R. U. Blasingame, "The Spread of Power Farming in Ohio," *Power Farming* (November 1927): 5.

45. Fletcher, "Real Effects of Mechanization," 361.

46. Ervin Rodabaugh, "How to Make a Tractor Last Longer," *Farm Quarterly* (Summer 1951): 38–41, 130.

47. E. A. Hunger, "Woman Drives Tractor and Does Work of Extra Hand," *Power Farming* (September 1925): 8.

48. Georgina Binnie Clark, a remarkable English gentlewoman with considerable capital, emigrated to Western Canada and farmed successfully in the era before tractors were common. Her experiences are required reading for anyone with an interest in both agriculture and women's history, *Wheat and Women* (Toronto: University of Toronto Press, 1979), 313.

49. The Success of a Woman Farmer," *Power Farming* (December 1917): 30.

50. Smith, "Users' Experience with Rubber-Tired Farm Tractors," 49.

51. Avis Gordon Vestal, "How to Save Woman Power on the Farm," *Power Farming* (May 1919): 30, 32; Dahl, "The Tractor that Never Tires," 321–39; "Woman Tames the Tractor," *The Practical Farmer* (June 1, 1918): 202; Glen T. Barton, "Increased Productivity of the Farm Worker," *Industrial and Labor Relations Review* (January 1948): 276.

52. "Farm Tractors, War, and Women," *Touchstone* (March 1918): 606–7.

53. Bureau of the Census, "A Statistical Portrait of Women in the United States," *Current Population Reports Special Studies Series*, P-23, No. 58 (Washington: United States Department of Commerce, April 1976): 35.

8
Tractors and Giantism

The tractor disrupted farm economics like a stray dog in a flock of guinea fowl. It certainly was *not* the only disturbance, but it was a major one. And when all the flutter and commotion died away, the countryside was as deserted as a roost that shows obvious signs of occupation in the recent past.

The depopulation of the American countryside was the result of numerous factors, but tractors played a conspicuous part in many of these factors. Mechanization promoted overproduction. It caused labor displacement. It increased farm size. And these trends had serious repercussions on the social and physical environments.

The tractor caused overproduction in three distinct ways. First, by displacing animal power, the tractor released millions of acres from the production of animal feed to commercial crop production. Second, the tractor increased the crop yields by a small but significant amount. Finally, the tractor increased the productivity of the individual farm operator. Each of these three factors contributed to the surpluses that have plagued farmers, and American society generally, since 1921, and even earlier.

Before farmers bought tractors, they had to use about one-quarter of their land to feed their horses or mules. As soon as they disposed of their draft stock, the land formerly used for producing fuel for mules was converted to commercial production. Many horse meadows became corn fields, and even untillable land was used differently. Rough ground, for example, that had carried horses now supported cattle, sheep, or hogs, and the resulting production that had formerly been used on the farm entered an already flooded food and fiber market. Fully one-half of the increase in farm produce for human consumption between the world wars came from acres that had formerly fed horses. In 1941 estimates of "re-leased" land came to about thirty-five million acres that had shifted into market production between 1918 and 1945[1] One observer noted that, "the sudden disappearance of about 16,000,000 horses in the thirties was a prominent factor in the depression of that period. By their removal, the farmer lost the market for the products of about 60,000,000 acres of land which had been used for the production of horse feed."[2] In addition, there was a marked decrease in the market demand for oats and hay.

Not only did the tractor release additional acres for market production, but it also increased the yield of each acre, whether new or old. Although there were numerous minor factors that allowed a tractor to increase yields, the overwhelming factor was timeliness.

The difference between harvesting an excellent crop and suffering a total loss may well be a matter of hours. The most obvious example of critical time can be seen at harvest, when combines and trucks may have to race furiously against an impending storm with its dark potential of destructive hail. But timeliness was important in less dramatic operations. Optimal yields come only from fields planted within a relatively brief period. Each day of delay reduces harvest by predictable average amounts. Horses had built-in limits to their use; tractors ran almost continuously. Horses were limited as to speed and the equipment size they could pull; tractors ran faster and pulled larger tools. By speeding up critical operations, tractors appreciably increased yields, both for the individual farmer and for the nation as a whole, although a few farmers claimed that they could get into the field earlier with horses in a wet spring than they could with tractors. The importance of timeliness has been a continuous refrain almost from the advent of the tractor.[3]

The third way in which the tractor increased production was through increased productivity per man hour. Such a change might not, at first, appear to influence the aggregate yield of the country as a whole—after all, when a farmer bought out his neighbor, he expanded his personal production but probably broke no new land nor increased the total acreage of the nation. In simple terms, by increasing productivity per man-hour, the tractor increased crop yields by allowing time for better management. "When labor was saved on particular farm jobs," one person wrote, "many of the 'saved' hours were used on other farm enterprises or on more intensive production."[4] Better management led to significant gains in production. Between the introduction of tractors like the Hart-Parr in the early teens and the widespread adoption of chemical agriculture in the mid-fifties, the productivity of the average farm worker more than dou-

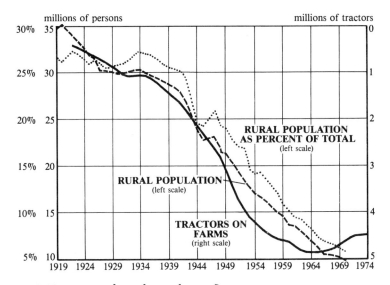

Figure 6. Tractors and rural population figures.

Sources. Historical Statistics I: 457; Durost and Black, "Changes in Farm Production," 31.

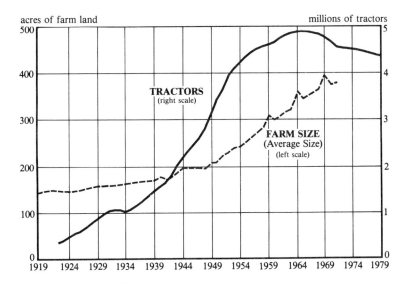

Figure 7. Tractors and farm size.

Sources. Historical Statistics I: 457; Durost and Black, "Changes in Farm Production," 31.

bled. Mechanization was a preeminent cause of increased productivity. Tractor-powered preparation, planting, and cultivating accounted for 10 percent of the savings in labor, while tractor-operated harvesting equipment added another 10 percent.[5]

Increased productivity, increased yields, and increased acreage combined to cause severe overproduction. The tractor alone was not responsible, of course, and actual increase in production because of the tractor was not and is not objectively measurable. The world's most patient econometrician would despair of achieving an accurate estimate. There were dozens of commercial crops in the United States, millions of farms, and unique weather patterns in each locality during each year. The data did not exist, or else was excessively complex. Figures on gross production do exist, however, but so many influences affected production that there was no way to derive from them the margin of increase that resulted from the tractor by itself. In the period since 1918, farmers have adopted chemical fertilizers and pesticides, and government has attempted to divert production during peace time and stimulate production in war time. New crops such as soybeans have become popular, while the popularity of others like flax or oats has declined. Crops such as cotton have migrated to new regions, while the old cotton belt has largely gone to grass and beef. The tractor's impact was probably almost negligible in 1919, but it undoubtedly increased steadily as tractor numbers increased. The tractor was never the only influence at work, but was intertwined with other factors throughout the era. Despite (or along with) all the other changes that were involved, however, it seems clear that tractors increased production through increased timeliness of operation. Further, it appears safe to conclude that the increase was significant.

The economics of increased production worked consistently within the principle of supply and demand. Bearing in mind that there were other factors at work, too, a historian must note that farmers began to oversupply the market only three years after the introduction of the mass-produced tractor. With varying severity, a price-depressing surplus has persisted in many farm commodities almost continually since 1921.

Of course, the tractor cannot be blamed for all aspects of the surplus. There had been periods of overproduction before the tractor. After the tractor was adopted in the United States, but before the rest of the world adopted it, there were frequent international surpluses. The extent to which the tractor was responsible for overproduction becomes a question. In reality, the tractor was a major factor that aggravated existing tendencies and created new ones. Considering the amount of land that was converted from raising horse feed to commercial crops, and allowing for small but appreciable boosts in production because of more timely operation and closer management, I estimate that by 1958 the tractor had increased production by at least 25 percent. If the tractor's contribution is prorated in those areas where it was used in conjunction with other new management techniques, the tractor's contribution to the surplus is much larger. By either estimate, the tractor was an element in overproduction.

The value judgments placed on the tractor and its role in overproduction have varied from time to time and from one viewer to another. In August 1929, before the stock market crash, a priggish writer in *World's Work* dismissed farmers' complaints about bulging elevators and low prices. He said that, "To the efficient producer a surplus has no terrors. His problem is already solved. The tendency of the surplus is merely to eliminate the footloose and inefficient producer—either that or to convert him to the machine system, wherein lies his salvation."[6]

Soon after the statement was made, the rest of the nation discovered the depression that had long plagued the farmer. Almost two years after the denunciation of the "inefficient producer," a popular magazine carried an eloquent description of the farmer's dilemma. It assured its readers that the farmer knew that mechanization led to overproduction, but that farmers had to produce more in order to meet the payments on their equipment. And machinery was essential in order to remain sufficiently competitive to continue farming.[7] The farmer was caught in a vicious cycle. A die-hard horse-defender made the same point, emphasizing the damage done to hay and grain prices by the tractor's displacement of draft animals. He wrote that "lowered prices for farm products are part of tractor costs."[8]

Not only did the tractor help produce a price-depressing surplus, but it also sharply reduced the need for human effort in farm fields. By 1935, the tractor was saving some 165 million man-hours per year in the United States in field operations alone. The total amount of human labor that was displaced between 1909 and 1938 was estimated at 785 billion man-hours annually—about 10 percent of the labor required for crop production. In some operations such as corn planting, as much as 60 percent of labor's time was eliminated. The introduction of the power-lift alone saved one million man-hours annually. And, after most farms had converted to tractor power, the machine again reduced labor requirements as farmers exchanged small tractors for larger ones.[9]

The tractor reduced labor requirements so dramatically that some people blamed the tractor for the depression. A fairly typical example declared, "Combined with the harvester-thresher, the tractor . . . has certainly been one of the most important factors in the structural trans-formation of agriculture and in the creation of these maladjustments and dislocations which are largely responsible for the present depression."[10]

Such an analysis undoubtedly overstated the *direct* influence of the tractor in labor replacement. Peak unemployment in 1933 amounted to some 12.8 million people, while the reduction in the agricultural work force between 1920 and 1940 was only 2.2 million. Such raw figures, of course, do not tell the entire story, for during the depression a significant number of unemployed workers migrated back to the farm, where they were chronically underemployed. When counted as employed, these peo-ple inflated the statistics on agricultural workers and deflated the unem-ployment figures. Even with that caveat in mind, however, it was clear that the displacement of workers by tractors did contribute to the unem-ployment problem during the depression era. Had they not disappeared, the 2.2 million jobs lost in agriculture between 1920 and 1940, might have absorbed well over one-sixth of the unemployment during the depths of the depression, or one-third of the average annual unemployment from 1920 to 1940. But, again, it must be remembered that not all of the farm jobs that were lost between 1920 and 1940 were lost to tractors or mech-anization, even though mechanization was a major cause. Still, workers displaced by tractors can safely be listed as an identifiable, if unquantifi-able, cause of depression-era unemployment.[11] But labor displacement was not a phenomenon restricted to the decade of the Great Depression. Mechanization generally—and the tractor specifically—reduced the num-ber of jobs available in agriculture over a long period of time. The results of the tractor's labor displacement is reflected, along with other labor-saving factors, in the following data.[12]

Year	Total Labor Force*	Ag. Labor Force*	% Total Labor Force
1910	38,167	12,388	32.5
1920	41,614	10,666	25.6
1930	48,830	10,472	21.4
1940	53,011	8,449	15.9
1950	59,643	6,876	11.5
1960	69,877	4,257	6.1
1970	83,049	2,750	3.4

*In 1,000s, 16 and over.

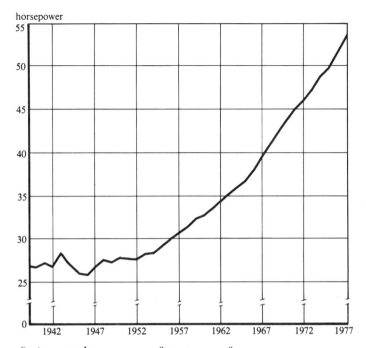

Figure 8. Average horsepower of tractors on farms.
Source. Durost and Black, "Changes in Farm Production," 31.

The number of jobs available on the farm has decreased consistently.

The forced shrinkage of the agricultural work force touched every level of farm worker, from owner to migrant laborer. Tractors, along with other economic forces, made small farms uncompetitive, and often forced small holders to abandon their land to seek more rewarding jobs in the city. A 1941 survey reported that, "Almost every farmer who at length migrated to the city blamed the tractor for his fate."[13] Yet many Americans either seemed unaware of the migration or misunderstood it.

The arrival of tractors and the reduced need for labor made large farm families uneconomic. Older children and other relatives made less contribution to the family's success or failure. Because three-fourths of the labor on farms was furnished by the family, the tractor's impact on family labor was greater—in sheer numbers—than on any other aspect of labor reduction.[14] No wonder the rural birthrate continued to fall—children were far less of an economic asset than they had been in the days of hay, horses, and hoes.[15]

In economic terms the greatest displacement of labor by the tractor probably came in the elimination of hired labor and sharecroppers. A

Georgia investigator discovered that the purchase of a tractor had profound consequences. On tractorless farms he found an average of slightly more than three families of sharecroppers and twelve wage hands. On farms with tractors, the labor force averaged two families of croppers and six hired hands. That represented a decrease of 35.5 and 50 percent, respectively. Later, after most farmers had adopted tractors, larger four-row tractors replaced the original two-row size and displaced still more workers. A Texas researcher estimated that the introduction of four-row equipment expelled one farm family in every three. In one locality a crossroads supported a population of seventeen mailboxes before mechanization. After machinery replaced workers, three lonely mailboxes remained.[16]

On the bottom of the economic scale in farm work was the migrant laborer. The migrant was a prerequisite of mechanization and often a casualty of it.

The migrant farm worker was necessary to fill gaps that resulted from the uneven pace of mechanization. The tractor, for example, minimized the amount of labor needed for most aspects of cotton production, especially plowing, planting, and cultivating. But the tractor did little to reduce the need for hoe hands or cotton pickers. So in hoeing season and picking season, there was at least as much demand for hand labor as in the days before tractorization. Incomplete mechanization had thus created a seasonal imbalance in labor requirements, and the migrant filled the need.

Migrant labor was an unsatisfactory solution from virtually every perspective. The migrant was almost always underemployed and frequently unemployed. By definition, migrant labor was mobile, and therefore unable to establish roots or develop stable resources or accumulate any permanent equity. It is not surprising that a sociologist wrote recently that migrant laborers are worse off than the impoverished residents of Appalachia or the inner-city ghettos.[17]

Despite the migrant's cheap wages, however, his labor was no bargain. The supply of migrants was not dependable, and if the requisite amount of labor was unavailable, the farmer lost money from the delay. And when there was a large amount of work to be done or a long season for hand labor, the farmer's cost for migrant help was high, despite the fact that the worker was underpaid relative to other wage rates. For this reason, when tractor-mounted machinery became available to replace migrant workers, such equipment was often a wise investment, even if it did not reduce the cost of the production process. Migrant-displacing machinery was dependable, and its costs were predictable.[18] Thus the initial machinery—that which displaced year-round labor—might induce temporary untimeliness, but was ultimately replaced with machinery that replaced migrants and that increased overall timeliness. Migrant labor offered uncertain rewards to migrant and employer alike.

Not all of the farm people displaced by the tractor immigrated to the city or became wanderers. Many owners of small farms gradually accepted more and more off-farm work until they became part-time farmers. Such a course was possible and practicable only with "a mechanical power plant."[19] By 1945, approximately one-fourth of the farms in the United States were worked by part-time farmers, a proportion that has held relatively constant since that time.[20]

Any generalized value judgment about part-time farming is difficult. As early as 1921, personnel from the Department of Agriculture noted that there were certain positive social benefits to part-time farming. It was far more efficient to have a mechanized part-time farmer operating a small farm—while supporting his family with a regular salary or wages—than to have a whole family working the land by hand in return for a pittance.[21] Later, as government economists pointed out, the move from full-time to part-time farming was a fairly smooth transition in good times, "If opportunities for employment are freely open in the cities, many small and unproductive farms will shift from full-time to part-time operations or even become rural homes where little or no farming is done."[22] In a similar way, Henry Ford and Harry Ferguson both professed faith in the transition to part-time farming as the solution to "the farm problem" and portrayed the part-time farm as the inevitable institution of the future.[23]

On the other hand, many who would have liked to concentrate on farming for their livelihood were forced to seek additional employment, because small farms would not support them and machinery payments. Not all of the farmers who engaged in part-time work would freely choose to farm full-time if that were a viable option. But many would.

By contrast, some small farms ceased any significant production and became little more than rural residences. Some became "hobby farms," which operated at a loss but provided recreation for the owner. A great many small farms became a source of secondary income to owners whose primary livelihood came from off the farm. These part-time farms and their accompanying nonfarm incomes were not possible without labor-saving machinery. As a result, these part-time farmers have purchased a surprisingly large percentage of the tractors that have been sold. In 1965

for example, an Ohio study showed that one-half of the equipment purchased by part-time farmers was new equipment. The part-time farmer
was a significant purchaser of tractors.[24]

The same machinery that allowed a farm to be operated by a part-
time farmer allowed a full-time farmer to continue working into old age.
The average age of farmers steadily increased after 1945. While part of
the reason for the increased average age of farmers was a reflection of
fewer young men starting to farm, it was also a result of older men deferring
retirement. And late retirement was impossible in the strenuous days
before the tractor.

Since the earliest days of the Industrial Revolution, there has been
a considerable debate over the replacement of human labor with machines.
Both sides tended to oversimplify. Opponents of mechanization were
likely to be called "Luddites," with the unflattering implication that they
were as feebleminded as poor Ned Lud, who allegedly smashed his employer's textile machinery in Scotland at the end of the eighteenth century
because it displaced workers. Proponents of labor-saving devices risked
being portrayed as greedy brutes with no concern for society in general
or their fellow man in particular. Both cases have been argued passionately
with reference to the tractor, but neither argument has been sufficiently
persuasive to be accepted in a fairly universal manner. Both advocates and
opponents of mechanization seemed better supplied with rhetoric and
opinion than with facts. Yet the crux of the argument devolved upon the
question of whether the tractor destroyed more old jobs than it created
new ones. Generally speaking, those who defended mechanization insisted
that the net result of the tractor was the creation of new jobs.[25] Although
the results of the tractor should not be extrapolated into other areas of
mechanization, it is possible to estimate the legitimacy of the claim of the
tractor as a job creator.

The *Statistical Abstracts of the United States* counted the number
of employees engaged in the manufacture of agricultural equipment. Between 1920 and 1970, the number of employees fluctuated from 40,000
to 180,000. Of that number it is safe to estimate the number that worked
on tractors as 49 percent plus or minus 4 percent.[26] That would indicate
that not more than 95,000 people were ever directly employed in tractor
manufacture. Even if twice that number were employed in tractor advertising, sales, and repair, the total *direct* employment figure would be
relatively small. There were also indirect employment figures—that is,
additional employees hired to produce the steel, rubber, fuel, and trans-

portation needs required by tractors. But even if one estimated these at several times the number needed for production, the total number of jobs created by tractors at periods of peak employment could not have exceeded one million jobs—and a much smaller figure is more reasonable. During the same 1920–70 period, the number of people employed in agriculture decreased by eight million, and while not all of these jobs were eliminated by the tractor, a sizable proportion were. It seems safe to conclude that the tractor did not create more jobs than it abolished.[27]

In this context, it would be noted many of the hours that the farmer "saved" were in fact merely transferred from farm to city. While the farmer no longer used his time to produce hay and oats, for example, he now paid workers in oil fields, refineries and offices to produce his fuel. Thus, while there may have been a net reduction in labor, the major factor was a change in the location of fuel production.

It would be naive to assume that the number of jobs destroyed is, by itself, a complete indicator of the tractor's impact. That figure is, at best, a partial and purely quantitive measure. Human values are both quantitative and qualitative.

The question about the tractor's displacement of labor is controversial. Was it good—for the farmer, for his family, for his employees, and for society—or was it bad? The issue was a complex one and has never produced unanimity. The verdict often depended more upon the context of the time and the presuppositions of the judge than upon the facts of the case.

Expulsion from the farm and attraction to the city were complementary forces that were probably inseparable. The dominance of one or the other force was largely the result of the economic climate at the moment. When times were good, farm labor was often lured to the city by high industrial wages and promises of modern conveniences. The farmer replaced lost labor with a tractor. When hard times came, and mechanization seemed to offer the only hope for farm solvency, labor was sometimes expelled from the countryside to compete for scarce urban employment. In either case, farm labor was simultaneously pulled toward the city and pushed off the farm. But the process was far less traumatic when the reasons for the exodus were positive.[28]

Even in hard times, the role of the tractor in labor displacement is far from simple. In 1933, at the depth of the depression, a farmer looked beyond statistical tables and raised basic questions of human values. He wrote:

> We should determine just what is the all-important function of labor. If the
> essential thing is to put everybody to work full time just for the sake of
> keeping them busy, then we may well consider a plan of putting one group
> of men to digging holes, another group to filling them. Another way of
> accomplishing the same results would be to junk our modern machinery.
> . . . One method is just as sensible as the other . . . just as much a needless
> waste of human labor. . . . Machines were originally invented for the pur-
> pose of relieving human beings from the back-breaking and soul-blighting
> drudgery of long hours at hard, manual labor.[29]

The farmer continued that increased productivity by the farmer should
lead to an increase in his standard of living. If the farmer's increased
productivity did not lead to better conditions, the problem lay in the
[economic] system.

Nor were farmers the only ones to realize that the problem of labor
displacement was only partially technological in nature. In 1930, an economist wrote that despite the prevailing pattern of mechanization, machines
should result in farm families enjoying the leisure and culture that were
available to other consumers. Three years later, an engineer at the World's
Grain Exhibition stated that the purpose of mechanization was leisure.
The same basic concept was echoed in 1934 and 1949.[30] Indeed, these
examples are typical of a continuous chorus that glorified leisure and urged
tractors and other machinery as the means to more free time. Its actual
results may not have produced leisure time.

The tractor's displacement of agricultural labor resulted in fewer
jobs. Although, perhaps, to a lesser degree than predicted, it also gave
the farmer more free time. To the ghetto dweller whose old life was
destroyed by adoption of the tractor during the depths of the depression,
the tractor may be a mechanical monster. To the farmer who has time to
fish when his father would have been feeding mules, the tractor is a minor
mechanical messiah. For most, the consensus rests between.

The tractor's impact on the American economy certainly did not end
with the displacement of a few million workers. It fully justified the
expectations of an economist who wrote in 1930 that, "Mechanical power
farming has already made certain demands in terms of units of area,
financial arrangements, labor force, and so forth, considerably at variance
with those which had been so well worked out both empirically and
scientifically for our accustomed horse-power technique. It is much too
soon to say just how we shall revamp our economic organization to meet
these new ideas."[31] Unfortunately, little revamping was forthcoming, and

the impact of the tractor settled on an American economy that was not only unprepared, but also oblivious.

Mechanized farming made a drastic increase in the amount of capital required to begin farming. By thus raising the ante, it reduced the number of individuals who could enter farming. In doing this, the tractor did not start a new trend so much as it intensified and accelerated existing tendencies. But such intensification and acceleration produced severe results. By 1952, the cost of a tractor, equipment, and other purchases necessary to begin farming were far greater than the potential life savings of an average individual. The middle-class American was shut out of farming, and, of course, ethnic minorities had even less access to capital. The traditional "agricultural ladder" by which an energetic young person pulled himself up was destroyed. He could no longer climb from hired hand to tenant to part owner to full owner.[32] From 1880 on, tenancy gained percentage points while ownership lost.

Along with larger capitalization, farms also grew in economies of scale and in physical size. It was an already familiar pattern that began

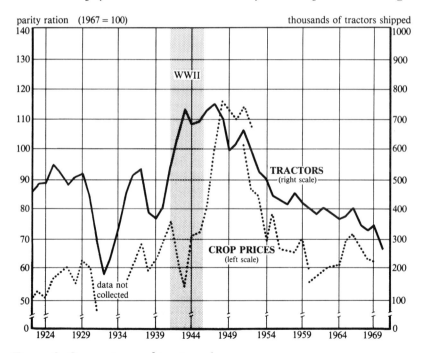

Figure 9. Crop prices and tractor sales.

Sources. Current Industrial Reports/Facts for Industry, 1953-70; *Historical Statistics* I: 488-89.

before the tractor but that became more acute with increased machinery. A Georgia survey noted that after purchasing a tractor, the farmer expanded his acreage. The pre-tractor average was 319 acres per farm. After adding mechanical power, the farmer purchased an average of 23.7 percent more land for an average of 394.5 acres. And the same trend is obvious in other studies and in the gross statistics of the United States as a whole.[33] In 1924, when the Farmall made its unobtrusive debut, the average-sized farm encompassed 144 acres. By the time American boys were called for service in World War II, the average size was 171 acres. After the war, came the most rapid period of mechanization, and by 1950, the average had grown to 216 acres—twice the size of the provisions of the Homestaed Act of 1862.[34] And while the statistical average was growing, it was diluted by the inclusion of ever-greater numbers of rural homes and hobby farms.

The rapid growth in farm size took place on a continent of essentially static size. Because of the finite nature of the land available, larger farms could only emerge by engulfing smaller neighbors. And again, despite the growth of rural residencies and status farms that dilute the census figures, there is nevertheless an absolute decrease in the total number of farms. Between 1920 and 1945 the United States lost 9 percent of its farms. By 1965, there were only 3.5 million farms for a population of over two hundred million. And the number of farms capable of supporting a family decreased faster than the gross number of farms.

The newer, larger farms were not always the property of traditional farm families. As early as 1921, low crop prices were forcing families to abandon their farms, and opportunistic businessmen were cashing in on the misfortune. The new owners used tractors for power and consolidated small farms into more viable units of considerably larger size. They probably would have been unable to follow such a procedure without the tractor.

Speculation in land has a long history in the United States, but the tractor allowed it to take a new turn. The previous large landholder rented to tenants who hoped to purchase the land; the new owner was often a doctor or executive who used the farm as a hobby or tax write-off. The tractor was his toy, and he hired the remainder of the work done by custom operators thus dispensing with tenants. Paul S. Taylor, professor of economics at the University of California at Berkeley, described the situation to a congressional committee, "On my train enroute to Washington, the sales manager of a national manufacturing corporation . . . told me that among businesses in his part of the country 'it's now the rage' to buy farms, partly for diversion instead of golf, partly as a safe place to put funds; indeed in some cities businessmen have formed 'farmers luncheon clubs'."[35] The testimony was given before a committee investigating the migration of destitute Americans. Many of the migrants were formerly farm tenants.

But not all of those who profited from the dislocations caused by mechanization and low farm prices were merely urban investors dabbling in farming. The pressure to constantly expand forced large farmers to swallow up their smaller neighbors. Ever-larger tractors demanded ever-larger farms if they were to be operated efficiently. The largest single group in bidding up land prices has consistently been farmers who desired to expand their holdings.

Large farmers' resources are minute, however, when compared to large corporations, which have often seen land as a tax shelter or speculative investment. In 1927, *Power Farming* described an investment company that had swallowed up nineteen farms totaling 2,900,000 acres. It was farmed with a handful of tenants and eight employees. In the following years, the phenomena became more common. With the coming of the depression, financial institutions and insurance companies found themselves in possession of even more land after many farmers, both mechanized and unmechanized, were forced to default on their mortgages. In some cases, the banks and insurance companies were unwilling owners and disposed of their farms to any buyer available. In other cases, the corporations farmed their land directly or through tenants. Equitable Life Assurance Society seized thousands of acres during the protracted crisis, farming while it awaited an upturn in real estate prices. In the meantime, the depression notwithstanding, the corporation purchased tractors to work its farms, mechanization undoubtedly essential for success. Eventually, when disposition of the land was complete, only 2 percent of the foreclosed debtors recovered their land, while 26 percent of the new owners were speculative investors. Equitable did not only lose money on the farms during the depression period, it even managed to show a small profit.[36] By late 1985, many farmers and rural editors predicted that a similar series of events were beginning again in the wake of several years of disastrous commodity prices and an indifferent-to-hostile administration.

Corporate farms remained relatively few in number. In 1974, corporations—including family corporations—accounted for only 28,656 units out of a total of 1,695,074 farms with sales of $2,500 or more.[37] Nonfamily corporate farms, however, are concentrated in the most capital-intensive and most profitable segments of agriculture. With tractors and other equipment becoming larger and more expensive, such corporations may enjoy increasing advantages.

Some companies have used those advantages. Tenneco, a huge conglomerate best known for its oil interests, was a good example. Not only did Tenneco purchase J. I. Case Tractor and Implement Company, but it also developed an agricultural division, Tenneco West. In 1979 this subsidiary owned 864,350 acres. The company farmed 27,176 acres and leased out an additional 89,392 acres of developed farmland. It boasted a "leading position in the grape industry," and produced everything from carrots and potatoes to almonds and pistachios. The giant corporation's resources allowed it to install expensive linear-move irrigation systems and develop a considerable degree of vertical integration—for example, controlling an almond from the orchard to the retail consumer.[38] Although the company's report did not mention the fact, Tenneco West may have been able to buy Case tractors well below the competitive market price.

At first glance, it would appear that such corporate farming ventures indicated poor judgment, because the return on an investment involved in farming has been notoriously poor in recent history. One observer noted this fact when day-dreaming about the farm of the future. After describing the fully automated, push-button farm of some future Utopia, he pondered briefly the capital requirements, then concluded, "Heck, if I had that much money, I would not even push buttons; I would just sit!"[39] But corporate farmers did not rely solely on the return from farming operations when they calculated expected profits, for not only did such corporations reap huge checks from government programs designed to help the small farmer, but their farms were also often tax dodges and real estate investment ventures. It seems highly improbable that Tenneco would have engaged in farming had the company lacked the real estate ventures that made consistent profits for both the subsidiary and mother company.

Corporations have not rushed into agriculture and swallowed up everything in sight. But the trends toward larger tractors, larger farms, and larger capital requirements gave large corporations a potential advantage. Apparently the major factor that discourages corporate farming is the anemic potential for profit in a competitive market.

The tractor—along with other forms of mechanization and other new technologies in farming—created an economic no-man's land in rural areas. It demanded more capital than most individuals could afford, yet did not attract corporate investment. It displaced rural residents by eliminating their livelihoods, yet through overproduction it reduced the selling price of farm products. Only those who were both very sharp managers and very lucky operators benefited from the changes. Thousands of family farms did not benefit.

The family farm has an almost sacred place in traditional American values. Yet *family farm* is a complex concept. Certainly it is based in the Jeffersonian ideal of an upstanding, independent yeomanry. Gradually this ideal has come to be understood as a sort of agrarian bourgeoisie, and few contemporary Americans—no matter how Hamiltonian or industrialized or urbanized—would condone the destruction of that ideal. It is popularly conceived as an indispensable part of whatever it is that America is.

If the agricultural jobs that the tractor and other factors destroyed were marginal or poverty-level jobs, then they clearly would not fit the American ideal. And such employment is a part of American history. The exploitation of the sharecropper in the post-bellam South is almost as unconscionable a disgrace as was ante-bellum slavery. The Populists were correct in raising it as a moral issue, and were both ethically and economically correct in linking the system with emergent industrialism.

Unlike the Populists, however, most recent commentators have seen no possible alternatives other than huge mechanized farms or an industrial establishment served by an archaic rural serfdom. But were gigantic mechanized farms and destitute tenancy the only alternatives? From a strictly historical perspective all that can be said is that no *tertium quid* emerged in the United States. Such an answer may be unsatisfactory philosophically to most Americans. But the historian is imprisoned at this point by his discipline to relate what was, and not what could have been. Yet historians can point to some European countries that have succeeded in retaining a larger percentage of families on their own farms without impoverishing either farm or industry. Comparative studies of the history of European and American farms and the public policy should benefit farmers, historians, economists, political scientists, sociologists, and the American public.

NOTES

1. Barton, "Increased Productivity," 267; McWilliams, "Farms into Factories," 411; Sherman E. Johnson, "Changes," 3; A. N. Johnson, "The Impact of Farm Machinery," 59.
2. J. F. Booth, "Some Economic Effects of Mechanization of Canadian

Agriculture with Particular Reference to the Spring Wheat Area," *Proceedings of the World's Grain Exhibition and Conference* 1 (Regina, Saskatchewan: Canadian Society of Technical Agriculturalists, July 24 to August 5, 1933): 359–60.

3. Rutenik, "Efficiency of the Farm Tractor," 5; Dahl, "Mobilizing Farm Machinery," 274; Capper Farm Press, *The Tractor*, 12–13; Reynoldson and Tolley, "What Tractors and Horses Do," 5; McCuen, "Dividends From Your Tractor," 8, 76; Pearse, "Power on the Farm," 376–77; Martin R. Cooper, Glen T. Barton, and Albert P. Brodell, "Progress of Farm Mechanization," *Miscellaneous Publications* No. 630 (Washington: United States Department of Agriculture, October 1947): 18–19; Sherman Johnson, "Changes," 13; T. S. Thorfinson and A. W. Epp, "Cost of Operating Tractors in Nebraska, 1961," *Nebraska Agricultural Experiment Station Bulletin* SB480 (February 1964): 8–9.

4. Barton, "Increased Productivity," 267.

5. Barton, "Increased Productivity," 267, 270–72; Hecht and Barton, "Gains in Productivity," 1; Marx, *Mechanization and Culture*, 80.

6. Silas Bent, "Machine—Master or Slave," *World's Work* (August 1929): 65–66.

7. Carlson, "The Wheat Farmer's Dilemma," 211–16. This was written by a farmer's wife.

8. "Horses, Mules and Tractors in Farming," *Journal of the American Veterinary Medical Association* (November 1940): 444.

9. James H. Shideler, *Farm Crisis 1919–1923* (Berkeley: University of California Press, 1957): 79–80; Walter W. Wilcox, *The Farmer in the Second World War* (Ames: Iowa State College Press, 1947): 290; Cooper, Barton, and Brodell, "Progress of Farm Mechanization," 18–19; McKibben and Griffin, "Changes in Farm Power and Equipment," 15–16; H. R. Tolley and L. M. Church, "Tractors on Southern Farms," *Farmers' Bulletin* No. 11278 (Washington: United States Department of Agriculture, August 1922): 12, 20; Chennaredy and Jones, "Labor," *The Overproduction Trap in Agriculture* [eds., Johnson and Quance] 123.

10. Fletcher. "Effects of Mechanization on Wheat Production," 361.

11. Farm laborers were not the only workers displaced by tractors; harness makers, horse breeders, and even some veterinarians found the market for their services reduced as tractors became more common. One can assume, however, that new jobs created by the tractor (salesmen, mechanics, etc.) more than replaced the lost jobs—at least on the macroeconomic level. Given the relatively small number of such old and new jobs, they seem to have had little impact on the economy.

12. Bureau of the Census, *Historical Statistics of the United States [from] Colonial Times to 1970*, Part 1 (Washington: United States Department of Commerce, September 1975); percentage column calculated from two columns to left.

13. Arnold P. Yerkes, "Tractors Nurture Abandoned Farms," *Power Farming* (May 1921): 6; Marx, *Mechanization and Culture*, 66.

14. Barton, "Increased Productivity," 265.

15. Marx, *Mechanization and Culture*, 64–65.

16. J. C. Elrod, "Cost and Utilization of Tractor Power and Equipment on

Farms on the Coastal Plain," *Georgia Experiment Station Bulletin* 260 (June 1949): 1–21; Marx, *Mechanization and Culture*, 63.

17. Mildred Pratt, "Effects of Mechanization on Migrant Farm Workers," *Social Casework* 54 (February 1973): 106–8.

18. Josephson and Blasingame, "Farm Power and Labor," 5.

19. Yerkes, "Tractors Nurture," 6.

20. W. I. Drummond, "Outside Earnings and Competition in Agriculture," *Agricultural Review* (September 1927): 3; Sherman Johnson, "Changes," 51; Kenneth L. Bachman, "Changes in Scale in Commercial Farming and Their Implications," *Journal of Farm Economics* 34 (May 1952): 158; McElveen, "Family Farms," 61; Bachman and Jones, "Sizes of Farms," 1–2; Bureau of Census, *1974 Census of Agriculture*, vol. 1, Part 51 (Washington: Department of Commerce, 1975), 1/13.

21. Yerkes, "Tractors Nurture," 6.

22. Sherman and Johnson, "Changes," 61.

23. Ford and Ferguson talked to reporters at length on this. "Mr. Ford's Only Partner," 66–67, 153–57. For extensive comments on the two men's common interests in the farmer and faith in mechanization, see Fraser, *Tractor Pioneer*; Nevins, *Ford*; and Ford and Crowther, *My Life and Work*.

24. J. Patrick Madden, "Agricultural Mechanization, Farm Size and Community Development," *Agricultural Engineering* 59 (August 1978): 15; William F. Johnstone, "You Can't Ignore the Part-time Farmers," *Implement & Tractor*, (May 21, 1965): 28–29.

25. Theo Brown, "How the Use of Farm Machinery Creates Employment," *Agricultural Engineering* 15 (July 1934): 233–37; Fletcher, "Real Effects," 363; R. U. Blasingame, "Discussion by R. U. Blasingame", *Agricultural Engineering* 15 (July 1934): 238–39; Cavert, "The Technological Revolution," 25–26.

26. This estimate is based on the fact that 49 percent of the companies' revenue came from tractors. Some implements (such as combines) require more labor per unit than tractors, some (like plows) require less. Thus, for economic purposes, the tractor's proportion of sales is closely related to its proportion of the work force.

27. Barton assigned 60 percent of labor savings to mechanization in the 1917/1921–39 period and 28 percent in the 1939–44 period, for a 1917/1921–1944 average of 48 percent labor savings. Such labor savings may or may not be comparable to job reductions, "Increased Productivity," 271.

28. Marx, *Mechanization and Culture*, 53–91; Yerkes, "The Tractor and Farm Management," 8; Arthur Huntington, "Engineering-Economics Relationships in the Agricultural Industries," *Agricultural Engineering* 12 (June 1931): 198; Barton, "Increased Productivity," 265.

29. Fred W. Hawthorn, "Discussion by Fred W. Hawthorn," *Agricultural Engineering* 15 (July 1934): 239.

30. C. H. Alford, "How to Succeed with Farm Tractors," *Progressive Farmer* (July 12, 1919): 6; Nourse, "Economic and Social Accompaniments," 125; Fletcher, "Real Effects of Mechanization," 367; Hawthorn, "Discussion," 239; Sherman Johnson, "Changes," 75.

31. Raymond C. Smith, "New Conditions Demand New Opportunities," *The Yearbook of Agriculture 1940: Farmers in a Changing World* (Washington: United States Department of Agriculture, 1940): 811.

32. Smith, "New Conditions," 813; Bachman, "Scale Changes," 171–72.

33. Elrod, "Cost and Utilization," 1–21; O. G. Lloyd and L. G. Hobson, "Relation of Farm Power and Farm Organization in Central Indiana," *Indiana Agricultural Experiment Station Bulletin* 332, (June 1939): 20; Nourse, "Economic and Social Accompaniments," 119; B. A. Russell, "Farm Power Utilization and Costs [in] South Carolina," *South Carolina Agricultural Experiment Station Bulletin* No. 280 (September 1931): 5, 41; Booth, "Economic Effects of Mechanization," 356; Yerkes, "The Tractor and Farm Management," 44; Elrod and Fullilove, "Cost and Utilization of Tractor Power and Equipment on Farms in the Lower Piedmont," 34–35; Robert T. McMillan, "Effects of Mechanization on American Agriculture," *Scientific Monthly* (July 1949): 25; Bachman and Jones, "Sizes of Farms," 2.

34. Bureau of the Census, *Historical Statistics,* 457.

35. U. S. Congress, House, *Hearings Before the Select Committee to Investigate the Interstate Migration of Destitute Citizens Pursuant to House Resolutions 63, 491, and 629,* 76th Cong., 34th sess., December 2, 1940, 3249.

36. "Are We Coming to Corporation Farming?" *Power Farming* (February 1927): 5, 9; Yerkes, "Tractors Nurture," 5–6; Skogvold, "Farm Loans and Farm Management," 116–18.

37. Bureau of the Census, *1974 Census,* 1/13.

38. Tenneco, Inc., *1979 Annual Report* (Houston: Tenneco, 1980): 6–7, 23.

39. Johnson, "Impact of Farm Machinery," 62.

9
The Tractor:
Farm, Industry, and Society

Any study of the tractor has to plow in several fields of history. Because it is a machine, it belongs in the territory of the historian of technology. The tractor created a new industry and transformed the old implement industry, so the business historian presses a legitimate claim to the tractor. Because the tractor is a major factor in modern farm production, agricultural historians also press a strong suit for it. So do social historians and economic historians. Exhaustive exploration of any one of these aspects of the tractor's past is beyond the scope of this study. Yet certain salient facts emerge from all of these areas.

The first tractor emerged as soon as the technical ability was developed to produce such a machine. Its development kept pace with the progress of improved engineering techniques of the times. The tractor industry seldom remained far ahead or far behind comparable industries.

There has been a consistent pattern in tractor development, however that may not continue. The growth of tractors into larger and larger sizes was steady after World War II, but this trend cannot continue indefinitely. Greater horsepower can only be utilized in one of two ways—either by pulling larger implements or by higher speeds. Wider implements are limited by highway rights-of-way and by the physics of plow design. The wider the implement, the greater the distance between the center of draft and the outermost plows or shovels, thus the greater the leverage on the implement frame. Similarly, there are limits to the speed with which field work may be done. Five or six miles-per-hour is about the maximum practical speed. Faster rates place excessive shock loads on equipment

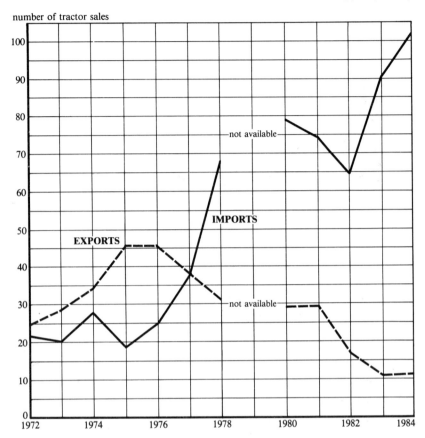

Figure 10. Imports, exports, and the domestic market.

Sources: Bureau of the Census. *Current Industrial Reports: Farm Machinery* (1959) and *Farm Machinery and Lawn and Garden Equipment* (1980). Washington: U.S. Department of Commerce.

and make the in-soil part of the tool wear too quickly. Work speeds faster than five miles per hour are also detrimental to operator comfort and safety. One engineer observed that while tractor horsepower increased, "The size and physical strength of the tractor haven't changed, nor have the load bearing properties of the soil."[1] He did not have to remind his colleagues that soil compaction was a growing problem.

Yet while engineers foresee problems with ever-larger machinery, farmers feel pressured to move to larger equipment. Labor requirements are not much larger for a twelve-row tractor than for a two-row one, but labor costs per acre are cheaper, and generally unit-production cost decreases as tractor size increases.[2]

One fairly consistent complaint that farmers have directed at tractor and implement engineers suggests that the engineers who designed tractors should have to drive them.[3] It was and is a sound concept. The same comment might also be made by mechanics who repair the engineer's handiwork. Perhaps the manufacturers should implement a program wherein engineers enjoy sabbaticals in the repair shop or actually plowing in the field.

The tractor industry itself occupies a distinctive position in the economy of the United States. It is small, highly concentrated, and has been studied intensely by government investigations.

Tractors almost seem to have been a by-product of American industry. In the five years preceding 1958, when the tractor industry was approaching its zenith, it annually converted an average of 1.8 million tons of steel into tractors. During the same period, the steel industry produced an average of almost 108 million tons of raw steel annually. The tractor industry thus absorbed something less than 2 percent of the nation's steel.[4] Between 1912 and 1939, wholesale tractor sales seldom amounted to much more than 10 percent of wholesale sales of automobiles. In many years, more than ten times as many dollars went for automobiles as for tractors.[5]

Yet tractors are the bread and butter of the farm equipment industry, for the whole farm equipment industry is based upon a small market, and tractors are a major component of that small market·due to their versatility.

The small market for farm equipment is easily demonstrated. The 1974 *Census of Agriculture* enumerated fewer than 1.7 million farms with an income of $2,500 per year or more. Farms with enough income to be potential purchasers of significant amounts of farm equipment numbered in the tens of thousands. And figures for 1974 were gathered in an era when farm prices were relatively high.

The size of the potential market was further reduced by specialization. There was obviously little market for cotton strippers in North Dakota or for Irish potato machinery in Florida. In fact, according to 1979 *Agricultural Statistics*, in 1977 there were only 1,676 cotton strippers manufactured in the United States, and only 1,006 potato harvesters. Even so versatile a tool as a moldboard plow has a fairly limited market, with only 46 thousand units built in 1977. Poor prices for farm products in the eighties slashed sales figures to far smaller numbers.

By contrast, the tractor has been fairly adaptable. The same tractor could cultivate cotton in Georgia, pull a corn picker in Iowa, and drive a baler in Oregon. Because it alone had a mass market, the tractor has furnished a large share of the income of farm machinery companies. Since the 1930s, tractors have produced an average of more than 40 percent of the manufacturers' income.[6]

Not only was the tractor a large segment of a small market, it was also subjected to unusual sales problems. An editor for the industry complained about the indirect effect of low farm prices on the industry and the tractor's role in the problem when he wrote:

> Tractor manufacturers build their machines too well and for too long an expectancy. When farmers get mulish and desire to punish Big Business for the economic woes of agriculture, they need only shop up their ancient tractors in winter and have new tractors come spring, without spending the price of new tractors.
>
> Tractor frames and engine blocs should be made out of plastics. In time they might warp enough to require junking. Now they are as eternal as ancient Roman plumbing.[7]

One can only hope the writer was writing tongue-in-cheek. The durability of tractors gave the farmer a vestige of economic leverage in a business world where for the most part he was at the mercy of those around him. The wholesale introduction of planned obsolescence into tractors would complete the process of reducing farmers to industrial serfs.

But the problem of tractor market volatility is a serious consideration for the manufacturers. Sales are closely tied to farm prosperity, and prosperity ultimately depends on commodity prices. The tractor plant, like the farmer, is badly hurt by an unpredictable crop market that constantly threatens to perform a world-class high dive. Unlike the farmer, the corporate executive can raise prices as insurance against fluctuations. But the farmer also has an insurance policy. Because tractors are well built and can be repaired, the farmer may choose to repair and boycott. In planning for that eventuality, industry and dealers may charge higher prices in good times. Yet for all the domestic squabbling between tractor maker and tractor user, they are joint hostages of commodity prices.[8]

Friction between the farm equipment industry and its customers is at least as old as the tractor. The formation of International Harvester Company at the turn of the century produced an almost absolute monopoly. Farmers reacted quickly and compelled the government to act as arbiter. By the time the issue dragged through the courts, a semblance of competition had returned to the industry. But the cycle has often been repeated.

The farmer's complaints were not irrational attacks proceeding from blind rage. Farmers were alert and aware of anomalies in the economy. To the farmer, there was something exceedingly sinister about Interna-

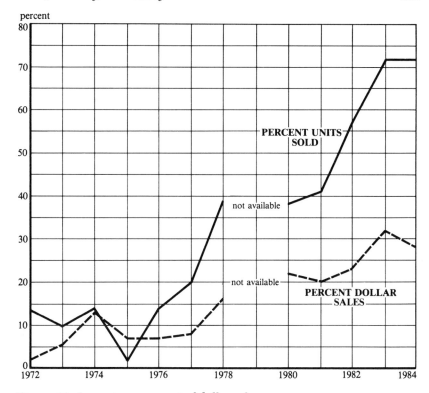

percent

Figure 11. Imports as percent of dollar sales.

Sources: Bureau of the Census. *Current Industrial Reports: Farm Machinery* (1959) and *Farm Machinery and Lawn and Garden Equipment* (1980). Washington: U.S. Department of Commerce.

tional Harvester's report that it had made higher profits in the deeply depressed economy of 1937 than it had in the generally prosperous year of 1929. Subsequently, in fact, the Federal Trade Commission attributed the matter to monopoly.[9]

The use of the term *monopoly* appears strange at first in reference to the tractor industry. From the time of the widespread acceptance of the row-crop tractor in the early thirties until the early eighties, there have been seven to nine firms engaged in tractor making. International Harvester, John Deere, Allis-Chalmers, J. I. Case, Oliver, Minneapolis-Moline, and Massey-Harris were all well established by the thirties. By the Second World War, Ford had reentered the tractor business, and shortly after the war, Harry Ferguson split from the Ford octopus and established the Ferguson Tractor Company. Thus, by 1947, there were nine manufacturers in the industry. Eventually, Massey-Harris absorbed

Ferguson in the late fifties, and in 1969 White Motor Corporation swallowed up Minneapolis-Moline, Oliver, and the Canadian firm of Cockshutt. By the seventies, there were still seven tractor builders. An agreement in 1980 between Hesston Farm Equipment and Fiat's tractor division—if viable—would have returned the number to eight. But by 1984, the ultimate disposition of almost every firm except (possibly) Deere was open to question. Financial commentators pondered the possibility that the number of major North American tractor makers might be reduced to an all-time low. Bankruptcies and mergers seemed likely to reduce the number of companies to five or even three, a concentration that boded ill for competition.[10]

Historically, however, a plurality of tractor manufacturers, has not assured competition. In 1937 the three largest implement houses—International Harvester, Deere, and J. I. Case—sold three-quarters of the farm implements purchased in the United States. In 1967, Deere and Harvester together took in 41 percent of sales dollars. By 1982, Deere sold more than the next two companies combined and was approaching the point where it would sell more than all of its competitors combined. If International Harvester/Case (Tenneco) holds its pre-merger market share, it will have some 35 percent of the American market, giving the two largest firms an unparalleled share of the market.[11] Studies of the agricultural equipment industry in 1938, 1954, and 1970 indicated that the majority of the long-line corporations simply priced their tractors and implements to compete with the two largest concerns, then adjusted production techniques until costs were considerably below the industry-wide price.[12] A student of the industry summarized the process succinctly, "There are recognized 'market leaders' . . . very large firms whose leadership in setting prices is tacitly followed by others. Struggle between these giants takes the form of advertising, aggressive salesmanship, service and improvement of product, rather than price cutting."[13] The existence of seven or more manufacturers has not resulted in price competition in North America. Three separate, intense economic studies of the industry have declared that the farm equipment industry has been a classic example of oligopoly.[14]

The existence of an oligopoly in the tractor industry is not the result of a devious conspiracy so much as a result of intermittent apathy. The farmer's traditional weapon against trusts is the intervention of the federal government. But litigation is a very slow process, and suits begun in periods of low farm prices frequently languish away with the return of prosperity when farmers again become preoccupied with daily production problems. Government policy toward concentration in the tractor industry thus tends to fluctuate with farm prices and has seldom persisted in a steady course long enough to effect a change in the industry. And the farm industry has seldom engaged in conspiracy. In the initial days of the depression, for example, tractor makers cooperated closely with the New Deal. Such cooperation contradicts the common image of crusty, reactionary industrialists barricaded in their factory complexes fulminating against Franklin D. Roosevelt in particular and the twentieth century in general. But, in fact, in 1935 the Bureau of Labor Statistics congratulated the farm machinery makers for their cooperation—theirs was the first industry to complete price tabulations in the massive economic research program then underway.[15]

Three years later there was far less amity between the industry and the government. In 1938 the Federal Trade Commission criticized both the structure and the practices of the industry with a special rebuke for the then largest company, International Harvester.[16] At about the same time, the Farm Security Administration lent money to a coalition of farmers' cooperatives to build a tractor plant in West Virginia to supply tractors to members of cooperatives. Republican congressmen conveniently overlooked the fact that cooperatives were privately owned and denounced the idea as an attempt to "Sovietize American industry." In reality the project offered the prospect of real competition in the industry, but it never got a fair trial. The venture was poorly located and apparently was undercapitalized. It faced problems of distribution and suffered from its "short-line" nature. The effort at cooperative tractor manufacture apparently died unnoticed and unmourned while still an infant.[17] The industry changed very little as a result of the project.

The implement industry and the government collided again after the United States entered World War II. The larger farm equipment firms had tremendous potential as manufacturers of war supplies, so the government attempted to shift tractor and implement production to smaller firms. Undoubtedly some of the more reform-minded planners hoped that the move would strengthen the weaker producers and leave them in a stronger position after the war, as well as produce a more competitive industry. But the farm implement industry opposed the plan, and the system broke down. The little factories did not have an effective national distribution system.[18]

After the war, government policy toward the industry fluctuated greatly. In 1948, the Federal Trade Commission issued a report on farm machinery manufacturers that was largely sweetness and light. The com-

mission seemed delighted to find that International Harvester had fore-
sworn the practices that had been censured in the report of a decade
earlier, and, in addition, that the company had cut prices.[19]

The FTC report, however, did not totally exonerate the industry,
and complained that tractor manufacturers used their size to bully their
own dealers. The retailer was often forced to accept unwanted merchandise and compelled to sign exclusive contracts in which he agreed to sell
the manufacturer's product line alone. While such contracts were advantageous to the manufacturer, they were injurious to the small local dealer
and were, in fact, illegal.

In late 1948, the government named International Harvester, Case,
and Deere in an antitrust suit. The source of complaint in this action seems
to have been the manufacturers' own dealers—not disgruntled farmers—
and the implement dealers' trade magazine applauded the government
action.[20] Eventually the FTC dropped the complaints, and the industry
returned to business as usual.

Concentration within the industry continued. For example, in 1964
Ford discarded its independent distributor network in favor of a company-
owned distribution system. Although the discarded distributors complained, there was no public outcry and no antitrust action. In 1963 White
Motor Company stated that its newly acquired subsidiaries—Moline and
Oliver—would continue to operate separately. Later, purportedly because of friction within White between Moline partisans and Oliver partisans, the company consolidated the former competitors into a single
White farm equipment structure. The move occasioned little comment,
perhaps because of the relatively small share of the market that Moline
and Oliver held.[21]

In retrospect, it appears that trust-busting has never seriously
touched the tractor industry. David Schwartzman, a meticulous economist
who has studied the farm machinery industry, questioned whether breaking up the dominant firms would, in fact, lower prices. He asserted that
the largest factories failed to approach maximum economies of scale, and
that numerous smaller, weaker companies would probably be even less
efficient—and not likely to reduce the cost of presently overpriced tractors. Schwartzman advised Canada and the United States to lower tariff
rates on tractors and to arrange for credit for struggling importers, thus
inducing competition.[22]

Since Schwartzman's recommendations were published, a steadily
deteriorating balance of payments for the United States and high domestic

unemployment eroded much of the appeal of a policy encouraging foreign competition. European and Japanese traders have gained an ever larger share of the market. Most American manufacturers are in serious straits. A more attractive alternative might well be the purchase and conversion of a long-line company into a farmer-owned cooperative. Experience with dozens of other farm cooperatives (such as Farmland Industries) in the past half-century indicates that such a project is feasible, although one undercapitalized and poorly located attempt at cooperative manufacture failed in the 1930s, as described earlier. By purchasing an existing firm, the cooperative could start out with a product line, a dealership network, and a sufficient volume of business to allow it to be competitive. Such a co-op, if well managed, should have little trouble repaying its initial loan and should induce competition—including price competition—in the tractor and implement industry. The job would not be easy; many of the problems that Gilbert Fite cited in his definitive study of co-ops remain. But the idea might well be pursued.[23] Another alternative might be the sale of one or more of the tractor and implement companies to its former employees. Such enterprises have a good track record. Given the status of agriculture and the status of the farm equipment industry, it seems obvious that the status quo has not worked well.

The tractor had a profound influence on the physical and social environment of America. It changed the tilth of small soil samples and the population of the major cities.

The physical environment was perhaps most obviously altered by changes in the nature and size of farm fields. When horses were the prime source of motive power, farms were frequently divided into small irregularly shaped fields that were rotated through a variety of crops and were frequently enclosed in fences or occasionally hedges. The fence rows, weed patches, and hedges that surrounded such fields were important to many small animals and birds. Quail and other game birds often fed on weed seeds in odd corners and depended upon the fence rows for nesting sites. Even animals as large as deer used the cover for protected paths. But tractors required more turning room than teams, and the "point rows" on irregular fields were bothersome. Not surprisingly, as soon as the tractor arrived, the farmer often used it to pull up hedges, plow out fence rows, and to lay out generally larger, more regular fields.[24] Experts advised the farmer, "If the tractor doesn't fit in with your system of farming, try changing your system of farming."[25] In so doing, he often changed the environment even more than he realized.

The tractor also changed a less obvious element of the physical environment—the soil itself. In some cases, the use of a tractor allowed the farmer to engage in soil-conserving practices that would have been impossible earlier. North Carolina investigators asked farmers if they had increased the amount of soil-improving work done on their farms since purchasing a tractor. Many replied that they had.[26] Other farmers constructed terraces and waterways with tractor power which would not have been done with horses. There were undoubtedly thousands of miles of terraces built and maintained by tractors. In some areas, erosion would reach intolerable proportions without tractors. On the High Plains, for example, tractors became indispensable in breaking the sandy crust that formed on the surface of fields after each rain shower. If left unbroken, the crust blew insufferably, causing both wind erosion and smothering dust storms.[27] In other cases, the adoption of larger tractors and wider implements has encouraged farmers to abandon old terraces, plow out old "point rows," and thus contributed to erosion.

Tractors not only changed the contour of the soil, but often gradually changed the physical structure of the soil itself. The first advocates of tractor power often expressed very high hopes for the machine in this respect. One enthusiast—who obviously had more exuberance than knowledge of soil science—assured farmers that deep plowing "virtually brings to the surface a new farm, a farm of virgin soil"[28] Farmers soon learned better. Subsoil, even "virgin" subsoil, is seldom fertile. By 1930 an agricultural engineer warned farmers that because tractor plows turned and mixed the soil better, they contributed to a rapid exhaustion of soil nutrients. Others warned that where unmechanized man depleted the soil in a generation, men with machinery stripped it of fertility in as few as five years.[29] The farmer's response—and perhaps the only one available— was to rely ever more heavily on chemical fertilizers, even though standard nitrogen-phosphorus-potassium (NPK) compounds did nothing to restore the humus necessary for good soil texture. Crop rotation, which helped soil structure in some cases, was often uneconomical because it required too varied an assortment of implements, each of which might be specialized to both crop and model of tractor, and because of the farmer's heavy dependence on his specialized cash crop upon which he depended for his mortgage payments.

The destruction of the soil's humus aggravated another tractor-related soil problem—soil compaction.[30] The passage of a tractor over the surface of the ground often packed the soil many inches below. With surprisingly little traffic, the soil became virtually impenetrable, blocking drainage and root penetration alike. Unfortunately, the worst compaction occurred under the same conditions that made for the best plowing. Soil compaction was a problem even before tractors, but mechanization intensified it.[31] In spite of ever more powerful tractors and even deeper plows, no definitive answer has been discovered. Meanwhile, as tractors grow more powerful, they also grow heavier.

After the fuel shortage of the mid-seventies, farmers and the agricultural research establishment turned to experimenting with concepts of "minimum tillage" or various similar concepts with similar names. Such practices generally (although not always) reduced the demand for tractor power and frequently reduced erosion. But their story is more closely tied to implement development than to the story of the tractor.

The advent of the tractor helped relocate crops more rapidly on a fairly massive scale, although Americans have always shifted around somewhat from time to time. The magnitude of such a nationwide geographical change may easily be observed in two crops: wheat and cotton.

In the early days of the depression, an economist described the shift in wheat acreage as succinctly as could any later writer, "Between 1914 and 1929 there was a decline in the wheat acreage of Ohio, Indiana, Illinois, Missouri and Minnesota from 13.6 million to 9.2 million acres and a decline of four hundred thousand acres under wheat in New York, Pennsylvania, Maryland, and Virginia; whereas the wheat acreage of Texas, Oklahoma, Kansas, Colorado, North Dakota, and Montana rose from 20.9 million to 33.2 million acres."[32]

Wheat had been slowly easing its way westward before the tractor, but to no small extent, the later migration of wheat production was because of the fact that the fields in the more western areas were larger and better adapted to tractors.

Even more dramatic was the rapid juxtaposition of the cattle and cotton regions of Texas. In the first decades of the twentieth century, the plains of West Texas had been devoted almost exclusively to cattle ranching, while East Texas concentrated on cotton. In the 1930s, the High Plains suddenly shifted to cotton production, and East Texas converted many fields to improved cow pastures. The economic motivation for that change can be dramatically illustrated in the lives of two men who ultimately retired in Lubbock County. Sterling Jerden was a Wolfforth, Texas, farmer who donated a tractor to the Lubbock County Museum in the late 1970s. The tractor—a four-row 1936 Massey-Harris Challenger—had been purchased new. It was his first tractor. The first year he used it, he farmed a quarter-section with little hired labor except at harvest time. He produced about eighty bales, total.

At the time Sterling Jerden was farming in West Texas, Ernest Wallace taught school in the winter and farmed in the summer in East Texas. He used mules on his small farm and produced one of the best crops in his area—a total of less than a half-dozen bales. The two men were more than four hundred miles apart and unknown to each other, but they typify the unequal regional competition. With about the same amount of labor, one produced roughly seventy bales more than the other—more than 1,000 percent. Soon the East Texas schoolmaster advised his students to forget cotton, plant grass, and raise cattle. Ultimately, he abandoned farming for graduate school and a career as a college professor at Texas Tech University.[33]

There can be little doubt that tractors and implements initiated the geographical change, although the development of irrigation technology accelerated the shift at a later time. In five years, the four southwestern states purchased enough machinery to equal 115 percent of the value of the machinery counted in the 1925 census. In 1937, the Texas High Plains derived 79 percent of its field power from tractors, almost all of it harnessed to multirow equipment. Six years earlier, the figure had been 26 percent.[34] Seldom has so large an area mechanized so completely so quickly. And the consequences of that area's mechanization were felt nationwide. One writer described the statistical indications of that change, "The total number of farms counted in the census of agriculture decreased 9 percent from 1920 to 1945. On the other hand, the 'land in farms' increased 19 percent." But such change was not evenly distributed, "the latter change occurred mostly in the 17 Western States. In fact, the land in farms decreased in most of the Eastern States during this period."[35] In fact, although wheat and cotton were typical moving crops in the era of "tractorization," they were not unique, but only one of several moving specialties.

As various areas became increasingly specialized—whether with traditional crops or new ones—the local economy gradually became more and more dependent on distant sources. A family in rural Illinois ate lettuce from California, beef from Iowa, apples from Washington state, potatoes from Idaho, and flour from wheat grown in South Dakota. Produce from the Illinois family's farm was shipped to equally distant points. Such a system—while superficially efficient—was both fuel intensive and fuel vulnerable. The consumer lost the alternative of a local source of supply, while the farmer lost a direct market and also found his eggs placed in fewer baskets. Specialization simultaneously increased and decreased the variety of food available. The Illinois family that now had access to Florida oranges was lucky to find two varieties of summer squash, where earlier farmers' markets might have carried a half-dozen.

By fostering specialization and urbanization, the tractor made the nation distinctly more susceptible to the ravages of economic downturns. In earlier days, when the population lived on semi-subsistence farms, panics and depressions were annoying and sometimes financially ruinous, but people could still eat—vegetables grew, hens laid, cows gave milk, and sows farrowed without regard to the Dow-Jones average or the unemployment rate. In subsequent urban life, acquisition of food was an economic exchange, and eating was dependent on income. Even many farm families exchanged their garden spot for an extra half-acre of cotton or corn and purchased their food in the same manner as city dwellers.

Some apologists for the status quo have argued that the low crop prices that resulted from mechanization brought low food prices. The evidence does not support such a contention. As early as 1941, an economist pointed out that fluctuations of 50 percent in the price of wheat did not influence the retail price of bread by a single cent.[36] Farmers complained that a rise in the price of wheat was sometimes used as a pretext for raising bakery prices—but dropping wheat prices seldom if ever lowered food prices. In his study of farm prices, Willard W. Cochrane credited the U. S. government with maintaining relatively stable farm prices in the period from 1950 to 1970 and implied that in so doing it held consumer prices slightly higher than would have otherwise been the case.[37] While few would quibble with the effect of price supports upon the farmer's income, there is some question about whether it influenced retail prices in an appreciable way. The agricultural raw materials that go into a consumer's groceries are a negligible part of the total cost. Wheat farmers, for instance, have repeatedly pointed to the fact that bakeries pay more for the loaf's plastic wrapper than they do for its flour. Transportation, retail overhead, labor and other costs are also proportionately larger.

The tractor's role in furthering the development of the cities also included the transfer of capital to urban areas. The *Yearbook of Agriculture* observed that, "Much rural wealth has migrated to the cities through ownership of equities in farms by people in cities and interest payments to such holders. With only 9 percent of the nation's income, farmers subsidize urban education because they rear and educate 31 percent of the nation's children, many of whom later migrate to cities; and this, too, has been equivalent to migration of wealth from the farm to the city."[38]

The writer did not explain that much of the wealth that migrated to the cities, particularly during the depression, was the patrimony of generations, a patrimony seized and expropriated by blind market forces that enriched the urban elite. Although similar migrations occurred earlier in American history (as in New England in the 1830s and 1840s), the twentieth-century phenomenon was unmatched in scale, speed, and severity.

As both human capital and financial capital migrated to the city, it left behind weakened rural institutions. Urbanization weakened community values and reduced the concern in rural areas for social services.[39] The phenomenon was not localized. One observer noted that "In studies both in the midwest and on the west coast, the trend in areas with fewer but larger farms was toward social services (elementary schools, dentists, pharmacies, etc.) which were less adequate than in towns surrounded by small-scale cropping operations. Various studies concluded that hired farm laborers on large and highly specialized agricultural operations seem to have less interest and [a] lower level of participation in functions that involve the quality of life than do farmer owner-operators.[40]

Unfortunately, studies on the effect of mechanization came too late to prevent the damage that occurred before or during the studies. Much of the harm to rural life had already been done and was not reversible. Once a village died, it was seldom revived.

Although agricultural mechanization has sometimes injured American society, the injury was not deliberate. At times, the injury was the result of naiveté. Raymond Moley, a member of the New Deal's Brain Trust, expected tractors and machinery to reverse the migration to the cities by reducing the drudgery of farm work and thus making country life more attractive. The people who stayed on the farm would become "capitalists," a term by which Moley meant "small businessmen." His wishful thinking proved as inaccurate as his terminology.[41]

On rare occasions, social disruption was postponed, at least at the local level, by sensitive individuals who foresaw the effects of new machinery. Elmer J. Baker, Jr., the articulate, entertaining, and responsible editor of *Implement & Tractor*, described one such instance in which a Cajun priest persuaded the plantation owners in his parish to refrain from buying combines because of the consequences to the local labor force. The old editor concluded his story with the statement that "Chàrlie Aspenwall returned to Chicago and had a long talk with company officials on sociology."[42] Apparently the company discontinued efforts to mechanize rice harvest until a more propitious time. Eventually, of course, the area was forced to mechanize.

The injury done by some carelessly conceived mechanization was dissected and damned in a pungent address that was widely reprinted in 1970. The speech reviewed some of the unwise dislocations that machinery had caused. It demanded that engineers and implement company executives anticipate the consequences of proposed machinery upon the environment and upon society. The message was not delivered by one of the antiestablishment radicals of the day, but by Brooks McCormick, the president of International Harvester Company. His concern followed the lines defined three years earlier by an engineer from John Deere. Both men were widely read within the farm machinery industry, and others echoed the same concerns.[43] In 1978, the American Society of Agricultural Engineers adopted the following statement as a part of the organization's official goals, "To Develop Public Understanding of the Consequences both Positive and Negative, of Existing and Proposed Engineering-Technology-for-Agriculture, the Environment, Economy, and Natural Resources."[44] The society courageously proposed for itself a high standard, and one which has the potential of creating considerable tension between the short-term economic interests of the employers of engineers and the long-term interests of American society. Yet there was room for mild optimism. If the professional society pledged itself to publicizing the consequences of mechanization, and if one of the largest equipment makers called attention to the problem, then it seemed possible that a combination of public and private action might eventually retard further deterioration of rural society as a result of machinery. Unfortunately, with less than 3 percent of the population left on the farm, there were few people left to preserve.

The profound changes engendered by mechanization in general, and the tractor in particular, have prompted honest people to pronounce widely divergent verdicts upon the machinery. Some of those value judgments were based upon analysis, others upon pure emotionalism. Viewpoint and circumstances were seldom the same for any two observers. Because the negative consequences of mechanization were so much more obvious in hard times, criticism of the tractor was most severe during the depression and other financially precarious periods. There are some general observations, however, that seem valid for the whole history of the machine.

The tractor and the modern agricultural system that it produced were unquestionably incompatible with the Jefferson philosophy that the nation espoused until the twentieth century. In a startling comparison in 1953, an article in *Agricultural History* contrasted the Jeffersonian concept of an independent small farmer with Lenin's idea of a disciplined proletariat. While American agriculture fitted neither pattern, it had many characteristics much more similar to Lenin's idea than to Jefferson's.[45] There was little reason to assume, the article implied, that a giant corporation in the Imperial Valley was inherently more solicitous of the needs of its hired laborer than was a huge collective in the Ukraine.

More recently a geographer commented on the difference between Jefferson's ideal and modern reality. He noted such characteristics of mechanical agriculture as crop specialization, advanced cultivating and harvesting techniques, large operating units, management specialization, labor specialization, large-scale production, and heavy capital investment. These characteristics, he observed, were once considered the hallmarks of the tropical plantation, but they have been increasingly associated with extra-tropical farms.[46] There was, of course, a distinct difference between a society structured around plantations and that idealized in American social tradition.

Had Americans continued to agree upon Jeffersonian values, or agreed to reject them in favor of a new consensus, subsequent policy decisions would have been far easier. But almost from the days of the first tractor, opinions were widely divided. In 1930, early in the depression, one cold-blooded economist called for the "culling out [of] three quarters of our farmers."[47] And as late as 1952, well after most Americans were urbanized, a farm editor still assumed a common consensus when he wrote, "How far the replacement of farmers by machinery can go remains a question. The American concept of relatively small farms with sufficient income to assure a good standard of living is thoroughly ingrained in the national thinking. The clash between economic and social objectives is bound to come."[48] In fact, there does not seem to have been any active consensus in the country, therefore there was no consistent public policy toward the tractor, mechanization or social changes.

Even though American society never reached a unanimous verdict on the tractor, several conclusions seem relatively clear about the machine. They are quite paradoxical. First, the tractor caused discernible suffering by displacing workers in hard times. One researcher who wrote during the depression claimed that every single farmer in his study who was displaced by the tractor moved down the economic ladder.[49] Results, of course, were probably not so devastating in periods of full employment. Second, the tractor was a good investment for a few farmers, and they enjoyed a better life because of the tractor. This was particularly true in prosperous years when labor was virtually unobtainable. Third, there is little doubt that the statement of a 1941 observer is true for most of the period. He wrote, "If mechanization in our country were forced to bear the expense of the social cost involved, evidently it would not pay."[50] Americans did not have to be overly religious to quote the words of the prophet Isaiah, when almost three thousand years ago he said of his own society:

> Woe to those who add house to house
> and join field to field
> until everywhere belongs to them
> and they are the sole inhabitants of the land.
> Yahweh Sabaoth has sworn this in my hearing,
> 'Many houses shall be brought to ruin,
> great and fine, but left untenanted;
> ten acres of vineyard will yield only one barrel,
> ten bushels of seed will yield only one bushel.[51]

Unrestrained greed is no more attractive in the United States in the last decades of the twentieth century A.D. than it was in Israel in the early eighth century B.C.

The impact of the tractor was exacerbated by governmental policies that have remained relatively consistent throughout the lifetime of the tractor and actually antedate it by several decades. Carey McWilliams, who wrote about mechanization on the eve of World War Two, asserted that the "Old Populists" had a clearer perception of reality than his contemporaries.[52] McWilliams had a legitimate point. Recent studies—such as Lawrence Goodwyn's *Democratic Promise*—chronicle the way in which American economic policy systematically expropriated rural wealth and showered it upon urban corporations.[53] Goodwyn's study concluded well before the widespread adoption of the tractor, yet there is little to indicate that subsequent policy was any less generous to corporate America or any less pillaging of rural resources.

Government policy, however, could still be reversed if popular sentiment could be mobilized. Subsidies could—and should—be reserved for family farms, which also deserve a predictable and reasonable price for their goods, not the crumbs from the table of commodity oligopolies. Tax breaks could—and should—be denied to corporate giants and perhaps the largest family plantations, but expanded for family farmers. Such policies would not only offset some of the persisting pain of mechanization, but would also help in a small way to reduce federal expenditure and increase revenue. The giants have been the greatest beneficiaries of both subsidy and loophole, even though they have had the least justification for receiving it.

Critics of mechanization may legitimately be asked what alternatives were available. It is not apparent that anyone has yet develped a practical thoroughgoing alternative to mechanization, or even a feasible method of slowing its adoption. That does not prove that no such solution could exist, or, that mechanization had to be taken to the level of *reductio ad absurdium*. Recent studies show that production efficiency, as measured by unit cost, is reached at a far smaller scale than commonly assumed. Such a scale is also far smaller than many of the cannibalistic farms that now enjoy the glutton's share of government subsidy. Indeed, in 1983 and 1984 virtually every farm magazine carried frequent stories of farmers who were cutting back acreage and improving their management techniques. By doing so such farmers reduced their dependence on borrowed capital, which was available only at usurious interest rates, and freed themselves of some management restraints imposed by the lending institutions. Unfortunately, such a course was only available to those who had, or could salvage, some equity in their operations.[54] Some proponents of largeness point to the United States' production surpluses as an indication of efficiency. It is a convoluted justification for largeness. European farms, which are smaller and on a more human scale, now produce comparable surpluses. While such surpluses cause problems for goverment policy on both sides of the Atlantic, one side has avoided some of the social trauma that afflicted the other.

In the United States, mechanization was essential and relatively innocuous in those eras when an expanding economy drew rural workers away from farm chores. It was compatible with American ideals so long as the scale of machinery and cost of it were adaptable to moderate-sized farms. In hard times, inanimate objects have often been portrayed as villains. In fact, tractors and other machinery are but scapegoats for a society that has never been able to address the unconscious centralization of economic power into ever fewer, but ever bigger, heedless corporations.

NOTES

1. Melvin E. Long, "Designing the Big Tractor," *Implement & Tractor* (August 7, 1967): 30; Hansen, "Engineering a New Line of Tractors," 604.

2. Mark Zimmerman, "How Much Does Tractor Power Cost," *Implement & Tractor* (September 7, 1967): 22–25.

3. Fletcher, "Factors Influencing Tractor Development," 179; "10 Farmers Talk Frankly About Equipment," *Implement & Tractor* (January 21, 1968): 22, 23.

4. George M. Seferovich, "Steel and the Price of Tractors," *Implement & Tractor* (August 23, 1958): 27; Bureau of the Census, *Historical Statistics*, 693.

5. *Historical Statistics*, 700, 791.

6. In 1977 tractor sales were $3,220,659,000 out of $7,773,546,000 total for the farm equipment industry—about 41 percent, *Agricultural Statistics 1977* (Washington: United States Department of Agriculture, 1979): ix-614; more recent analysts put it at about 40 percent, see Greenhouse, "Farm Equipment Sales Still Hurting," D-11; "Farm Implement Demands Increase," 40; "Farm Horsepower," *Fortune* (October 1948): 99; Neufeld, *A Global Corporation*, 13.

7. "Planned Obsolescence Should Be Built In," *Farm Implement News* (February 10, 1957): 43.

8. W. G. Phillips, *The Agricultural Implement Industry in Canada: A Study in Competition* (Toronto: University of Toronto Press, 1956), 118.

9. Marx, *Mechanization and Culture*, 71.

10. "Farm Tools Boom," 33; "Farm Implement Rivals Are Rarin'," *Business Week* (March 6, 1937): 20; Everett, "Big Expansion Ahead in Tractor Industry," 54, 62; Michael Conant, "Competition in the Farm-Machinery Industry," *The Journal of Business of the University of Chicago* (January 1953): 26; White Motor Corporation, *Progress*; Hesston Corporation, *Tractors, Productivity & Fuel Efficiency Hesston—The Prime Line* [advertising brochure], (Hesston, Kansas: Hesston Corporation, 1980), 26 pp. Greenhouse,"Farm Equipment Sales Still Hurting," D-11; Petzinger and Morris, "Tenneco Buys Farm Gear Unit," 2; Richards, "Allis-Chalmers Could Be First Big Loser," 6.

11. Betner and Gass,"Planting Deep and Wide at John Deere," 122; "Demands Increase," 40; Phillips, *Implement Industry in Canada*, 90.

12. Federal Trade Commission, *Report on the Agricultural Implement and Machinery Industry* (Washington: Federal Trade Commission, 1938), hereafter cited as FTC *Report*; Phillips, *Implement Industry in Canada*; David Schwartzman, *Oligopoly in the Farm Machinery Industry* (Ottawa: Royal Commission on Farm Machinery, 1970). These three books are essential reading for anyone interested in agricultural machinery and economics in the United States and Canada. Anglo-America is essentially a single market, and studies by either government are pertinent to the other.

13. Cauley, *Agriculture in an Industrial Economy*, 41.

14. FTC *Report*, 1938; Phillips, *Implement Industry in Canada*; Schwartzman, *Oligopoly*. See also McWilliams, "Farms into Factories," 406–31.

15. Jesse M. Cutts, "Revised Index of Wholesale Prices of Farm Machinery," (Bureau of Labor Statistics), *Monthly Labor Review* 41 (August 1935): 526.

16. FTC *Report*, 1938.

17. "Tractor 'Co-ops' Get U. S. Blessing," *Newsweek* (September 5, 1938): 33–34.

18. "WPB's Hot Potato," *Business Week* (April 24, 1943): 16, 16.

19. Federal Trade Commission, *Report of the Federal Trade Commission on Manufacture and Distribution of Farm Implements* (1948).

20. "New Anti-Trust Suit," *Farm Implement News* (September 23, 1948): 43; "Deny Any Basis for Trust Charges," *Farm Implement News* (October 1948): 73, 112, 114.

21. "An Industry Bombshell," *Implement & Tractor* (January 21, 1964): 30–31, 58; J. P. Dragin, "Why We Bought Moline," *Implement & Tractor* (January 21, 1963): 30.

22. Schwartzman, *Oligopoly*, 148, 205–16.

23. Gilbert C. Fite, *Farm to Factory* (Columbia: University of Missouri Press, 1965): 123–24.

24. H. R. Tolley, "Laying Out Fields for Tractor Plowing," *Farmers' Bulletin* No. 1045 (Washington: United States Department of Agriculture, May 1919 [Revised 1926, 1945, 1954]), 1–40; Gilbert, "Tractors on New York Farms," 69; Schwantes and Pond, "Tractor in Minnesota," 82; Hecht and Barton, "Gains in Productivity," 13.

25. Wheeler McMillen, "Making the Farm Fit the Tractor," *Power Farming* (January 1921): 9.

26. Elrod and Fullilove, "Cost and Utilization of Tractor Power and Equipment on Farms in the Lower Piedmont," 36, 37.

27. The task of "crust busting" can be onerous. Farmers in the Texas Panhandle enjoy telling about a retiree who sold all his equipment at a farm sale except for a sand fighter and a trailer. When curious neighbors asked why he retained those particular items, he replied that he planned to place the sand fighter on the trailer and head east. "When people begin asking me about that damn sand fighter, then I'll have found a place to retire!"

28. H. A. Crofts, "Plowing Deeper and Deeper: The Gasoline Tractor and the Science of Subsoiling," *Scientific American* (November 22, 1919): 516; Crossman, "The Gasoline Horse in the West,"

29. C. A. Bacon, "Relation of Farm Machinery to Maintenance of Soil Fertility," *Agricultural Engineering* (June 1930): 214; Marx, *Mechanization and Culture*, 55.

30. This should not be taken to mean that hooves cannot cause soil compaction. Road construction crews who use a sheeps-foot packer may not realize that their machine deliberately mimics the packing action of animals, yet that is exactly what it does. The horsedrawn plow, however, has only six or ten feet walking down the rows, not a herd of hooves nor a pair of rollers.

31. Yerkes and Church, "Tractor Experience in Illinois," 6; Schwantes and Pond, "Tractor in Minnesota," 58–59; I. F. Reed, "A Method of Studying Soil Packing by Tractors," *Agricultural Engineering* 21 (July 1940): 285; Holekamp,

Thomas, and Frost, "Cotton Cultivation with Tractors," 5; L. D. Doneen and D. W. Henderson, "Compaction of Irrigated Soils by Tractors," *Agricultural Engineering* (February 1953): 94; S. J. Bourget, J. G. Kemp, and B. K. Dow, "Effect of Tractor Traffic on Crop Yields and Soil Density," *Agricultural Engineering* (October 1961): 554.

32. Nourse, "Economic and Social Accompaniments," 117.

33. Sterling Jerden, interview, Wolfforth, Texas, 1978, cassette and transcript in Lubbock County Museum Archive; Ernest Wallace, informal interview, Texas Tech University, April 1979.

34. Stephens, "Mechanization of Cotton Farms," 27; Marx, *Mechanization and Culture*, 58.

35. Sherman E. Johnson, "Changes," 51.

36. Marx, *Mechanization and Culture*, 89.

37. Willard W. Cochrane, *The Development of American Agriculture* (Minneapolis: University of Minnesota Press, 1979), 404–5.

38. Smith, "New Conditions Demand New Opportunities," 811.

39. Marx, *Mechanization and Culture*, 62–63; Nourse, "Economic and Social Accompaniments," 114.

40. Madden, "Agricultural Mechanization," 13–14.

41. Raymond Moley, "More Democracy Through More Machinery," *Newsweek* (October 29, 1945): 112; Walter M. Carleton and Glen E. Vanden Berg. "That 'Hidden' Migration: History Now," *Agricultural Engineering* 51 (October 1970): 597–98.

42. Elmer J. Baker, Jr., "Charlie and the Padre," *Implement & Tractor* (August 9, 1958): 50, 52, 86.

43. Earl D. Anderson, "Engineering Planning for a Rebirth of the Countryside," *Agricultural Engineering* 47 (January 1966): 15, 32–33; Brooks McCormick, "One Cloth to be Worn Intact," *Agricultural Engineering* 51 (June 1970): 368–70; Wayne Worthington, "Engineer's Tractor History, VIII: We Engineers Are Involved in Humanity," *Implement & Tractor* (May 7, 1967): 38–39, 62–63.

44. "ASAE Adopts Complete Goals Program," *Agricultural Engineering* 59 (April 1978): 48.

45. Geroid T. Robinson, "Small Farms and Big Machines," *Agricultural History* 27 (April 1953): 69–71. Robinson proposed equipment-sharing pools as a solution to the high cost of machinery. It is an idea with little record of success in past experiments.

46. Howard F. Gregor, "The Large Industrialized American Crop Farm: A Mid-Latitude Plantation Variant," *The Geographical Review* 60 (April 1970): 115–75.

47. John T. Schlebecker, "Agriculture in Western Nebraska 1906–1966," *Nebraska History* 48 (Autumn 1967): 253; Nourse, "Economic and Social Accompaniments," 114–32.

48. Kirc Fox, ed., *New Farm Horizons* (Des Moines: Successful Farming, 1952), 47.

49. Marx, *Mechanization and Culture*, 65.

50. Marx, *Mechanization and Culture*, 89.

51. Isaiah 5:8–10, *Jerusalem Bible*.

52. McWilliams, "Farms into Factories," 425.

53. Lawrence Goodwyn, *Democratic Promise: The Populist Movement in America* (New York: Oxford University Press, 1976).

54. "Down on The Farm," "Nova" (Boston: WGBH, broadcast March 27, 1984); typical of such articles are: "Cut Back and Do Better: 'Smaller is More Efficient'," *Progressive Farmer* (October 1984): 64; "You Don't Have to Be Big to Be Profitable," *Progressive Farmer* (October 1984): 54; Bill Johnson, "Cut Back and Do Better: Why the Brakes Are Slowing Down," *Progressive Farmer*, (December 1984): 58; see also "Corporate Farms Disliked," *Progressive Farmer* (December 1984): 16.

Bibliography

BOOKS

Barger, Harold, and Landsberg, Hans H. *American Agriculture, 1899–1939: A Study of Output, Employment, and Productivity.* New York: National Bureau of Economic Research, Inc., 1942.

Berry, Wendell. *The Unsettling of America.* New York: Avon Books, 1972.

Bidwell, Percy Wells, and Falconer, John L. *History of Agriculture in the Northern United States, 1620–1860.* New York: Peter Smith, 1941.

Binnie-Clark, Georgina. *Wheat and Women,* Toronto: University of Toronto Press, 1979.

Borgan, Donald E., Hainline, Everette, and Long, Melvin E. *Fundamentals of Machine Operation: Tractors.* Moline, Ill.: John Deere Service Publications, 1974.

Broehl, Wayne. *John Deere's Company.* Garden City, N. Y.: Doubleday and Co., 1984.

Capper Farm Press. *The Tractor: Selling It as an Agricultural Implement and Fitting It to Midwest Crop Areas,* 4th ed. Topeka: Capper Farm Press, 1920.

Carrier, Lyman. *The Beginnings of American Agriculture.* New York: McGraw-Hill, 1923.

Cauley, Troy J. *Agriculture in an Industrial Economy: The Agrarian Crisis.* New York: Bookman Associates, 1956.

Cochrane, Willard W. *The Development of American Agriculture: A Historical Analysis.* Minneapolis: University of Minnesota Press, 1979.

Cummins, C. Lyle, Jr. *Internal Fire.* Lake Oswego, Ore.: Carnot Press, 1976

Danbom, David B. *The Revisited Revolution: Urban America and the Industrialization of Agriculture, 1900–1930.* Ames: Iowa State University Press, 1979.

Danhof, Clarence H. *Changes in Agriculture: The Northern United States, 1820–1870.* Cambridge, Mass.: Harvard University Press, 1969.

Denison, Merrill. *Harvest Triumphant: The Story of Massey-Harris.* New York: Dodd, Mead and Co., 1949.

Drache, Hiram M. *The Day of the Bonanza: A History of Bonanza Farming in the Red River Valley of the North.* Fargo, N.D.: Institute for Regional Studies, 1964.

Ellis, L. W., and Rumely, Edward A. *Power and the Plow.* Garden City, N. Y.: Doubleday, Page, 1911.

Farm Implement News. *The Tractor and Field Book, 1935–1936.* Chicago: Farm Implement News, 1936.

———. *The Tractor Field Book, 1938–1939.* Chicago: Farm Implement News, 1939.

———. *The Tractor Field Book, 1948–1949.* Chicago: Farm Implement News, 1949.

Fite, Gilbert C. *The Farmers' Frontier, 1865–1900.* New York: Holt, Rinehart & Winston, 1966.

———. *Farm to Factory.* Columbia: University of Missouri Press, 1965.

———. *George N. Peek and the Fight for Farm Parity.* Norman: University of Oklahoma Press, 1954.

Ford, Henry, and Crowthers, Samuel. *My Life and Work.* Garden City, N. Y.: Garden City Publishing Co., 1922.

Fox, Kirc, ed., *New Farm Horizons.* Des Moines: Successful Farming, 1952.

Fraser, Colin. *Tractor Pioneer: The Life of Harry Ferguson.* Athens: Ohio University Press, 1973.

Fussell, G. E. *The Farmer's Tools.* London: Andrew Melrose, 1952.

Gates, Paul W. *The Farmer's Age: Agriculture 1815–1860.* White Plains, N. Y.: M. E. Sharpe, 1960.

Gittins, Bert S. *Land of Plenty.* Chicago: Farm Equipment Institute, 1950.

Gold, Bela. *Wartime Economic Planning in Agriculture.* New York: Columbia University Press, 1949.

Goldschmidt, Walter. *As You Sow.* New York: Universe Books, 1978.

Goodwyn, Lawrence. *Democratic Promise: The Populist Movement in America.* New York: Oxford University Press, 1976.

Gray, R. B. *Development of the Agricultural Tractor in the United States.* St. Joseph, Mich.: American Society of Agricultural Engineers, 1974.

Griliches, Zvi. "The Demand for a Durable Input: Farm Tractors in the United States, 1927–1957. *The Demand for Durable Goods.* Arnold C. Harberger, ed. Chicago: University of Chicago Press, 1960, 179–207.

Harlan, Jack R. *Crops & Man.* Madison, Wisc.: American Society of Agronomy, 1975.

Hayter, Earl W. *The Troubled Farmer: Rural Adjustment to Industrialism, 1850–1900.* DeKalb: Northern Illinois University Press, 1968.

Hesston Corporation. *Tractors, Productivity & Fuel-Efficiency: Hesston—The Prime Line* [advertising brochure]. Hesston, Kan.: Hesston Corporation, 1980.

Holbrook, Stewart. *Machines of Plenty.* New York: MacMillan Co., 1955.

Hutchinson, William T. *Cyrus Hall McCormick.* New York: DaCappo Press, 1968. Reprint New York: Appleton-Century Co., 1935.

J. I. Case Threshing Machine Co. *Case Threshing Machinery* [catalog]. Racine, Wisc.: J. I. Case Threshing Machine Co., 1914.

John Deere Co. *Greater Earning Power on the Farm: John Deere Quality Implements* [catalog]. Moline, Ill.: John Deere, n.d.

Johnson, Glenn L., and Quance, C. Leroy. *The Overproduction Trap in Agriculture.* Baltimore: Resources for the Future, 1972.

Kirkendall, Richard S. *Social Scientists and Farm Politics in the Age of Roosevelt.* Columbia: University of Missouri Press, 1966.

Kolko, Gabriel. *The Triumph of Conservatism.* New York: Macmillan Publishing Co., 1977.

Kranzberg, Melvin, and Pursell, Carroll, Jr. *Technology in Western Civilization.* Vol. 2, *The Twentieth Century.* New York: Oxford University Press, 1967.

Mangelsdorf, Paul C. *Corn: Its Origin, Evolution and Improvement.* Cambridge, Mass.: The Belknap Press, 1974.

Marx, Walter John. *Mechanization and Culture: The Social and Cultural Implications of a Mechanized Society.* St Louis: B. Herder Book Co., 1941.

McCormick, Cyrus. *The Century of the Reaper.* Boston: Houghton Mifflin Co., 1931.

McEwan, Grant. *Power for Prairie Plows.* Saskatoon, Saskatchewan: The Midwestern Producer, 1971.

Merrill, Richard, ed. *Radical Agriculture.* New York: New York University Press, 1976.

Neufeld, E. P. *A Global Corporation: A History of the International Development of Massey-Ferguson Limited.* Toronto: University of Toronto Press, 1969.

Nevins, Allan. *Ford: The Times, the Man, the Company.* New York: Charles Scribner's Sons, 1954.

New Departure Manufacturing Co. *Tractor Manual: The Horse vs. the Tractor on the Farm Comparative Cost Data.* Bristol, Conn.: Engineering Service Department, New Departure Manufacturing Co., 1920.

Niemeyer, Glenn A. *The Automotive Career of Ransom E. Olds.* East Lansing: Michigan State University Business Studies, 1963.

Noble, David F. *America by Design: Science, Technology, and the Rise of Corporate Capitalism.* New York: Alfred A. Knopf, 1977.

Norbeck, Jack. *Encyclopedia of American Steam Traction Engines.* Glen Ellyn, Ill.: Crestline Publishing, n.d.

Perelman, Michael. "Efficiency in Agriculture: the Economics of Energy." *Radical Agriculture.* Edited by Richard Merrill. New York: New York University Press, 1976.

Phillips, W. G. *The Agricultural Implement Industry in Canada: A Study in Competition.* Toronto: University of Toronto Press, 1956.

Pursell, Carroll W., Jr. *Early Stationary Steam Engines in America.* Washington: Smithsonian Institution Press, 1969.

Roe, John B. *The American Automobile.* Chicago: University of Chicago Press, 1965.

Rosenberg, Nathan. *Technology and American Economic Growth.* New York: Harper & Row, 1972.

"Rumely, Edward A." *Who Was Who in America.* Vol. 4, *1961–1968.* Chicago: Marquis—Who's Who, Inc., 1968.

Schlebecker, John T. *Agricultural Implements and Machines in the Collection of the National Museum of History and Technology.* Washington: Smithsonian Institution Press, 1972.

———. *A Bibliography of Books and Pamphlets on the History of American Agriculture, 1607–1967.* Santa Barbara, Calif.: ABC-Clio Press, 1969.

———. *Whereby We Thrive: A History of American Farming, 1607–1972.* Ames: Iowa State University Press, 1975.

Schwartzman, David. *Oligopoly in the Farm Machinery Industry.* Ottawa: Royal Commission on Farm Machinery, 1970.

Shannon, Fred A. *The Farmer's Last Frontier: Agriculture, 1860–1897.* New York: Holt, Rinehart & Winston, 1945.

Shideler, James H. *Farm Crisis, 1919–1923.* Berkeley: University of California Press, 1957.

Shover, John L. *First Majority—Last Minority.* De Kalb: Northern Illinois University Press, 1976.

Simmonds, N. W. *Evolution of Crop Plants.* London: Longman, 1976.

Singer, Charles, Holmyard, E. J., Hall, A. R., and Williams Trevor I., eds. *A History of Technology.* Vol. 3 and 4. New York: Oxford University Press, 1957.

Smith, David Eugene. *Thomas Jefferson and Mathematics.* New York: Scripta Mathematica, n.d.

Stadtfeld, Curtis K. *From the Land and Back.* New York: Charles Scribner's Sons, 1972.

Stewart, Robert E. *Seven Decades that Changed America: A History of the American Society of Agricultural Engineers, 1907–1977.* St. Joseph, Mich.: The American Society of Agricultural Engineers, 1979.

Stone, Archie A. *Farm Tractors.* New York: John Wiley & Sons, 1932.

Tenneco, Inc. *1979 Annual Report.* Houston: Tenneco, Inc., 1980.

Thomas, Norman F. *Minneapolis-Moline: A History of Its Formation and Operations.* New York: Arno Press, 1976.

Turner, Frederick Jackson. *The United States, 1830–1850.* New York: W. W. Norton & Co., 1962 [1935].

White Motor Corporation. *Progress . . . [sic] in Tractor Power from 1898: Charles City Plant, White Farm Equipment, (Form No. R-1672).* Charles City, Iowa: White Motor Corporation, March 1975.

Wiebe, Robert. *Businessmen and Reform.* Cambridge, Mass.: Harvard University Press, 1962.

Wik, Reynold M. *Henry Ford and Grass-Roots America.* Ann Arbor: University of Michigan Press, 1972.

———. *Steam Power on the American Farm.* Philadelphia: University of Pennsylvania Press, 1953.

Wilcox, Walter, *The Farmer in the Second World War.* Ames: Iowa State College Press. 1947.

Williams, Michael. *Farm Tractors in Color.* New York: Macmillan Publishing Co., 1974.

Williams, Robert C., *Antique Farm Equipment: Researching and Identifying* [Technical Leaflet 101]. Nashville: American Association for State and Local History, November 1977.

GOVERNMENT PUBLICATIONS

Agricultural Statistics 1950. Washington: United States Department of Agriculture, 1950.

Agricultural Statistics 1977. Washington: United States Department of Agriculture, 1979.

Aitkenhead, William. "The Farm Tractor." *Indiana Agricultural Experiment Station Circular* No. 89 (January 1919).

Armstrong, David L., and Faris, J. Edwin. "Farm Machinery: Costs, Performance, Rates, and Combinations." *Gianni Foundation Research Reports* No. 273 [California Agricultural Experiment Station], 1964.

Atchley, F. M. "Tractor Costs in Michigan, 1938." *Michigan Agricultural Experiment Station Quarterly Bulletin* 22 (November 1939): 91–96.

Bachman, Kenneth L., and Jones, Ronald W. "Sizes of Farms in the United States." *Technical Bulletin* No. 1019 [Washington: United States Department of Agriculture], July 1950.

Brodell, A. P., and Kendall, A. R. "Life Span of Average Tractor Nearly Two Decades." *Agricultural Situation* 34 (August 1950): 11.

————, and Kendall. "Tractors Burn Less Fuel per Hour but Use More per Year." *The Agricultural Situation* 34 (January 1950): 8–9.

Brody, Samuel, and Cunningham, Richard. "Growth and Development with Special Reference to Domestic Animals: XL Comparison between Efficiency of Horse, Man and Motor with Special Reference to Size and Monetary Economy." *Missouri Agricultural Experiment Station Research Bulletin* No. 244, August 31, 1936.

Bureau of the Census. *1974 Census of Agriculture.* Vol. 1, Part 51. Washington: Department of Commerce, 1975.

————.*Fourteenth Census of the United States: Agriculture.* Washington: United States Department of Commerce, 1922.

————. *Historical Statistics of the United States [from] Colonial Times to 1970.* Part 1. Washington: United States Department of Commerce, September 1975.

————. "A Statistical Portrait of Women in the United States." *Current Population Reports Special Studies Series* P-23, No. 58. Washington: United States Department of Commerce, April 1976.

Bureau of Corporations. *Farm Machinery Trade Associations.* Washington: United States Department of Commerce, March 15, 1915.

Bureau of Labor Statistics. "Earnings in the Manufacture of Tractors, 1942." *Monthly Labor Review* 55 (November 1942): 1048–52.

————. "Mechanization of Agriculture as a Factor in Labor Development." *Monthly Labor Review* 33 (October 1931): 749–83.

———— *Monthly Labor Review* 32 (May 1931): 1072–75.

Butler, Charles P., and Crawford, D. C. "The Use and Cost of Tractor Power on

Small Farms in Anderson County, South Carolina." *South Carolina Agricultural Experiment Station Bulletin* 368, July 1947.

Cargill, B. F., and Schram, J. R. "The Tractor as an Emergency Source of Vacuum for Milking Machine Operation." *Michigan Agricultural Experiment Quarterly Bulletin* 31, November 1948.

Cavert, W. L. "Sources of Power on Minnesota Farms." *Minnesota Agricultural Experiment Station Bulletin* 262. February 1930.

Cooper, Martin R., Barton, Glen T., and Brodell, Albert P. "Progress of Farm Mechanization." *[United States Department of Agriculture] Miscellaneous Publication* No. 630, October 1947.

Cooper, M. R., and Williams, J. O. "Cost of Using Horses on Corn-Belt Farms." *[United States Department of Agriculture] Farmers' Bulletin* No. 298, 1922.

Cutts, Jesse M. "Revised Index of Wholesale Prices of Farm Machinery." Bureau of Labor Statistics' *Monthly Labor Review* 41 (August 1935): 526–32.

Davidson, J. Brownlee, Collins, Edger V., and McKibben, G. M. "Tractive Efficiency of the Farm Tractor." *Iowa Agricultural Experiment Station Research Bulletin* No. 189, September 1935.

Duncan, Marvin, and Webb, Kerry. *Energy and American Agriculture.* Kansas City: Federal Reserve Bank of Kansas City, February 1980.

Durost, Donald D., and Black, Evelyn T. "Changes in Farm Production and Efficiency." *[United States Department of Agriculture Economic Research Service] Statistical Bulletin* No. 581, November 1977.

Economics, Statistics and Cooperative Service. "Status of the Family Farm: Second Annual Report to Congress." *[United States Department of Agriculture National Economics Division Agricultural Economics Report]* No. 434. September 1979.

Elrod, J. C. "Cost and Utilization of Tractor Power and Equipment on Farms in the Coastal Plain." *Georgia Experiment Station Bulletin* 260, June 1949.

————, and Fullilove, W. J. "Cost and Utilization of Tractor Power and Equipment on Farms in the Lower Piedmont." *Georgia Experiment Station Bulletin* 256, January 1948.

Federal Trade Commission. *Report of the Federal Trade Commission on Manufacture and Distribution of Farm Implements.* Washington: Federal Trade Commission, 1948.

————. *Report on the Agricultural Implement and Machinery Industry.* Washington: Federal Trade Commission, 1938.

Fletcher, L. J., and Kinsman, C. C. "The Tractor on California Farms." *California Agricultural Experiment Station Bulletin* 415, December 1926.

Gilbert, G. W. "An Economic Study of Tractors on New York Farms." *New York Agricultural Experiment Station Bulletin* 506, June 1930.

Hecht, Reuben W., and Barton, Glen T. "Gains in Productivity of Farm Labor." *[United States Department of Agriculture] Technical Bulletin* No. 1020. December 1950.

Hoffman, A. H. "The Tendency of Tractors to Rise in Front, Causes and Remedies," *California Agricultural Experiment Station Circular* No. 267, June 1923.

Holekamp, E., Thomas, W. I., and Frost, K. R. "Cotton Cultivation with Tractors." *Arizona Agricultural Experiment Station Bulletin* 235, March 1951.

Holley, William C., Winston, Ellen, and Woofter, T. J., Jr. "The Plantation South, 1934–1937." *Research Monograph*, 22.

Hopkins, John A., Jr. "Horses, Tractors and Farm Equipment." *Iowa Agricultural Experiment Station Bulletin* No. 264 (June 1929): 373–404.

Humphries, W. R., and Church, L. M. "A Farm Machinery Survey of Selected Districts in Pennsylvania." *Pennsylvania Agricultural Experiment Station Bulletin* 237, March 1929.

Hurst, W. M., and Church, L. M. "Power and Machinery in Agriculture." *United States Department of Agriculture Miscellaneous Publication* No. 157, April 1933.

Johnson, Sherman E. "Changes in American Farming." *[United States Department of Agriculture Bureau of Agricultural Economics] Miscellaneous Publication* No. 707, December 1949.

Johnston, P. E., and Wills, J. E. "A Study of the Cost of Horse and Tractor Power on Illinois Farms." *Illinois Agricultural Experiment Station Bulletin* No. 395 (December 1933): 269–332.

Josephson, H. B., and Blasingame, R. U. "Farm Power and Labor." *Pennsylvania Agricultural Experiment Station Bulletin* 238, April 1929.

Kifer, R. S., Hurst, B. H., and Thornborough, Albert. "The Influence of Technical Progress on Agricultural Production." *Yearbook of Agriculture, 1940: Farmers in a Changing World*. Washington: United States Department of Agriculture, 1940.

———, and Stewart, H. L. "Farming Hazards in the Drought Area." *Research Monograph* 16. Washington: Works Progress Administration, 1938.

Lloyd, O. G., and Hobson, L. G. "Relation of Farm Power and Farm Organization in Central Indiana." *Indiana Agricultural Experiment Station Bulletin* 332, June 1929.

Long, Lewis E. "Farm Power in the Yazoo—Mississippi Delta." *Mississippi Agricultural Experiment Station Bulletin* No. 295, November 1931.

Mangus, A. R. "Rural Regions of the United States." *Special Report*. Washington: Works Progress Administration, 1940.

McElveen, Jackson V. "Family Farms in a Changing Economy." *[United States Department of Agriculture] Agricultural Information Bulletin* No. 171, March 1957.

McKibben, Eugene G., and Griffin, R. Austin. "Changes in Farm Power and Equipment: Tractors, Trucks, and Automobiles." *National Research Project Report* No. A-9. Philadelphia: Works Progress Administration, December 1938.

Miller, Frank, Ruden, W. L., and Smith, C. W. "Cost of Tractor Power on Nebraska Farms." *Nebraska Agricultural Experiment Station Bulletin* 324 [revised], September 1942.

Morison, F. L. "The Tractor on Ohio Farms." *Ohio Agricultural Experiment Station Bulletin* No. 383, May 1925.

———. "Tractors on Small Farms in Ohio." *Ohio Agricultural Experiment Station Bimonthly Bulletin* 26, November–December 1941.

————. "Tractors Reduce Demand for Horse Feed." *Ohio Agricultural Experiment Station Bimonthly Bulletin* No. 142, January–February 1930.

Muckley, Harry E., and Diller, Oliver D. "Increase Tractor Efficiency with Logging Sulky." *Ohio Farm and Home Research* 35 (September–October 1950): 70–71.

Musselman, H. H. "Selecting the Tractor." *The Quarterly Bulletin.* East Lansing: Michigan Agricultural College Experiment Station (August 1918): 110–11.

Nichols, W. D. "Tractor Experience in Kentucky." *Kentucky Agricultural Experiment Station Bulletin* No. 222 (September 1919): 45–68.

Office of the Secretary [of Agriculture]. "Proposed Farm Power Studies." *United States Department of Agriculture Circular* 149, March 1920.

Reed, I. F. "Laying Out Fields for Tractor Plowing."*[United States Department of Agriculture] Farmers' Bulletin* No. 1045 [revised], October 1954.

Reynoldson, L. A. "Influence of the Tractor on Use of Horses." *[United States Department of Agriculture] Farmers' Bulletin* No. 1093, May 1920.

————, and Tolley, H. R. "Changes Effected by Tractors on Corn-Belt Farms." *[United States Department of Agriculture] Farmers' Bulletin* No. 1296, 1922.

————, and Tolley. "Choosing a Tractor for a Corn-Belt Farm." *[United States Department of Agriculture] Farmers' Bulletin* No. 1300, n.d.

————, and Tolley. "Cost of Using Tractors on Corn-Belt Farms." *[United States Department of Agriculture] Farmers' Bulletin* No. 1297, 1922.

————, and Tolley. "Shall I Buy a Tractor? (For a Corn-Belt Farmer)." *[United States Department of Agriculture] Farmers' Bulletin* No. 1299, 1922.

————, and Tolley, "What Tractors and Horses Do on Corn-Belt Farms." *[United States Department of Agriculture] Farmers' Bulletin* No. 1295, January 1923.

Reynoldson, L. A., et al. "Utilization and Cost of Power on Corn-Belt Farms." *[United States Department of Agriculture] Technical Bulletin* No. 384, October 1933.

Riley, H. W. "Report of Committee on Tractors." [Department of Farms and Markets of the State of New York] *Agricultural Bulletin* No. 109: *Report of Farmers' Institute,* July 1918 [July 1, 1917 to June 30, 1918].

Russell, B. A. "Farm Power Utilization and Costs [in] South Carolina." *South Carolina Agricultural Experiment Station Bulletin* No. 280, September 1931.

Sauve, E. C. "Tractor Tests of Single Pneumatic Tires versus Dual Pneumatic Tires." *Michigan Agricultural Experiment Station Quarterly Bulletin* 22, November 1939.

————. "Tractor Operation Costs." *Michigan Agricultural Exeriment Station Quarterly Bulletin* 7, May 1925.

Schwantes, A. J., and Pond, G. A. "The Farm Tractor in Minnesota." *Minnesota Agricultural Experiment Station Bulletin* 280, September 1931.

Smith, Raymond C. "New Conditions Demand New Opportunities." *The Yearbook of Agriculture, 1940: Farmers in a Changing World.* Washington: United States Department of Agriculture, 1940.

Strickler, Paul E., and Hines, Charles A. *U. S. D. A. Statistical Bulletin* 258:

Numbers of Selected Machines and Equipment on Farms with Related Data. Washington: United States Department of Agriculture, February 1960.

Thorfinnson, T. S., and Epp, A. W. "Cost of Operating Tractors in Nebraska, 1961." *Nebraska Agricultural Experiment Station Bulletin* SB480, February 1964

Tolley, H. R. "Laying Out Fields for Tractor Plowing." *[United States Department of Agriculture] Farmers' Bulletin* No. 1045, May 1919.

———, and Church, L. M. "The Manufacture and Sale of Farm Equipment in 1920." *[United States Department of Agriculture] Department Circular* 212, April 1922.

———, and Church. "Tractors on Southern Farms." *[United States Department of Agriculture] Farmers' Bulletin* No. 1278, August 1922.

Washburn, R. S. "Cost of Using Horses, Tractors and Combines on Wheat Farms in Sherman County, Oregon." *United States Department of Agriculture Department Bulletin* No. 1447, December 1926.

Wooley, John C. "Power Farming in Idaho." *Idaho Agricultural Experiment Station Bulletin* No. 111, September 1918.

Wooten, O. B., Jr., Smith, W. R., and Meek, William E. "Cultivator Spray Rig for Farm Tractor." *Mississippi Agricultural Experiment Station Bulletin* 472, April 1950.

Wright, K. T. "1925 Tractor Costs in Michigan." *Michigan Agricultural Experiment Station Quarterly Bulletin* 19 (August 1926): 21–23.

Yerkes, Arnold P., and Church, L. M. "Tractor Experience in Illinois." *[United States Department of Agriculture] Farmers' Bulletin* 963, June 1918.

———, and Mowry, H. H. "Farm Experiences with the Tractor." *United States Department of Agriculture Bulletin* No. 174, April 15, 1915.

———, and Church, L. M. "An Economic Study of the Farm Tractor in the Corn-Belt." *[United States Department of Agriculture] Farmers' Bulletin* 719, May 5, 1916.

———, and Church. "The Farm Tractor in the Dakotas." *[United States Department of Agriculture] Farmers' Bulletin* No. 1035, 1919.

———, and Church. "The Gas Tractor in Eastern Farming." *United States Department of Agriculture Bulletin* No. 1004, September 1918.

———, and Church. "Tractor Experiences in Illinois: A Study of the Farm Tractor under Corn-belt Conditions" *[United States Department of Agriculture] Farmers' Bulletin* No. 963, June 1918.

JOURNALS

Adams, E. T. "Discussion of Modern Tendencies in Tractor Design." *Transactions of the American Society of Agricultural Engineers* 9 (March 1916): 68–73.

"Agriculturing Engineering: Recent Progress in Tractors." *International Review of Agriculture* 20 (September 1929): 359–65.

"Agricultural Tractor Equipment with Depth Control." *Engineering* 151 (March 7, 1941): 186–87.

Ahart, J. Leo. "Corn Planting and Cultivating with the General-Purpose Tractor." *Agricultural Engineering* 11 (February 1930): 61–63.

Aitkenhead, William. "Discussion by Wm. Aitkenhead." *Agricultural Engineering* 15 (July 1934): 243.

Anderson, Earl D. "Engineering Planning for a Rebirth of the Countryside." *Agricultural Engineering* 47 (January 1966): 15, 32–33.

Anderson, K. W. "Hydraulic Controls for Farm Implements." *Agricultural Engineering* 27 (August 1946): 355–66.

Ankli, Robert E. "Horses vs. Tractors in the Corn Belt." *Agricultural History* 54 (January 1980): 134–48.

"ASAE Adopts Complete Goals Program." *Agricultural Engineering* 59 (April 1978): 48–49.

"ASAE 10 Year Plan for Agricultural Safety." *Agricultural Engineering* 52 (January 1971): 17.

"Awaiting the Tractor Designed for Rubber Tires." *Agricultural Engineering* 5 (February 1934): 76–77.

Bachman, Kenneth L. "Changes in Scale in Commercial Farming and Their Implications." *Journal of Farm Economics* 34 (May 1952): 157–72.

Bacon, C. A. "Relation of Farm Machinery to Maintenance of Soil Fertility." *Agricultural Engineering* 11 (June 1930): 213–15.

Baker, E. J., Jr. "A Quarter Century of Tractor Development." *Agricultural Engineering* 12 (June 1931): 206–7.

Baldwin, Carliss Y., and Mason, Scott. "The Resolution of Claims in Financial Distress in the Case of Massey-Ferguson." *Journal of Finance* 38 (May 1983): 505–16.

Barger, E. L. "Power Alcohol in Tractors and Farm Engines." *Agricultural Engineering* 27 (February 1941): 65–67, 78.

Bartholomew, J. B. [The Avery Co.]. "Discussion on the Motor Contest." *Transactions of the American Society of Agricultural Engineers* 6 (December 1912): 87–91, 201.

Barton, Glen T. "Increased Productivity of the Farm Worker." *Industrial and Labor Relations Review* 1 (January 1948): 264–82.

Bassellmon, James. "New 1000-rpm Power Take-Off Standard Approved for Farm Tractors." *Agricultural Engineering* 39 (February 1958): 86–87.

Benjamin, B. R. "Farm Requirements of the Small All-Purpose Tractor." *Agricultural Engineering* 18 (May 1937).

Blasingame, R. U. "Corn Production Studies with the General Purpose Tractor." *Agricultural Engineering* 12 (March 1931): 89–90.

———. "Discussion by R. U. Blasingame." *Agricultural Engineering* 15 (July 1934): 237–38.

———. "Relation of Lug Equipment to Traction." *Agricultural Engineering* 3 (May 1922): 79–81.

———, and Josephson, H. B. "The General-Purpose Tractor in Potato Production in Pennsylvania." *Agricultural Engineering* 11 (February 1930): 58–60.

Bonnen, C. A. "Mechanization and Its Relation to the Cost of Producing Cotton in Texas." *Southwestern Social Science Quarterly* 22 (June 1941): 67–75.

————, and Magee, A. C. "Some Technological Changes in the High Plains Cotton Area of Texas," *Journal of Farm Economics* 20 (August 1938): 605–15.

Booth, J. F. "Some Economic Effects of Mechanization of Canadian Agriculture with Particular Reference to the Spring Wheat Area." *Proceedings of the World's Grain Exhibition and Conference* 1 (Regina, Saskatchewan: Canadian Society of Technical Agriculturalists, July 24 to August 5, 1933): 352–61.

Bowers, William L. "Country-Life Reform, 1900–1920: A Neglected Aspect of Progressive Era History." *Agricultural History* 45 (July 1971): 211–21.

Bourget, S. J., Kemp, J. G., and Dow, B. K. "Effect of Tractor Traffic on Crop Yields and Soil Density." *Agricultural Engineering* 42 (October 1961): 554.

Brackett, E. E. "The Nebraska Tractor Tests." *Agricultural Engineering* 12 (June 1931): 205–6.

Brown, Theo. "How the Use of Farm Machinery Creates Employment." *Agricultural Engineering* 15 (July 1934): 233–37.

————. "The Requirements and Design of Cultivating Equipment for the General-Purpose Tractor." *Agricultural Engineering* 11 (February 1930): 63–64.

Brunner, E. F. "Problems in the Design of Low-Pressure Tires for Farm Tractors." *Agricultural Engineering* 14 (February 1933): 45–46.

Buchele, Wesley F., and Collins, E. V. "Development of the Tandem Tractor." *Agricultural Engineering* 39 (April 1958): 232–34, 236.

Carleton, Walter M., and Vanden Berg, Glen E. "That 'Hidden' Migration: History Now." *Agricultural Engineering* 51 (October 1970): 597–99.

Cavert, William L. "The Technological Revolution in Agriculture, 1910–1955." *Agricultural History* 30 (January 1956): 18–24.

Chase, L. W. "The Motor Contest." *Transactions of the American Society of Agricultural Engineers* 6 (December 1912): 55–86.

Clark, Rex L. "Tractor Performance in Two- and Four-Wheel Drive." *Transactions of the American Society of Agricultural Engineers* 27 (January/February 1984): 8–11.

Clyde, A. W. "Mounted Plows and Their Effects on the Tractor." *Agricultural Engineering* 21 (May 1940): 167–70.

Collins, Arthur A. "General-Purpose Farm Equipment in Iowa." *Agricultural Engineering* 12 (November 1931): 416-18.

Collins, E. V. "Making a Tractor Drawbar Test." *Agricultural Engineering* 2 (January 1921): 19.

Conant, Michael. "Competition in the Farm Machinery Industry." *The Journal of Business of the University of Chicago* 26 (January 1953): 26–36.

" 'Daddy of Farmall Tractor' Dies at Age 98." *Agricultural Engineering* 50 (November 1969): 649.

Danhoff, Clarence. "Discussion." *Journal of Economic History* 22 (December 1962): 592–94.

"Developing Closed-Center Hydraulic Systems for Tractors." *Agricultural Engineering* 44 (January 1963): 18–21.

Dinsmore, Wayne. "Tractors Impoverish Farmers." *Journal of the American Veterinary Medical Association* 98 (June 1941): 469.

Doll, R. M. "Diesel Engines: The Next 15 Years." *Agricultural Engineering* 55 (October 1974): 27–28.

Dommel, H. K., and Race, K. W. "Design and Performance Characteristics of Four-Wheel-Drive Tractors." *Agricultural Engineering* 45 (August 1964): 424–27, 429.

Donaldson, G. F., and McInerney, J. P. "Changing Machinery Technology and Agricultural Adjustment." *American Journal of Agricultural Economics* 55 (December 1973): 829–39.

Doneen. L. D., and Henderson, D. W. "Compaction of Irrigated Soils by Tractors." *Agricultural Engineering* 34 (February 1953): 94–95, 102.

Duffee, F. W. "Wisconsin Observations of Rubber Tire Performance." *Agricultural Engineering* 15 (February 1934): 58–59.

Eason, C. M. "The General-Purpose Farm Tractor." *Journal of the Society of Automotive Engineers* 12 (June 1923): 597–609.

———. "Tendency of Farm Tractor Design." *Transactions of the American Society of Agricultural Engineers* 9 (March 1916): 59–67.

"Farmers Need Efficient Tractors." *Journal of the Society of Automotive Engineers* 12 (May 1923): 501.

Faulkner, Harold Underwood. "Farm Machinery and the Industrial Revolution." *Current History* 33 (March 1931): 872–76.

Fletcher, Leonard J. "Factors Influencing Tractor Development." *Agricultural Engineering* 3 (November 1922): 179–82.

———. "Mechanical Power—The Basis of the Next Agricultural Revolution." *Agricultural Engineering* 12 (June 1931): 199–200.

———. "The Real Effects of Mechanization on Wheat Production." *Proceedings of the World's Grain Exhibition and Conference* 1 (Regina, Saskatchewan: Canadian Society of Technical Agriculturalists, July 24 to August 5, 1933): 361–68.

———. "Tractor Service—Curative or Preventive—Which?" *Agricultural Engineering* 1 (December 1920): 71-72.

"Futuristic Fuel Cell Tractor." *Agricultural Engineering* 41 (October 1960): 685.

Geiger, M. Lynne. "Value of Differential Locks for Tractors." *Agricultural Engineering* 42 (March 1961): 124–27, 139–40.

Giebelhaus, August W. "Farming for Fuel: The Alcohol Fuel Movement of the 1930's." *Agricultural History* 54 (January 1980): 173–84.

Giles, William. "The Agricultural Revolution in the Delta." *Journal of Mississippi History* 31 (May 1969): 79–88.

Gray, R. B. "Alcohol-Gasoline Blends Are Engine Fuel." *Agricultural Engineering* 15 (March 1934): 106–9.

———. "Performance Tests of Alcohol-Gasoline Fuel Blends." *Agricultural Engineering* 14 (July 1933): 185.

Gregg, John B. "Noise Injuries to Farmers." *Agricultural Engineering* 53 (March 1972): 12–15.

Gregor, Howard F. "The Large Industrialized American Crop Farm: A Mid-Latitude Plantation Variant." *The Geographical Review* 60 (April 1970): 151–75.

Hahn, R. H. "Federal Safety Standards for Tractors." *Agricultural Engineering* 52 (March 1971): 108.

Hall, Carl W. "Energy and Agricultural Engineering." *Agricultural Engineering* 56 (March 1975): 13–14.

Hamilton, C. L. "Agriculture's Safety Challenge." *Agricultural Engineering* 26 (April 1945): 145–46, 148.

Hansen, Merlin. "Design Features of a New Diesel-Powered Tractor." *Agricultural Engineering* 31 (April 1950): 171–74.

———. "Engineering a New Line of Tractors." *Agricultural Engineering* 42 (November 1961): 602–5.

———. "Reducing Tractor Fatalities." *Agricultural Engineering* 47 (September 1966): 472–74.

Harvey, J. R., and Barnard, J. D. "Deere Announces Power Differential Lock." *Agricultural Engineering* 45 (December 1964): 664–66.

Hawthorne, Fred W. "Discussion by Fred. W. Hawthorne." *Agricultural Engineering* 15 (July 1934): 238–40.

Hennessy, Wesley J. "The Hidden Migration." *Agricultural Engineering* 51 (October 1970): 596–97

Higgs, Robert. "Tractors or Horses? Some Basic Economics in the Pacific Northwest and Elsewhere." *Agricultural History* 49 (January 1955): 281–83.

Hilliard, Sam B. "The Dynamics of Power: Recent Trends in Mechanization on the American Farm." *Technology and Culture* 13 (January 1972): 1–24.

Hornick, Richard J. "Effects of Tractor Vibration." *Agricultural Engineering* 42 (December 1961): 674–75, 696–97.

"Horses, Mules and Tractors in Farming." *Journal of the American Veterinary Medical Association* (November 1940): 444.

Huber, S. G., and Lamp, B. J. "One Way to Lower Tractor Power Costs: Operation of Optimum Engine Speeds." *Agricultural Engineering* 41 (August 1960): 508–10, 519.

Huntington, Arthur. "Engineering-Economic Relationships in the Agricultural Industries." *Agricultural Engineering* 12 (June 1931): 198–99.

Hurlbut, Lloyd W. "Comparative Test Results of Rubber Tires and Steel Wheels for Tractors." *Agricultural Engineering* 14 (August 1933): 217–18.

Ihrig, Harry K. "An Electric Powered Tractor." *Agricultural Engineering* 41 (April 1960): 232–33, 240.

Iverson, George W. "Possibilities of the All-Purpose Tractor." *Agricultural Engineering* 3 (September 1922): 147–49.

Jacobi, Louis. "Present-Day Tractor Well Engineered." *Agricultural Engineering* 14 (November 1933): 307–8.

Jensen, James K. "Are Tractors Noisy?" *Agricultural Engineering* 47 (October 1966): 532–34.

Johnson, A. N. "The Impact of Farm Machinery on the Farm Economy." *Agricultural History* 24 (January 1950): 58.

Jones, G. D. "General-Purpose Tractor Design." *Agricultural Engineering* 12 (March 1931): 91–92.

———. "Tractor Power in Relation to Agriculture." *Proceedings of the World's*

Grain Exhibition and Conference 1 (Regina, Saskatchewan: Canadian Society of Technical Agriculturalists, July 24 to August 5, 1933): 419–23.

Jones, Walter B. "A Summary: Pneumatic Rubber Tires on Farm Equipment." *Agricultural Engineering* 15 (February 1934): 49–50.

King, R. W., and Jessup, J. L. "Introduces New Line of Tractors at ASAE Meeting." *Agricultural Engineering* 54 (January 1973): 24.

Koeber, T. H. "The Styling of Farm Machinery." *Agricultural Engineering* 26 (January 1945): 17–18.

Kramer, Helen M. "Harvesters and High Finance: Formation of the International Harvester Company." *Business History Review* 38 (Autumn 1964): 283–301.

Kranich, F. N. G. "Is a Tractor Drawbar Needed." *Agricultural Engineering* 34 (March 1953): 186, 188.

———. "The Power Take-Off for Tractors." *Agricultural Engineering* 6 (September 1925): 204–8, 216–17.

Krieger, C. G. "Results of Recent Farm Tractor Fuel Studies." *Agricultural Engineering* 14 (July 1933): 177.

Larson, George H. "LP Gas as a Fuel for Farm Power Units." *Agricultural Engineering* 31 (May 1950): 215–18, 222.

Leviticus, Louis I. "Tractor Testing around the World." *Agricultural History* 54 (January 1980): 167–72.

Lewis, David C., and Williams, Douglas W. "Agricultural Engineers versus Agricultural Workers." *Agricultural Engineering* 51 (June 1970): 347, 351.

Madden, J. Patrick. "Agricultural Mechanization, Farm Size and Community Development." *Agricultural Engineering* 59 (August 1978): 12–15.

Manning, Mervyn H. "Future Technology and Foreign Competition." *Agricultural Engineering* 65 (March 1984): 13.

Mather, J. M., and Adams, K. C. "New 5-Plow 'One-Ninety' Tractor by Allis-Chalmers." *Agricultural Engineering* 45 (December 1964): 677–78.

McClure, Thomas A., and Scantland, D. Alan. "Energy: New Crop Sources." *Agricultural Engineering* 58 (September 1977): 17–20.

McCormick, Brooks. "One Cloth to be Worn Intact." *Agricultural Engineering* 51 (June 1970): 368–70.

McCuen, G. W. "Ohio Tests of Rubber Tractor Tires." *Agricultural Engineering* 14 (February 1933): 41–44.

Meile, Carl H. "Hydrostatic Drives for Tractors." *Agricultural Engineering* 43 (October 1962): 570–71.

Morrison, C. S., and Harrington, R. E. "Tractor Seating for Operator Comfort." *Agricultural Engineering* 43 (November 1962): 632–35, 650–52.

Murphy, Roy E. "Operating an Iowa Farm Without Horses." *Agricultural Engineering* 6 (March 1925): 59–60.

Murray, Donald A. "Tractor Implement Trends." *Agricultural Engineering* 45 (October 1964): 542–43, 561.

Neal, Ernest E. "The Education of the Southern Negro in a Changing Economy." *Journal of Negro Education* 22 (Spring 1953): 216–20.

"The New Tractors: Giants of the Earth." *Agricultural Engineering* 59 (July 1978): 38–44.

Newman, J. "Future Developments in Wheat Growing." *Proceedings of the World's Grain Exhibition and Congress* 1 (Regina, Saskatchewan: Canadian Society of Technical Agriculturists, July 24 to August 5, 1933): 350–52.

"News on Noise in Chicago." *Agricultural Engineering* 53 (July 1972): 11–12.

Nourse, E. G. "Some Economic and Social Accompaniments of the Mechanization of Agriculture." *The American Economic Review Supplement* 20 (March 1930): 114–32.

Nystrom, George H. "The Development of Pneumatic-Tired Tractors for Agriculture." *Proceedings of the World's Grain Exhibition and Conference* 1 (Regina, Saskatchewan: Canadian Society of Technical Agriculturalists, July 24 to August 5, 1933): 424–27.

Orelind, J. R. "Requirements of the Small All-Purpose Tractor from the Implement Engineer's Viewpoint." *Agricultural Engineering* 18 (May 1937): 211–12.

Patterson, H. L. "A Statistical Analysis of Farm Mechanization in Canada." *Agricultural Institute Review* 2 (March 1947): 87–88, 111.

Peace, C. G. "Power on the Farm." *Proceedings of the World's Grain Exhibition and Conference* 1 (Regina, Saskatchewan: Canadian Society of Technical Agriculturalists, July 24 to August 5, 1933): 368–75, 410.

Peck, H. W. "The Influence of Agricultural Machinery and the Automobile on Farming Operations." *Quarterly Journal of Economics* 41 (May 1927): 534–44.

Pfister, Richard G. "Do Tractors Last Too Long?" *Agricultural Engineering* 54 (May 1973): 12–13.

Pinches, Harold E. "Integrating Farm Machinery with the Tractor." *Agricultural Engineering* 25 (May 1944): 172–74, 176.

Pratt, Marianna, "A 'Sound Idea' from Deere." *Agricultural Engineering* 53 (September 1972): 23.

Pratt, Mildred. "Effect of Mechanization on Migrant Farm Workers." *Social Casework* 54 (February 1973): 105–13.

Pyle, Howard. "Setting ASAE Goals for Agricultural Safety." *Agricultural Engineering* 52 (January 1971): 15–16.

Rasmussen, Wayne D. "The Impact of Technological Change on American Agriculture, 1862–1962." *Journal of Economic History* 22 (December 1962): 578–91.

Reed, I. F. "A Method of Studying Soil Packing by Tractors." *Agricultural Engineering* 21 (July 1940): 281–82, 285.

Robinson, Geroid T. "Small Farms and Big Machines." *Agricultural History* 27 (April 1953): 69–71.

Ronayne, R. J. "Oliver Introduces Three New Tractors." *Agricultural Engineering* 45 (December 1964): 666–67, 676.

Rose, Philip S. "Gasoline Farm Tractors." *Engineering Magazine* 49 (August 1915): 750–52.

Ross, Earle D. "Retardation in Farm Technology Before the Power Age." *Agricultural History* 30 (January 1956): 11–18.

Rowan, James E. "Mechanization of the Sugar Beet Industry of Scottsbluff County, Nebraska." *Economic Geography* 24 (July 1948): 174–80.

Rushing, Karl. "Developing the Driverless Tractor." *Agricultural Engineering* 52 (May 1971): 260–62.

Ryan, K.E., and Terry, C.W. "Four Wheel Tractor Braking." *Agricultural Engineeering* 41 (November 1960): 746–47, 751.

Schlebecker, John T. "Agriculture in Western Nebraska 1906–1966." *Nebraska History* 48 (Autumn 1967): 249–66.

Schmidt, Louis Bernard. "The Agricultural Revolution in the Prairies and Great Plains of the United States." *Agricultural History* 8 (October 1934): 169–95.

———. "The Agricultural Revolution in the United States—1860–1930." *Science* 72 (Friday, December 12, 1930): 585–94.

Shawl, R. I. "Field Tests of Rubber-Tired Tractor Wheels." *Agricultural Engineering* 15 (February 1934): 57–58.

Shields, J. W. "Pneumatic Tires for Agricultural Tractors." *Agricultural Engineering* 14 (February 1933): 39–40.

Shiner, Neltje Tannehill, ed. "Tractor Shows and Demonstrations." *Agricultural Index* 1–3 (New York: H. W. Wilson Co., 1919): 940–41.

Sjorgren, Oscar W. "Nebraska Tractor Test Analysis." *Journal of the Society of Automotive Engineers* 12 (June 1923): 587–94.

———. "Tractor Testing in Nebraska." *Agricultural Engineering* 2 (February 1921): 34–37.

———. "Why Standardize Tractor Ratings." *Agricultural Engineering* 1 (November 1920): 67–68.

Skogvold, F. J. "Farm Loans and Farm Management by the Equitable Life Assurance Society of the United States." *Agricultural History* 30 (July 1956): 114–19.

Skromme, Arnold B. "The Growth of ASAE and the Farm Equipment Industry, 1907–1970," *Agricultural Engineering* 51 (April 1970): 181–84.

Smith, C. W. "A Study of Users' Experiences with Rubber-Tired Farm Tractors." *Agricultural Engineering* 16 (February 1935): 45–52.

———, and Hurlbut, Lloyd W. "A Comparative Study of Pneumatic Tires and Steel Wheels on Farm Tractors." *Agricultural Engineering* 15 (February 1934): 35–48.

———, Miller, Frank, and Ruden, W. L. "The Cost of Tractor Power." *Agricultural Engineering* 21 (September 1940): 348–50.

Sperry, L. B. "Farm Power and the Post-War Tractor." *Society of Automotive Engineers-Transactions* 52 (November 1944): 504, 510, 518.

"Standard Code for Tractor Testing." *Agricultural Engineering* 3 (May 1922): 82–83.

Steinbruegge, G. W., Schmer, Gary L., and Meier, Ned. "Measuring Tractor Noise at the Nebraska Tractor Testing Laboratory." *Agricultural Engineering* 51 (March 1970): 142.

Stephens, P. H. "Mechanization of Cotton Farms." *Journal of Farm Economics* 13 (January 1931): 27–36.

Stevenson, W. L. "Minneapolis-Moline Stresses Durability and Operator Comfort." *Agricultural Engineering* 45 (December 1964): 679–81.

Stewart, Robert E. "Social Responsibility—Then and Now." *Agricultural Engineering* 54 (August 1973): 25–27.

Strang, Peter M. "An Industrial Engineer Looks at Agriculture." *The Journal of Land and Public Utility Economics* 10 (August 1934): 268–74.

Tanner, P. Arthur. "Farm Tractor Ignition." *Agricultural Engineering* 2 (July 1921): 157–59.

Thomas, Edward Llewellyn. "The Subtle Pollutants." *Agricultural Engineering* 51 (March 1970): 127.

"Three-Point Tractor Hitch." *Agricultural Engineering* 34 (January 1953): 44.

Tower, J. Allen. "Cotton Change in Alabama, 1879–1946." *Economic Geography* 26 (January 1950): 6–28.

"Tractor Defects Summarized." *Journal of the Society of Automotive Engineers* 12 (May 1923): 499–501.

Trullinger, R. W. "Organization of Research in the Adaptation of the General-Purpose Tractor." *Agricultural Engineering* 11 (February 1930): 65–68.

Van Gerpen, Harlan W. "Evaluating Tractor Seating Comfort." *Agricultural Engineering* 37 (October 1956): 673–76.

Van Syoc, W. M., and Lemmon, N. F. "The ASAE Quick-Attaching Three-Point Hitch Coupler Standard." *Agricultural Engineering* 48 (February 1967): 80–81, 85.

Vaugh, Mason. "Subsistence Farming—A New Look." *Agricultural Engineering* 43 (November 1962): 631, 670–71.

Welty, A. B. "Considerations Affecting Belt Speeds." *Agricultural Engineering* 3 (July 1922): 115–16.

Wiggins, E. R. "Economics of the Farm Tractor," *Transactions of the American Society of Agricultural Engineers* 9 (March 1916): 79–92.

Wik, Reynold M. "Henry Ford and the Agricultural Depression of 1920–1923." *Agricultural History* 29 (January 1955): 15–22.

———. "Henry Ford's Tractors and American Agriculture." *Agricultural History* 38 (April 1964): 79–86.

Williams, D. G. "Economical Length of Time to Keep a Tractor." *Agricultural Engineering* 17 (June 1936): 254.

Wirt, F. A. "Experiences of Maryland Tractor Owners." *Maryland Agricultural Society Report* 3 (1918): 80–84.

———. "The General-Purpose Farm Tractor." *Agricultural Engineering* 5 (May 1924): 102–4.

Woolley, Edward Mott. "Secrets of Business Success." *The World's Work* 27 (January 1914): 346–52.

Yerkes, Arnold P. "Discussion of Tractor Economics." *Transactions of the American Society of Agricultural Engineers* 9 (March 1916): 93–103.

Young, O. W. "Tractor Industry in 1922." *The Journal of the Society of Automotive Engineers* 12 (February 1923): 188.

Zelle, William C. "What Form Will the Tractor Ultimately Take." *Agricultural Engineering* 1 (October 1920): 35–41.

Zink, Carlton L. "Safety in Farm Equipment: The Manufacturer's Concern." *Agricultural Engineering* 49 (February 1968): 74–75.

———. "Selecting a Farm Tractor." *Consumer's Research Bulletin* 1 (April 1941) [Consumer's Research, Inc.]: 20–23.

Zink, Frank Z., Barger, E. L., Roberts, June, and Martin, T. E. "Comparative Field Tests in Kansas of Rubber Tires and Steel Wheels." *Agricultural Engineering* 15 (February 1934): 51–54.

Zink, Leland. "The Agricultural Power Take-Off." *Agricultural Engineering* 12 (June 1931): 209–10.

Zink, W. Leland. "Standardization of the Power Take-Off for Farm Tractors." *Agricultural Engineering* 11 (February 1930): 75–79.

MAGAZINES AND NEWSPAPERS

"The Acid Test for Tractors." *Scientific American* (May 1923): 337.

Adams, E. T. "Is the Tractor to be a Horse Substitute?" *Power Farming* (May 1916): 12, 49–50.

"Advantages of Propane for Tractors." *Implement & Tractor* (May 17, 1958): 34–35.

"The Agricultural Application of the Gasoline Automobile." *Scientific American Supplement* (October 21, 1905): 24917.

Alford, C. H. "How to Succeed with Farm Tractors." *Progressive Farmer* (July 12, 1919): 6, 26.

"Allis-Chalmers, 'America's Krupp.'" *Fortune* (May 1939): 52–59, 148, 150–52.

Allis-Chalmers. "Here It Is! The New Allis-Chalmers General-Purpose Farm Tractor" [advertisement]. *Orange Judd Farmer* (November 30, 1918): 508–9.

"America: First in Farm Tractors." *Literary Digest* (November 23, 1918): 23.

"America to Restock the World with Farm Machinery." *Scientific American* (November 4, 1916): 424–25.

"American Peasantry." *Power Farming* (February 1926): 3.

"American Tractors to the Rescue." *World's Work* (February 1918): 363.

"Among the Manufacturers: The Avery Motor Corn Cultivator." *Power Farming* (July 1916): 62.

Anderson, Francis M. "Is the Ultimate Tractor Here?" *Power Farming* (May 1926): 6, 19.

"Are We an Endgame Industry?" *Implement & Tractor* (March 1983): 14.

"Are We Coming to Corporation Farming?" *Power Farming* (February 1927): 5, 9.

"An Army of Farm Tractor Operators Needed." *Power Farming* (June 1917): 8.

"ASAE Drafts Tractor Demonstration Rules." *Power Farming* (May 1919): 57.

Atteberry, R. H. "I.H. Hitch Not the Ferguson." *Farm Implement News* (August 10, 1953): 14, 124.

"Authoritative Statement on Farm Tractor Progress and Education." *Literary Digest* (January 4, 1919): 46.

"The Automobile as a Plow Horse." *Scientific American* (September 19, 1903): 201.

"Automobilism in Agriculture." *Scientific American Supplement* (March 16, 1901): 21078.

Avery Co. "The Most Efficient Tractor Transmission System Built" [advertisement]. *Power Farming* (February 1919): 5.

"Avery 2-Plow Tractor Has 6-Cylinder Engine." *Automotive Industries* (September 23, 1920): 604–5.

Bacon, C. A. "The Advantages of Tractor Plowing." *Power Farming* (December 1917): 22.

———. "What a Tractor Plow Did in a Small Field." *Power Farming* (February 1916): 7–8, 32.

Baker, E. J., Jr. "Charlie and the Padre." *Implement & Tractor* (August 9, 1958): 50, 52, 86.

———."Five Transcendent Developments." *Farm Implement News* (March 10, 1957): 76.

———. "From Allis-Chalmers: An Experimental Fuel Cell Tractor." *Implement & Tractor* (November 28, 1959): 24, 59.

———. "Harry Ferguson and the Mystery of 'Genius.' " *Implement & Tractor* (December 10, 1960): 36–37, 76–77.

———. "Tractor PTO Speeds under Reconsideration." *Farm Implement News* (January 10, 1957): 4.

"The Bank Eyes Changes in the Farm Equipment Market." *Implement & Tractor* (February 20, 1960): 106.

Barden, R. D. "Ohio Fruit Growers Prove Tractors Pay." *Power Farming* (October 1925): 5, 19.

Beecroft, David. "Fifty Tractors in National Demonstration at Salina." *Automotive Industries* (August 1, 1918): 175–78, 213.

———. "Specialization Helps Tractor Industry: Automobile Practice Exerting its Influence on Tractor Design. . . ." *Automotive Industries* (February 21, 1918): 393–96.

———. "Tractor Makers Assert They Can't Cut Their Price Now." *Automotive Industries* (October 26, 1922): 804–6.

———. "Tractor Problems That Are Awaiting Solution." *Automotive Industries* (March 13, 1919): 583, 601.

Bellinger, Page L. "Man-Machine Compatibility." *Agricultural Engineering* (January 1969): 17–19, 21.

Bent, Silas. "Machine-Master or Slave." *World's Work* (August 1929): 62–67.

Betner, Jill, and Gass, Linda. "Planting Deep and Wide at John Deere." *Forbes.* (March 14, 1983): 123–26.

"The Big Auto Tractor Attachment." *Automotive Industries* (March 6, 1919): 528–29.

"Big Changes in New Tractors." *Better Farming* (May 1955): 66.

Bird, J. M. "A Steel Mule That Drives Like a Horse." *Scientific American* (February 2, 1918): 109, 119.

Blasingame, R. U. "Power and Production." *Hoard's Dairyman* (March 18, 1921): 360, 394.

———. "The Spread of Power Farming in Ohio." *Power Farming* (November 1927): 5.

———. "Tractors Replace Hay and Oat Burners." *Power Farming* (December 1925): 5.

Boyer, Jacques. "An Automobile Hoe." *Scientific American* (November 28, 1908): 376.

Brantingham, C. S. "A Threatened Implement Shortage." *Power Farming* (July 1917): 23, 24.

Brinton, Bradford. "Some Suggestions for Tractor Plowmen." *Threshermen's Review and Power Farming* (March 1914): 7.

Buckingham, Frank. "The Current Picture on Wheel Diesel Tractors." *Implement & Tractor* (May 28, 1960): 22–26.

———. "4-Wheel Drive." *Implement & Tractor* (March 21, 1963): 46–49.

———. "The Future Tractor." *Implement & Tractor* (August 7, 1963): 48–51.

"Building McCormick-Deering Tractors." *The American Machinist* (July 30, 1925): 183, 186; (August 6, 1925): 223–28.

Buntin, J. L. "Views on Tractors." *The Breeder's Gazette* (December 26, 1918): 1228.

Burnett, Fred W. "Rice Farmer Uses a Gas Tractor." *Power Farming* (November 1917): 34.

"Buy a Tractor and Raise Better Horses." *Power Farming* (April 1917): 8, 34.

"Can a Farm Be Worked With Tractors Alone." *Rural New Yorker* (February 19, 1921): 267–68.

Carlson, Avis D. "The Wheat Farmer's Dilemma: Notes From TractorLand." *Harper's Magazine* (July 1931): 208–16.

Carlson, Lowell. "Remember the 'Tractivators?' " *Grain Producer's News* (October 1977): 4–8.

[Cartoon.] *Farm Implement News* (September 25, 1952): 36, reprinted from *Farm Implement News* (February 1, 1917): n.p.

Carver, W. L. "Narrow View of Power Farming Blights Tractor Trade." *Automotive Industries* (August 16, 1923): 309–13.

"Case Anti-Trust Suit Dismissed" *Farm Implement News* (October 25, 1951): 64.

Cavert, William L. "Farm Tractors in the Red River Valley." *The Breeder's Gazette* (July 17, 1919): 98.

"Chandler to Make Tractors for Government." *Automotive Industries* (February 21, 1918): 425.

Chase, Herbert. "International Brings Out Advanced Design of Tractor." *Automotive Industries* (March 23, 1922): 651–54.

Chew, Peter. "If Fuel Is Too High Down on the Farm—Just Get a Horse." *Smithsonian* (February 1980): 76–92.

Clapper, J. S. " 'The All-Purpose' Tractor on the Modern Farm." *Automotive Industries* (March 16, 1922): 622–23.

Clark, Florence L. "Marker Erected to Iowan Who Built First Tractor." *Hoard's Dairyman* (October 25, 1939): 566.

Clark, Neil M. "The American Farmer Wakes Up." *World's Work* (November 1926): 49–56.

"Comfort in Tractor Operation." *Automotive Industries* (March 13, 1919): 603.

Conger, C. S., Jr. "A Tractor Relieved His Mules." *Power Farming* (January 1917): 32.

"Corporate Farms Disliked." *Progressive Farmer* (December 1984): 16.

Cox, Meg. "Horses Are Pulling Their Weight Again with Some Farmers." *Wall Street Journal* (December 14, 1978): 1, 33.

Cozens, Harry. "A Farm, a Farmer, and a Tractor." *Rural New Yorker* (June 3, 1922): 738.

Crofts, H. A. "Plowing Deeper and Deeper: The Gasoline Tractor and the Science of Subsoiling." *Scientific American* (November 22, 1919): 516.

Crossman, Edward C. "The Gasoline Horse in the West." *Scientific American* (January 5, 1918): 17, 44, 46.

Crozier, Wilmot F. "Father of Nebraska's Tractor Law Explains It." *Implement & Tractor Trade Journal* (September 1919): 58, 70.

Cushing, F. L. "A Nebraskan's Power Farming Experience." *Power Farming* (October 1916): 9, 36.

Cusick, R. L. "Tractor Industry Is Completing Record-Breaking Year." *Automotive Industries* (December 8, 1928): 817–19.

"Cut Back and Do Better: 'Smaller Is More Efficient'." *Progressive Farmer* (October 1984): 64.

Dahl, Arthur L. "Mobilizing Farm Machinery." *Scientific American* (October 13, 1917): 274.

———. "The Tractor's Place in the Rice Fields." *Power Farming* (July 1918): 13.

———. "The Tractor That Never Tires." *The Independent* (May 25, 1918): 321, 339.

Davis, Harry G. "Farm Problems and the Machine." *Scientific American* (November 1933): 222–23.

Davis, J. Irwin. "Tractor Production of Peanuts." *The Country Gentlemen* (April 1929): 39.

"Dealers Delivered More Horsepower in 1966." *Implement & Tractor* (November 21, 1967): 30–35.

"Dealers Gather for Implement Convention." *Automotive Industries* (November 14, 1918): 853.

De Graff, A. H. "Horses and Tractors." *Hoard's Dairyman* (August 1, 1919): 61.

Demaree, F. H. "A County Agent's Opinion of the Tractor." *Power Farming* (December 1916): 7–8.

"Deny Any Basis for Trust Charges." *Farm Implement News* (October 7, 1948): 73, 110.

"Detroit's Tractors." *Business Week* (June 16, 1945): 32–34.

"Detailed Technical Specifications of Gasoline Farm Tractors for 1919." *Automotive Industries* (January 16, 1919): 176–79.

"Deutz Buys Allis-Chalmers." *Progressive Farmer Soybeans Midmonth [Supplement]* (May 1984): 21.

Dickey, E. E. "Tractor Much Cheaper Than Horses." *Power Farming* (October 1917): 13, 47.

Dies, J. Edward. "How Farm Tractor Saved the Spring Crop in Storm Area." *Power Farming* (May 1923): 5.

"A Diesel Succeeds the 'D' for Deere." *Farm Implement News* (January 13, 1949): 62, 98.

Dietz, Grace. "An Ideal Horse-Tractor Power Combination." *Power Farming* (April 1917): 7–8.

"Different Kind of Tractor." *Farm Journal* (March 1951): 39.

Dimock, Julian A. "The Farm Horse Doesn't Pay." *The Independent* (May 29, 1916): 337.

Dinsmore, Wayne. "Horsepower vs. Horse Power." *Breeder's Gazette* (October 8, 1914): 585.

Dodd, William E. "Shall Our Farmers Become Peasants." *Century Magazine* (May 1928): 10–44.

Domonoske, Arthur B. "Tractor Design from an Operator's Viewpoint." *Automotive Industries* (June 12, 1919): 1309–11, 1359.

"Do They Want Quality Most or Does Price Still Dominate." *Implement & Tractor* (February 7, 1971): 222–23.

"Doughnut Tires Enter Farm Field." *Business Week* (October 12, 1932): 8.

Dragin, J. P. "Why We Bought Moline." *Implement & Tractor* (January 21, 1963): 30.

"The Drought in Farm Equipment Isn't Over Yet." *Business Week* (April 23, 1984): 36.

Drummond, D. R. A. "Timely Hints for War Time Power Farming: Let Every Tractor Work." *Power Farming* (July 1917): 7.

Drummond, W. S. "Outside Earnings and Competition in Agriculture." *Agricultural Review* (September 1927): 3.

Dumas, Paul L. "Progress in Transmissions." *Implement & Tractor* (January 23, 1960): 90–94, 96.

"Dusty Fields." *Literary Digest* (August 30, 1919): 26.

Dyer, J. F. "Experience With Tractors." *Breeder's Gazette* (February 10, 1916): 307–08.

"E. A. Rumely Dies; Foe of New Deal." *New York Times* (November 28, 1924): 21.

Eason, C. M. "Efficiency of Farm Tractors A Standard System of Testing Needed." *Scientific American* (July 29, 1916): 96–97.

———. "The Tendency in Farm Tractor Design." *Power Farming* (February 1916): 9, 28, 30–31.

———. "The Tendency in Tractor Design (concluded)." *Power Farming* (March 1916): 42–44.

———. "Tractors to Increase Farm Resources." *Power Farming* (June 1917): 22, 24, 36, 40.

"The Effect of the War on Power Farming." *Power Farming* (August 1917): 7–8, 20.

"$875 for Ford Tractor with Plow." *Automotive Industries* (March 28, 1918): 654.

Ekblaw, K. J. T. "How Long Will a Tractor Last?" *Power Farming* (April 1928): 9.

Elam, F. Leland. "Hydraulics—Hard-Working Farm Hand." *Popular Mechanics* (June 1954): 134–37, 218, 220.

Ellis, John G. "A Light Tractor on a Dairy Farm." *Hoard's Dairyman* (July 10, 1926): 698, 730.

Ellis, L. W. "Economic Importance of the Farm Tractor." *The Engineering Magazine* (May 1911): 335–38.

———. "The Problem of the Small Farm Tractor." *Scientific American* (June 7, 1913): 518–19, 525, 528.

————. "The Winnipeg Tractor Trials Sixth Annual Event Shows Farmers Ready for General-Purpose Engines." *Scientific American* (September 6, 1913): 201–4.

Erwin, R. L., and O'Harrow, C. T. "Tractor Transmission Responds to Finger-Tip Control." *Agricultural Engineeering* (April 1959): 198–203, 207.

Eustis, John R. "On the Trail of the Tractor." *The Independent* (September 21, 1918): 388–89, 399.

Everett, Howard E. "Big Expansion Ahead in Tractor Industry." *Automotive Industries* (July 1, 1947): 28–30, 54, 62.

"Extension Controls for Clutch, Throttle and Steering." *Power Farming* (November 1919): 56.

"The Farm Backlog Is Rolling In." *Business Week* (May 5, 1934): 14–15.

"Farm Equipment Companies Are Bigger and Fewer." *Business Week* (May 6, 1931): 22, 25.

"Farm Horsepower." *Fortune* (October 1948): 92–100.

"Farm Implement Comeback." *Business Week* (December 15, 1934): 22.

"Farm Implement Demands Increase: Manufacturers' Earnings High as Tractors Supplant Horses." *Literary Digest* (March 6, 1937): 40.

"Farm Implement Rivals Are Rarin'." *Business Week* (March 6, 1937): 20, 22.

"Farm Tool Rush." *Business Week* (July 12, 1941): 26, 28.

"Farm Tools Boom." *Business Week* (June 6, 1936): 32–33.

"The Farm Tractor Instruction Book: Send It in the Period Between Purchase of Tractor and Its Delivery. . . ." *Automotive Industries* (February 21, 1918): 419.

"Farm Tractor—A National Necessity." *Horseless Age* (April 1, 1918): 42, 43.

"Farm Tractors, War and Women." *The Touchstone* (March 1918): 606–11.

"Farmall Model A Tractor with Adjustable Wheel Track." *Automotive Industries* (February 1, 1940): 119–20.

"Farmers Get Aid." *Business Week* (April 24, 1943): 28–30.

"Farmer's Power Plant." *Literary Digest* (November 27, 1915): 1219–20.

"Farms Go Mechanical." *Business Week* (July 1, 1939): 34–35.

"Favors U.S. Tractors in Europe: Italy, Switzerland, New Zealand and South Africa Buying American Products." *Automotive Industries* (March 7, 1918): 529.

"Filling the Place of Thousands Gone 'Over There'. . . ." [caption]. *Literary Digest* (November 23, 1918): 23.

Floyd, Charles S. "Cab Makers Confer on DOT Manifesto." *Implement & Tractor* (June 21, 1971): 12–14.

————. "Dust, Noise, Cold and Heat Are Out, Cabs Are In." *Implement & Tractor* (June 21, 1971): 15–17.

————. "The 1970's—Era of the Four Wheelers?" *Implement & Tractor* (May 1970): 6–9.

Fogarty, Bill. "Spotting the Adoption Leader." *Implement & Tractor* (July 25, 1958): 28–29, 73.

————. "Tractor Imports, Tractor Exports." *Implement & Tractor* (March 21, 1978): 20–22.

————. "What Banks Think About Financing Farm Equipment." *Implement &*

Tractor (August 23, 1958): 38–40.

Fogleman, Ralph M. "Tractor and Horses in War and Peace." *Breeder's Gazette* (July 10, 1919): 58.

"Food Prospects Grow Worse." *Business Week* (May 29, 1943): 15.

"Ford Makes a New Tractor and Implements." *Automotive Industries* (July 15, 1939): 66–67.

"Ford Pays Off." *Time* (April 21, 1952): 97, 98.

"Ford Selects Oakwood Site for Tractor Plant." *Horseless Age* (June 23, 1915): 835.

"Ford Settlement." *Newsweek* (April 21, 1952): 92.

"Ford to Buy Assets, Plant of Sherman Products, Inc." *Implement & Tractor* (May 28, 1970): 38.

"Ford to Make Tires and Operate Steamship Line." *Horseless Age* (July 7, 1915): 5.

"Ford Tractor-'53 Model." *Popular Mechanics* (January 1953): 120.

"Ford Tractors Move to Showrooms." *Business Week* (July 12, 1947): 28.

"Ford's New Tractor." *Business Week* (May 6, 1939): 30.

"Ford's Tractor." *Newsweek* (May 8, 1939): 42–44.

"A Four-Wheel Drive Tractor from the Pacific Coast." *Automotive Industries* (March 9, 1922): 554–55.

Foulkrod, G. M. "Meet the Tractor Half Way." *The Penn State Farmer* (January 1921): 117–38.

Fullenweider, H. N. "Mixing Common Sense With Tractor Operation." *Power Farming* (June 1917): 9, 41.

"Future Tractors: The Size and Shape of Things to Come." *Implement & Tractor* (January 1983): 12, 13.

Gage, Earle W. "Tractor Harvests Beet Crop." *Power Farming* (July 1920): 17.

"A Gasoline Steam Carriage." *Scientific American* (May 21, 1892): 329.

"General Utility Tractor Controlled with Reins." *Scientific American* (August 17, 1918): 132, 140–41.

Geschelin, Joseph. "Following Ford Tractors Down the Line." *Automotive Industries* (July 1, 1940): 4, 11, 43, 44.

———. "Oliver's Modernized Facilities for Producing Three Tractor Models." *Automotive Industries* (March 1, 1949): 34–36, 52.

"Get Through to the Good Times." *Forbes* (March 14, 1983): 123–26.

Gillette, G. M. "Tractor Service Has Been Neglected—It Must Be Improved." *Automotive Industries* (May 11, 1922): 1016–17.

Gilling, Tom. "England's Popular Perkins Diesel Engines." *Implement Tractor* (May 28, 1960): 32–34.

Godman, C. F. "The Limitations of Tractors." *Breeder's Gazette* (August 26, 1920): 347–48.

Goldberger, E. "The Most Economical Size of Tractor." *Automotive Industries* (March 7, 1918): 500.

"The Government Charges." *Farm Implement News* (October 7, 1948): 73, 112, 114.

"The Graham-Bradley Farm Tractor Described." *Automotive Industries* (July 31, 1937): 154–56.

"The Grand Tractor Circuit Ends." *Power Farming* (October 1916): 17.

Greene, P. H. "All This—And Cobweb Catchers, Too!" *California Citrograph* (December 1950): 49.

Greenhouse, Steven. "Farm Equipment Sales Still Hurting." Lubbock *Avalanche Journal* (December 7, 1984): D-11.

Grupp, George W. "Diesels in the Agriculture Industry." *Diesel Power and Diesel Transportation* (November 1950): 30–33.

Gunlogson, G. B. "General-Purpose Tractor Needed for American Farm Market." *Automotive Industries* (July 6, 1922): 4–7.

Hall, H. Scott, and Burford, H. G. "The Agrimotor: Present Failings, Future Prospects." *Automobile Engineer* (November 1921): 387–89.

Haystead, Ladd. "Can Farmers Afford Their New Tools?" *Fortune* (September 1946): 177, 179–80, 183.

———. "Machines That Weren't There." *Fortune* (June 1946): 195–96, 198.

Hazlett, Francis E. "The Farm Tractor in 1920." *Scientific American* (December 18, 1920): 612–13.

"Heavy Duty Power, Easy Duty Comfort" [advertisement]. *The Furrow* (November–December 1978): 6, 7.

"Heider Friction Drive Tractor." *Automotive Industries* (November 14, 1918): 831–32.

Heitshu, D. C. "Requirements of the Small All-Purpose Tractor from the Implement Engineer's Viewpoint." *Agricultural Engineering* (May 1933): 213–14.

Held, Frank. "The Tractor Age." *Market Growers Journal* (March 15, 1928): 250–52.

Heldt, P. M. "Avery 5–10 Orchard & Farm Tractor." *Automotive Industries* (October 24, 1918): 720–21.

———. "Case Designs Production Machines for Unit Frames." *Automotive Industries* (September 16, 1920): 563–68.

———. "Case 15–27 Hp. Tractor. *Automotive Industries* (January 30, 1919): 256–61.

———. "Cooling Capacity Increased in Samson Tractor." *Automotive Industries* (March 2, 1922): 502–5.

———. "Emerson Brantingham Model AA Tractor." *Automotive Industries* (June 13, 1918): 1128–33.

———. "J. I. Case Co. Announces New Model L Four-Plow Tractor with Engine Arranged Longitudinally." *Automotive Industries* (August 24, 1929): 268–70.

———. "Moline Model D Tractor." *Automotive Industries* (June 6, 1918): 1090–94.

———. "Motor Cultivators at Kansas City." *Automotive Industries* (March 13, 1919): 580–82.

———. "Tractor Activities in Illinois." *Automotive Industries* (November 21, 1918): 869–72.

———. "Tractor Activities in Northern Ohio." *Automotive Industries* (October 10, 1918): 619–21.

———. "Tractor Activities in Twin Cities." *Automotive Industries* (October 24,

1918): 702–5.

———. "Tractor Development in Iowa." *Automotive Industries* (October 17, 1918): 663–65, 696.

———. "Turning Out 100 Tractors Per Day." *Automotive Industries* (April 10, 1919): 788–92.

———. "The Twin City '16' Oil Tractor." *Automotive Industries* (February 14, 1918): 360–63.

———. "Twin City 12–20 Kerosene Tractor." *Automotive Industries* (April 17, 1919): 836–39.

———. "Varied Types of Farm Work Handled by Air-Tired, All-Purpose Tractors." *Automotive Industries* (December 28, 1935): 852, 854, 856–57.

Henderson, F. M. "Farming with a Gas Tractor in Indiana. *Power Farming* (September 1916): 7, 8, 53.

Hewitt, Edward R. "Principles of the Wheeled Farm Tractor." *Automotive Industries* (February 6, 1919): 312–15.

Hines, Paisley T. "Give the Tractor a Chance to Make Good." *Power Farming* (January 1919): 9.

———. "Southern Farmers Find Tractors Profitable." *Power Farming* (April 1918): 9, 20.

———. "When You Buy a Tractor, Buy Tractor Equipment." *Progressive Farmer* (July 12, 1919): 1142.

———. "Will a Tractor Reduce Overhead?" *Power Farming* (January 1918): 15.

"Historic Furrow." *Time* (July 3, 1939): 45, 50.

Hoag, M. E. "Manufacturing a Farm Tractor." *The American Machinist* (December 19, 1918): 1135–37.

Hobart, James F. "A Mississippi Plantation That Needs Tractors." *Power Farming* (September 1918): 11–12.

Hodsdon, F. G. "Does a Small Tractor Pack the Soil." *Power Farming* (August 1916): 52.

Holmes, John S. " 'What Is the Matter with My Tractor.' " *Power Farming* (October 1916): 9, 34.

Holman, Ross L. "A Big Expanding Market in the South." *Farm Implement News* (January 10, 1953): 72–73.

"The Hoosier Farm Tractor." *Automotive Industries* (January 10, 1918): 132, 133.

"The Horse as a Farm Tractor." *Literary Digest* (February 14, 1920): 98–101.

"Horse vs. Tractor." *Market Growers Journal* (September 1, 1926): 39.

"How Does a Turbocharger Work?" *Implement & Tractor* (July 15, 1962): 20.

"How Efficient Is the Farmer?" *Power Farming* (September 1927): 3, 14.

"How to Do Spring Work with the Tractor." *Power Farming* (March 1917): 7–9, 49.

"How to Look for Tractor Trouble." *Power Farming* (February 1917): 32, 50.

Hull, C. V. "Power Farming America's Vast Prairies." *Power Farming* (October 1916): 7.

Hunger, E. A. "Forestdale Said 'Good-Bye' to Dobbin." *Power Farming* (June 1926): 6–7, 12.

———. "Woman Drives Tractor and Does Work of Extra Hand." *Power Farming* (September 1925): 8.

Hutchinson, George L. "Pulls Stumps with His Tractor." *Power Farming* (December 1917): 25.

"IH Brings Out New Tractor Models." *Farm Implement News* (March 25, 1952): 52.

"Implement Dealers Losing Tractor Sales." *Automotive Industries* (October 17, 1918): 684, 696.

"Implement Pinch." *Business Week* (August 29, 1942): 17.

"Implements Freed." *Business Week* (October 7, 1944): 20.

"Imports of Farm Equipment by Product, 1975–1976." *Implement & Tractor* (November 7, 1977): 100.

"An Industry Bombshell: Ford Sheds Its 24 U. S. Distributors." *Implement & Tractor* (January 21, 1964): 30–31, 58.

International Harvester Co. "Women Join the 'Field Artillery'" [advertisement]. *Business Week* (August 22, 1942): 35.

"The Iron Horse Designed for General Farm Work." *Automotive Industries* (November 27, 1919): 1081.

"Is the Packing Effect of Tractor Harmful?" *Power Farming* (April 1917): 12–13, 51–55.

"It Solves the Farm Help Problem" [advertisement]. *Literary Digest* (November 23, 1918): 40.

Jandosek, Joseph. "Farm Tractor Design." *Automotive Industries* (June 12, 1919): 1265–73.

Johnson, Bill. "Cut Back and Do Better: Why the Brakes Are Slowing Down." *Progressive Farmer* (December 1984): 58.

Johnstone, William F. "You Can't Ignore Part-time Farmers." *Implement & Tractor* (May 21, 1965): 28–29.

Jones, W. B. "Exposed Tractor Gears Should Not be Oiled." *Power Farming* (August 1918): 47.

———. "A Rhapsody—Chiefly Raps—on the Horse." *Power Farming* (September 1918): 13.

Juengel, Carl E. "Experience with a Tractor." *Rural New Yorker* (April 16, 1921): 587.

Justice, J. L. "Canvas Covers for Tractors." *Power Farming* (July 1920): 16.

———. "Comparing Horse and Tractor Costs." *Hoard's Dairyman* (September 2, 1921): 160, 184.

———. "Quality in Tractor Work." *Hoard's Dairyman* (April 22, 1921): 580.

———. "The Tractor a Power Unit." *Hoard's Dairyman* (May 21, 1920): 1119.

"Keen Tractor Rivalry." *Business Week* (March 18, 1939): 34–35.

"Keep the Farm Tractor at Work." *Power Farming* (October 1918): 34.

Kirk, E. "Letter to Editor." *Thresherman's Review and Power Farming* (March 1913): 9.

Kramer, Dale. "Eviction by Machinery." *The Nation* (April 19, 1941): 497–99.

Larson, [no first name given]. "Letter to Editor." *Thresherman's Review and Power Farming* (March 1913): 9.

"Lauson 'Full Jeweled' Tractor." *Automotive Industries* (May 2, 1918): 874–75.

"Latest in New Jobs for a Tractor. *Power Farming* (June 1917): 18.

"Life of the Farm Tractor." *Farm Implement News* (July 10, 1951): 110–11.

"Light-Weight Gas Tractor for the Farm." *Scientific American* (January 15, 1916): 80.

Lockwood, Warren S. "Rubber Tired Farm Tractors." *India Rubber World* (March 1, 1939): 43–45.

Long, Melvin E. "All About Tractor Hitches." *Implement & Tractor* (January 21, 1964): 23–25, 54.

———. "Cabs for Tractors and Combines." *Implement & Tractor* (August 21, 1965): 34–37.

———. "Designing the Big Tractors." *Implement & Tractor* (August 7, 1967): 30–33.

———. "New Emphasis on Operator Comfort, Convenience." *Implement & Tractor* (May 21, 1965): 24–26.

———. "Power-Adjusted Rear Wheels." *Implement & Tractor*, (December 7, 1963): 28–29.

———. "Supercharging the Diesel Engine." *Implement & Tractor* (February 21, 1965): 26–28.

"Lost Retail Sales: The Horsepower Went Up." *Implement & Tractor* (August 7, 1967): 30.

Luman, R. R. "A Farmer's Views on Tractors." *Breeder's Gazette* (September 9, 1920): 466–67.

"Making Tractors Roll-Over Safe." *Farm Implement News* (February 25, 1957): 53.

Mally, R. T. "The Farm Tractor and the Renter." *Power Farming* (September 1916): 8, 29.

———. "Sidelights on the Tractor Business." *Power Farming* (October 1916): 14, 39.

———. "Why a Tractor Pays—The Investment Side." *Power Farming* (May 1916): 9, 56.

"Manufacturing of Worm Gear and Assembly Methods in Fordson Tractor Success." *Automotive Industries* (April 25, 1918): 810–14.

"Many Tractor Schools." *Power Farming* (May 1919): 57.

Marx, Walter John. "Farms, Machines, and the Good Society." *The Commonweal* (December 24, 1948): 271–74.

"Massey-Harris." *Fortune* (June 1946): 108–15, 246, 248, 251.

"The Massey-Harris-Ferguson Announcement." *Farm Implement News* (September 10, 1953): 154, 156.

Matthieson, J. F. "How I Save Money with a Tractor." *Power Farming* (July 1916): 28–29.

"Maxwell Develops 3-Plow, Enclosed Transmission Farm Tractor." *Automotive Industries* (February 7, 1918): 336–37.

"Mayer Little Giant Agricultural Tractor." *Horseless Age* (May 1, 1916): 352–53.

McCuen, G. W. "Dividends from Your Tractor." *The Ohio Farmer* (January 19, 1924): 9, 76–77.

———. "The Present Status of Tractor Farming." *Ohio Farmer* (January 11, 1919): 2–70.

McMillan, Robert T. "Effects of Mechanization on American Agriculture." *Scientific Monthly* (July 1949): 23–28.

McMillen, Wheeler. "Making the Farm Fit the Tractor." *Power Farming* (January 1921): 9–10.

McWilliams, Cary. "Farms Into Factories: Our Agricultural Revolution." *Antioch Review* (Winter 1941): 406–31.

"Mechanical Details of the $650 Samson Tractor." *Automotive Industries* (October 16, 1919): 772–73.

"A Mechanical Plow Horse." *The Literary Digest* (March 21, 1914): 617.

"Mechanizing the Small Farm." *Popular Mechanics Magazine* (April 1940): 536–39, 140A-43A.

Meir, F. A. "Tractors and Horses." *Breeder's Gazette* (October 22, 1914): 692.

Merrill, Robert D. "Tractor Production Lags 24 Percent Behind '51." *Farm Implement News* (January 10, 1953): 75.

Metcalf, H. J. "The Farm Tractor in Iowa." *Hoard's Dairyman* (October 1919): 545, 562–63.

"Michigan Buys 1,000 Tractors." *Automotive Industries* (March 14, 1918): 563.

Miller, Henry J. "The Tractor and Horse in the South." *Breeder's Gazette* (November 18, 1915): 905.

"Mr. Ford's Only Partner." *Fortune* (January 1942): 66–67, 153–57.

Moley, Raymond. "More Democracy through More Machinery." *Newsweek* (October 29, 1945): 112.

"More Work from the Tractor." *Power Farming* (June 1918): 14.

Morganthau, Henry, Jr. "Farm Tractor Expedition to France." *Power Farming* (March 1918): 46–47.

———. "Tractor Expedition to France." *Jersey Bulletin and Dairy World* (February 27, 1918): 307.

Moses, B. D., and Frost, K. R. "Tractive Performance of Pneumatic Tires and Steel Wheels." *Agricultural Engineering* (February 1934): 55–57.

"The Motorized Farm" [editorial]. *Automotive Industries* (March 20, 1919): 657.

"Motorizing the Farm." *Scientific American* (August 3, 1918): 92.

"Much Opposition to Liberty Tractor." *Automotive Industries* (February 21, 1918): 422, 425.

"Nebraska Tractor Tests: Help or Hindrance." *Farm Implement News* (September 25, 1952): 30–31, 78–80.

"The New Anti-Trust Suit." *Farm Implement News* (September 23, 1948): 43.

"New Case 9–18 Tractor of Simpler Design." *Automotive Industries* (April 18, 1918): 767–68.

"New Farm Tractor Burning Kerosene." *Scientific American* (January 19, 1918): 76.

"New Field Plowed." *Time* (July 21, 1947): 88.

"New Ford Tractors." *Business Week* (June 24, 1939): 38–39.

"New Fordson Tricycle-Type Tractor Passes Nebraska Test." *Automotive Industries* (August 27, 1938): 267–68.

"New Models and Strong Representation of Parts Makers at K. C. Tractor Show." *Automotive Industries* (February 27, 1919): 494, 506.

"New One-Man Hook-Ups." *Farm Journal* (July 1956): 37.

"New Samson Tractor at $650." *Automotive Industries* (November 28, 1918): 939.

"New Star Rises in Far East." *Progressive Farmer* (May 1984): A-4.

"New York State Investigates Its Tractors." *Automotive Industries* (November 28, 1918): 942–43.

Nichols, G. A. "Harvester and Ford in Finish Fight for Tractor Market." *Printer's Ink* (March 30, 1922): 25–28.

"$956 Season's Saving with Small Tractor." *Power Farming* (November 1927): 12.

"1965 Retail Sales: The Horsepower Went Up." *Implement & Tractor* (April 21, 1966): 40.

" 'Offset' Tractor Allows a Clear View of Row." *Popular Mechanics* (November 1939): 703.

"Oilpull Tractors Redesigned: Weight Reduced and Working Parts Enclosed." *Automotive Industries* (March 5, 1925): 466–68.

"Oliver 500 Tractor Made by David Brown." *Implement & Tractor*, March 5, 1960): 4, 30.

"Oliver Starts Its Second 100 [Years]—with a New Tractor Line." *Farm Implement News* (July 1, 1948): 120–22, 160, 162–63.

"Oliver Unit is 'Streamlined.' " *Automotive Industries* (January 11, 1936): 48–49.

Olney, Raymond. "Adapting the Tractor to Power Farming." *Power Farming* (November 1918): 11, 13.

———. "Farm Tractor Spells Doom of Mule in Dixie." *Power Farming* (August 1916): 7–8, 34.

———. "How Much Will This Tractor Pull?" *Power Farming* (May 1916): 7–9, 50–52.

———. "How to Care for the Tractor in Winter." *Power Farming* (December 1916): 38.

———. "How to Do a Good Job of Tractor Plowing." *Power Farming* (February 1916): 8, 32.

———. "A New Chapter in Farm Tractor Development." *Power Farming* (September 1917): 7–9.

———. "Power Farming and the Farm Boy Problem." *Power Farming* (February 1917): 8.

———. "Power Farming Solves Crop Production Problems." *Power Farming* (May 1917): 9, 14.

———. "Shall We Have More Public Tractor Shows." *Power Farming* (September 1916): 9.

———. "Signs of Progress in the Farm Tractor Field." *Power Farming* (October 1918): 9–11.

———. "A Standard Drawbar Rating for Gas Tractors." *Power Farming* (August 1916): 9, 50–52.

———. "Standardization of Tractor Ratings." *Power Farming* (February 1917): 13–14.

———. "The Tractor and the Boys." *Power Farming* (May 1919): 7.

———. "Tractor to Solve the Food Problem." *Power Farming* (June 1917): 6, 38, 40.

"150,955 Tractors in 2 Years." *Automotive Industries* (November 14, 1918): 859.

"Overland Completes Moline Purchase." *Automotive Industries* (November 21, 1918): 894.

Page, Victor W. "Modern Agricultural Tractor Designs." *Scientific American* (July 29, 1916): 100.

————. The Motor Driven Commercial Vehicle: Distinctive Agricultural Tractor Design." *Scientific American* (May 18, 1918): 458.

"Parade of Progress." *Farm Implement News* (August 10, 1953): 66–67, 116–17.

Patterson, J. M. "Tractor vs. Mule Power in Nut Production." *American Nut Journal* (January 1930): n.p.

Peddie, Donald. "Production Control as Applied in a Farm Tractor Plant." *The Iron Age* (January 29, 1948): 56–61.

"Pennsylvania Buys 40 Tractors." *Automotive Industries* (February 28, 1918): 470.

Perkins, Frank C. "A Gasoline Tractor of 100 Horse-power Capacity." *Scientific American Supplement* (March 18, 1911): 168.

————. "The Modern Farmer's Tireless Horse." *Scientific American* (June 27, 1908): 453, 458.

Peterson, Walter F. "Barney Oldfield Turns a Plowhorse Into a Racehorse." *Northwest Ohio Quarterly* (Summer 1963): 122–28.

"Petroleum on Farms of the U. S." *National Petroleum News* (February 5, 1936): 130–41.

Petzinger, Thomas, Jr., and Morriss, Betsy. "Tenneco to Buy Farm-Gear Unit from Harvester." *Wall Street Journal* (November 27, 1984): 2.

"The Place of the Tractor in Cotton Belt Farming." *Progressive Farmer* (August 31, 1918): 962.

"Plan for Distributing Fordson Tractors." *Automotive Industries* (April 4, 1918): 667–68.

"Planned Obsolescence Should Be Built In." *Farm Implement News* (February 10, 1957): 43.

Port Huron Engine & Thresher Co. "Attention! Steam, the Dependable Power" [advertisement]. *Power Farming* (October 1916): 46.

"Port Huron Friction Drive Tractor." *Automotive Industries* (November 28, 1918): 928, 946.

Poulton, Ralph W. "The Farm Tractor on Parade." *Breeder's Gazette* (December 1937): 16–17, 19.

Pound, Robert T. "Machine vs. Muscle." *Breeder's Gazette* (September 16, 1920): 512.

"Power Costs." *Power Farming* (February 1921): 10.

Power Farming (April 1917): 12–13, 51–55.

"Power Farming at O.S.U." *Power Farming* (November 1916): 26.

Price, Theodore S. "Gasoline and Agriculture." *The Outlook* (June 27, 1917): 334–35.

————. "Gasoline and Agriculture." *The Outlook* (July 28, 1915): 760-67.

A Reader. "Draft Horses for Farm Work." *Breeder's Gazette* (November 11, 1915): 862.

"Remy System Combines Governor with Generator." *Automotive Industries* (May 2, 1918): 862–63.

"Requirements of Tractors for Use in Southern States." *Automotive Industries* (March 20, 1919): 662.

Richards, Bill. "Allis-Chalmers Could Be First Big Loser As Harvester Leaves Farm-Gear Business." *Wall Street Journal* (December 7, 1984): 6.

Richardson, John L. "When the Tractor Comes the Barberry Goes." *Power Farming* (October 1925): 12.

Roberts, H. P. "What It Costs to Run the Tractor." *Progressive Farmer* (July 12, 1919): 1142.

Rockwell, F. F. "Adapting the Farm to Tractors." *The Field* (February 1919): 81–85, 122.

Rodabaugh, Evin. "How to Make a Tractor Last Longer." *Farm Quarterly* (Summer 1951): 38–41, 130–31.

Rogers, Everett M. "How Farmers Make Decisions." *Implement & Tractor* (July 26, 1958): 26–27, 80–81.

Rose, Philip S. "Economics of the Farm Tractor." *Scientific American* (February 1, 1913): 114–15.

———. "Farm Tractors and Their Motors." *Horseless Age* (June 16, 1915): 799–800.

———. "Farm Tractors: A Review of Their History, Conditions of Use and Methods of Construction." *Scientific American Supplement* (April 29, 1916): 282–83.

Rose, Raymond. "Tractor Makes Up for Delays." *Power Farming* (May 1919): 48.

"A Rubber Tired Tractor." *Scientific American* (February 8, 1919): 122.

Rutenik, B. J. "The Efficiency of the Farm Tractor." *Hoard's Dairyman* (July 28, 1916): 5, 14.

———. "The Small Tractor." *Breeder's Gazette* (February 10, 1916): 307.

Rumely, Edward A. "The Passing of the Man with the Hoe." *World's Work* (August 1910): 1324–58.

"Rumely Adds Smaller Tractor Model." *Automotive Industries* (January 24, 1918): 208, 210.

"Running Tractors on LP Gas." *Breeder's Gazette* (August 1951): 24.

R. W. B. "The Displacement of Horses." *Breeder's Gazette* (November 18, 1915): 905.

R. W. C. "Horses, Mules, and Tractors." *Breeder's Gazette* (October 14, 1915): 660.

Salmon, Edward. "Four Years of Farming with a Tractor." *Power Farming* (March 1916): 8, 49.

The Samson Tractor Co. "The Samson Tractor Company" [advertisement]. *Power Farming* (December 1918): 28–29.

Sauve, E. C. "Horsepower of Tractors and Horses." *Breeder's Gazette* (November 16, 1916): 935.

Scarratt, A. W. "The Influence of Hitches and Drawbar Location on Tractor Design." *Automotive Industries* (June 12, 1919): 1334–35, 1359.

Schipper, J. Edward. "Ford Tractor Production Plan Unchanged in Growth." *Automotive Industries* (March 28, 1918): 621- 24.

———. "Fordson Assembly Wholly on Progressive Plan." *Automotive Industries* (May 1, 1919): 960–66.

———. "Handling Parts in the Shop and on the Assembly Floor." *Automotive*

Industries (May 8, 1919): 1008–12.

———. "Machining Operations on the Backbone of the Fordson Tractor." *Automotive Industries* (April 11, 1918): 717–23.

"The Scott Gasoline-Motor-Propelled Agricultural Tractor." *Scientific American Supplement* (November 4, 1905): 24948–49.

Seferovich, George H. "Dealer Location: Where Do Farmers Shop." *Implement & Tractor* (October 1, 1960): 22–25.

———. "Deere's Engineered New Line of Tractors." *Implement & Tractor* (September 17, 1960): 66–69.

———. "Steel and the Price of Tractors." *Implement & Tractor* (August 23, 1958): 26, 29, 36, 58.

———. "Tractors: The Surge in Imports." *Implement & Tractor* (May 28, 1960): 28–30.

"The Seventies Are Over." *Implement & Tractor* (July 1983): 30.

Shaver, W. J. "A Tractor and Horses Combined." *Power Farming* (February 1917): 15, 16.

Shellabarger, Ira G. "Tractor Experience." *Hoard's Dairyman* (October 31, 1919): 657.

"Show New Tractors." *Business Week* (February 25, 1939): 41, 43.

"The Small Farm Tractor." *Scientific American* (April 3, 1915): 304.

"Small Farmers Will Have Small Tractors to Fit." *Business Week* (October 12, 1932): 8.

"The Small Tractor." *Scientific American* (October 4, 1914): 254.

"Small Tractor Derby." *Business Week* (October 14, 1939): 42.

"Small Tractor Increases Potential Market From 7% to 60% of Farms." *Automotive Industries* (January 16, 1919): 182–83.

"Small Tractors, Adapted Chiefly to Plowing, Are Increasing in Popularity." *Breeder's Gazette* (February 10, 1916): 305.

"Smaller Tractors." *Business Week* (October 20, 1945): 21–22.

"Sound-Gard Body Gives You Staying Power to Handle Big Tractor Power" [advertisement]. *The Furrow* (July-August 1979): 6, 7.

Spencer, W. "Farms More Cheaply With a Gas Tractor." *Power Farming* (November 1917): 20, 33.

"Standardized Fordson Equipment." *Automotive Industries* (May 16, 1918): 971.

"Steering and Controlling Devices for the Four Wheeled Tractor." *Scientific American* (November 2, 1918): 358.

Stone, Archie A. "Putting Tractors on the Night Shift." *Power Farming* (May 1919): 26, 28.

Storm, Bill. "How Frick Co. Is Distributing England's Nuffield Tractor." *Implement & Tractor* (December 21, 1964): 14–15.

Strite, George T. "Fundamentals of Tractor Design." *Automotive Industries* (February 14, 1918): 354–56.

"The Success of a Woman Farmer." *Power Farming* (December 1917): 30.

Taylor, H. C. "Difficulties in Using Tractors." *Breeder's Gazette* (May 16, 1918): 1036.

Taylor, Paul Schuster. "Good-bye to the Homestead Farm." *Harper's Magazine*

(May 1914): 589–97.

"10 Farmers Talk Frankly About Equipment." *Implement & Tractor* (January 21, 1968): 21–23.

"A Test for Tractors." *Power Farming* (October 1918): 14.

"Texas Has 4144 Tractors." *Automotive Industries* (November 28, 1918): 943.

"That U.S.D.A. Tractor Census." *Power Farming* (April 1917): 10.

"This Must Make It Unanimous." *Farm Implement News* (July 10, 1953): 59.

Thornton, W. B. "Revolution by Farm Machinery." *World's Work* (August 1903): 3766–79.

"Those Tractor Tests." *Power Farming* (April 1919): 16.

"A Threatened Implement Shortage." *Power Farming* (July 1917): 22, 24.

"Three Reasons for Tractor Farming." *Power Farming* (August 1916): 52.

"Through the Watching Glass, Part III." *Implement & Tractor* (February 21, 1968): 30–31.

Tigner, Louis L. "Six Cylinders and a New 60 HP Tractor Highlights I-H's 1959 Challenge." *Implement & Tractor* (August 23, 1958): 70–73.

Tisiner, P. G. "Using the Liberty Motor." *Scientific American* (July 5, 1919): 9.

Tolley, H. R., and Church, L. M. "Southern Farmers Say What They Think About Tractors." *Automotive Industries* (February 8, 1923): 276–77.

"Tractor a Modern Necessity." *American Fruit Grower* (October 1918): 4

"Tractor Attachment for Pleasure Car Chassis." *Scientific American* (September 15, 1917): 196.

"Tractor 'Co-ops' Get U. S. Blessing." *Newsweek* (September 5, 1938): 33–34.

"Tractor Costs and Profits." *Power Farming* (May 1921): 10.

"Tractor Curtailment Order Is Modified." *Automotive Industries* (November 14, 1918): 849.

"Tractor Dealers Get Plow Sales: Oliver Company Gives Ohio Agency to Automobile Agency—Others May Follow." *Automotive Industries* (May 16, 1918): 971.

"The Tractor Demonstration." *Power Farming* (June 1917): 10.

"Tractor Demonstrations." *Power Farming* (June 1916): 34–35, 54.

"Tractor Demonstrations." *Power Farming* (February 1919): 14.

"Tractor Demonstrations for 1916." *Power Farming* (January 1916): 30. 32.

"Tractor Makers Protest Curtailment." *Automotive Industries* (October 17, 1918): 657–59, 696.

"Tractor Men Need 3,000 Cars." *Automotive Industries* (February 21, 1918): 432.

"Tractor Most Reliable." *Power Farming* (July 1926): 3.

"Tractor of Good Design and Construction." *Scientific American* (December 14, 1918): 482.

"Tractor Operation Data." *Scientific American* (November 2, 1918): 358.

"Tractor Power Plant Improvements." *Scientific American* (November 16, 1918): 396.

"Tractor Production Past and Present." *Automotive Industries* (January 16, 1919): 175.

"Tractor Progress." *Power Farming* (April 1919): 55.

"Tractor Ratings." *Automotive Industries* (March 7, 1918): 513.

"Tractor Saves Half Expense." *Orange Judd Farmer* (February 17, 1917): 20.

"The Tractor with Drive Wheel in the Furrow." *Scientific American* (May 13, 1916): 512.

"The Tractors Are Running Hot." *Business Week* (July 15, 1939): 17–18.

"Tractors: Ferguson's Fight." *Newsweek* (May 19, 1947): 76.

"Tractors for '44." *Business Week* (November 13, 1943): 19–20.

"Tractors Show Mechanical Refinement." *Automotive Industries* (February 21, 1918): 396–99.

"Tractors Take Special Tooling." *American Machinist* (June 15, 1938): 493–95.

"Tractors: Where the Horsepower Went in 1977." *Implement & Tractor* (April 21, 1978): 26–27.

Trumbull, Horace Niles. "Why Use Anti-Friction Bearings on the Tractor." *Power Farming* (September 1916): 34.

Turner, Charles W., Jr. "Why It Pays to House the Farm Tractor." *Power Farming* (September 1918): 10.

Tuttle, R. Ray. "Lighting Tractor for Night Work." *Power Farming* (July 1920): 15.

"Two or Three Plow Rating for Massey." *Automotive Industries* (January 11, 1936): 49.

"Two-Plow 12–20 Hp. Tractor Added to Massey Harris Line." *Automotive Industries* (December 1, 1928): 802–3.

Universal Tractor Manufacturing Co. "Automobile Dealers Are Winning Trade with the Universal" [advertisement]. *The Horseless Age* (April 14, 1915): 22.

Underwood, W. H. "My First Experience with a Tractor." *Power Farming* (September 1916): 16, 45.

Vestal, Avis Gordon. "How to Save Woman Power on the Farm." *Power Farming* (May 1919): 30, 32.

Waddel, A. F. "As Public Works Buying Slackens Returning Farm Prosperity Lifts Production of Adaptable New Models." *Automotive Industries* (December 28, 1935): 853, 855, 857, 861.

Wallace, Henry A. "Report from Minnesota." *New Republic* (March 22, 1948): 12.

Warren, C. K. "I Cannot Afford to Farm Without Tractors." *Power Farming* (August 1921): 5–6.

Warren, Howard. "The Trend of Tractor Development." *Scientific American* (December 28, 1918): 516, 532, 534.

Watson, E. Lloyd. "The Farm Tractor and Horse Production." *Power Farming* (January 1917): 8.

———. "Save the Corn Crop with a Tractor." *Power Farming* (November 1917): 22, 27.

Wells, Jennifer. "Jilted." *Canadian Business* (May 1984): 73–76.

Wennergran, E. "His Neighbors Laughed, but John Froelich Invented a Tractor Anyway." *Wallace's Farmer and Iowa Homestead* (March 18, 1950): 380–81.

Wentworth, Edward N. "Horses and Tractors in Army Service." *The Breeder's Gazette* (July 10, 1919): 58.

Wentworth, G. E. "Horsepower and Horse Power." *Breeder's Gazette* (September 14, 1916): 412.

Whallon, Archer P. "Farming with Tractors the Cheaper Way." *California Citrograph* (January 1920): 79.

"What Can I Learn at the Tractor Show." *Power Farming* (July 1916): 7–8, 51.

"What Farmers Say of Tractors." *The Ohio Farmer* (January 18, 1919): 14–82.

"What Farmers Want and Need from Their Machinery." *Farm Implement News* (March 10, 1952): 62–63, 130, 132, 134.

"Wheel Tractor Imports, 1975." *Implement & Tractor* (November 7, 1977): 102.

"Wheel Tractor Imports, 1976." *Implement & Tractor* (November 7, 1977): 102.

"Wheel Tractors on Farms by Age and Fuel Type." *Implement & Tractor* (November 21, 1963): 120–21.

White, E. A. "The Farm Power Problem." *Breeder's Gazette* (August 1, 1918): 156–57.

———. "Market Research Essential to Development of Tractor Design." *Automotive Industries* (June 8, 1922): 1210–13.

White, Frank M. "The Cost of Keeping a Tractor." *Orange Judd Farmer* (December 28, 1918): 596, 601, 603.

"Why Farmers Buy Tractors." *Power Farming* (April 1916): 40.

Wiggins, E. R. "The Economics of the Farm Tractor." *Power Farming* (February 1916): 16, 45, 48.

———. "The Farm Power Plant." *Power Farming* (March 1916): 14–15.

———. "Peak Loads on a Mechanical Power Farm." *Power Farming* (April 1917): 9, 49.

Wilcox, W. F. "Tractor Alfalfa Combination Promises Big Return." *Power Farming* (September 1920): 12–14.

Williamson, Paul. "Cost of Farm Power." *Hoard's Dairyman* (August 10, 1939): 434.

"The Winnipeg Motor Contest: A Motor Show for Farmers." *Scientific American* (June 29, 1912): 583.

Witter, S. R. "Retired Farmer Goes Back—With a Tractor." *Power Farming* (February 1917): 7.

"Woman Tames the Tractor." *The Practical Farmer* (June 1, 1918): 202.

Wooley, John C. "Striking Survey Shows Success of Farmer-Owner with Tractor." *Automotive Industries* (April 12, 1921): 866–67.

Wormley, George W. "Brand New Line of Tractors." *Farm Journal* (October 1960): 44.

Worthington, Wayne. "The Engineer's History of the Farm Tractor." *Implement & Tractor* (January 21, 1967): 34–35, 43.

———. "The Engineer's History of the Farm Tractor II: World War I: Confusion, Development." *Implement & Tractor* (February 7, 1967): 33, 56.

———. "Engineer's Tractor History [III]: The 1920's: Eliminating and Consolidating." *Implement & Tractor* (February 21, 1967): 46, 73–74.

———. "Engineer's Tractor History [IV]: Depression and Recovery—Rubber Tires, Fuel, Ferguson." *Implement & Tractor* (March 7, 1967): 44–45, 63–64.

———. "Engineer's Farm Tractor History, V: Post War Standards Progress—and the Beginning of the Businessman Farmer." *Implement & Tractor* (March 21, 1967): 34–37.

———. "Engineer's Tractor History, VII: Manufacturers, Customers and Safety." *Implement & Tractor* (April 21, 1967): 16, 22.

———. "Engineer's Tractor History, VIII: We Engineers Are Involved in Humanity." *Implement & Tractor* (May 7, 1967): 38, 39, 62, 63.

"WPB's Hot Potato." *Business Week* (October 31, 1942): 16, 17.

Wright, John T. "Why Power Farming Short Courses Are Needed." *Power Farming* (November 1918): 13, 35.

Yerkes, Arnold P. "The Present Status of Power Farming." *Power Farming* (August 1923): 5–7.

———. "The Tractor and Farm Management." *Power Farming* (March 1916): 7–8, 44, 66.

———. "The Tractor and Farm Management." *Power Farming*, (April 1916): 44–45.

———. "The Tractor and Farm Management." *Power Farming* (May 1916): 15–16.

———. "The Tractor—A Farm Management Viewpoint." *Power Farming* (October 1917): 12–13.

———. "The Tractor's Influence on Crop Production." *Power Farming* (May 1918): 7–8.

———. "Tractors Nurture Abandoned Farms." *Power Farming* (May 1921): 506.

"You Don't Have to Be Big to Be Profitable." *Progressive Farmer* (October 1984): 54, 55.

Zimmerman, Mark. "The Farm Tractor." *Implement & Tractor* (November 21, 1964): 28–31.

———. "How Much Does Tractor Power Cost?" *Implement & Tractor* (September 7, 1967): 22–27.

———. "Profile: Today's Heavyweight Tractors." *Implement & Tractor* (February 21, 1965): 18, 20.

———. "Why Alternators." *Implement & Tractor* (February 7, 1964): 50–51.

Index

Jeffersonian ideals versus Leninism, 184
Jerden, Sterling, 179–80
J. I. Case Co., experimental tractor, 16; row-crop tractor proposal, 78, 87; Tenneco farming and land speculation, 164, 165; market share, 174
John Deere tractors, Model D, 66; GP, 89; A, 90; multicylinder line introduced, 113–14
John McGinty, 116
John N. Willys, 31
Johnson, Ed [IH engineer], 62–64
Johnson, Hugh S., 31

Kerosene, use as fuel, 29
Kolko, Gabriel, 68
Kubota, 118, 120

Labor savings, 131–35; 149–65; 158–60
La Crosse Plow Co., 95
Legge, Alexander, 53, 120
Liberty tractor proposal, 45
Long-line implements need to go with tractors, 79 n4
Luddites, 158

Mally, R. T., 66
Market leaders, 174
Mass production of tractor, 47–56
Massey-Ferguson, formation, 105; problems, 116
Massey-Harris Co., first tractor unsuccessful, 46; Ferguson merger, 105
Massey-Harris tractors, GP, 89, 114; Challenger, 89, 179
Maxwell Automobile Co., 51
McCormick, Brooks, on social responsibility, 183
McCormick, Cyrus, on early tractor, 19, 27; Ford price war, 53; obituary for Fordson, 55–56; on Farmall, 86
McCormick-Deering tractors, 10–20, 66; 15–30, 66; Farmall [Regular], 86–89; F-20, 90; F-30, 90; F-12, 94; A, 94, 101; Super M, 112

McWilliams, Carey, 185
Mechanization, pre-tractor, 8
Merrit and Kellogg Co., 9
Merritt, Harry C., and ruber tires, 92; and "baby tractor" [B], 94; Allis-Chalmers growth, 94–96, 120
Migrant Labor, 156–57
Minneapolis-Moline, Comfortractor, 121; acquired by White, 174, 176
Mogul [IH], 18
Moley, Raymond, 182
Moline Plow Co., Universal, 30–31; in WWI, 44–45
Monarch Tractor Co., 95
Monopoly, oligopoly and concentration, 173–77
Montgomery Ward, early Graham-Bradley cab tractor, 121
Morgan Engine Works, 19
Motorized cultivators, 32
Mowry, H. H., 20, 33

Nebraska Tractor Tests, 67–70
Nichols, Shepard & Co., 12
Number of tractor makers, 173–74

Oliver, Ford and plow, 49, 50; Super 55, 106; early cab, 121; acquired by White, 174, 176
Olney, Raymond, 26–27, 44
Operator comfort, 66, 120
Otto four-cycle engine, 14
Otto Gas Engine Co., 16
Overproduction, of tractors, 71, 112, 117; of commodities, 149–54

Parr, Charles H., 16–17
Parret Tractor Co., 46
Part-time farming, 157–58
Peek, George N., 31
Plows, development of, 4–6
"Poppin' Johnnys," 113
Populism, 165
Port Huron Co., 34
Power lift, first 91; Ferguson three-point, 105–6
Power steering, 121